Praise for *Denial*

"The history of industry is rich with such cases, a number of which Tedlow examines with thorough understanding of both business and psychology."
—*Publishers Weekly*

"*Denial*'s case studies span from 1916 through the present, but its lessons are particularly urgent for today's business leaders, who face increased scrutiny in challenging times."   —*Worth*

"Tedlow's book forces the business executive to ask: 'Is this about me?' If the answer is yes, you've got a problem. The stories presented here can help you work your way out of it."   —Suzy Welch, author of *10-10-10*

"Tedlow's book is a fascinating look at the phenomenon of denial. It's a great explanation of why smart leaders act dumb, and what you can do about it."   —Scott Adams, creator of *Dilbert*

PORTFOLIO / PENGUIN

DENIAL

Richard S. Tedlow is the Class of 1949 Professor of Business Administration Emeritus at Harvard Business School. His previous books include *Andy Grove* (one of *BusinessWeek*'s ten best books of 2006), *Giants of Enterprise* (one of *BusinessWeek*'s ten best books of 2001), and *The Watson Dynasty*. He has written articles for *The Harvard Business Review*, *Fortune*, and many other publications.

DENIAL

*Why Business Leaders Fail
to Look Facts in the Face—
and What to Do About It*

RICHARD S. TEDLOW

PORTFOLIO / PENGUIN

PORTFOLIO / PENGUIN
Published by the Penguin Group
Penguin Group (USA) Inc., 375 Hudson Street, New York, New York 10014, U.S.A.
Penguin Group (Canada), 90 Eglinton Avenue East, Suite 700, Toronto, Ontario,
Canada M4P 2Y3 (a division of Pearson Penguin Canada Inc.)
Penguin Books Ltd, 80 Strand, London WC2R 0RL, England
Penguin Ireland, 25 St. Stephen's Green, Dublin 2, Ireland (a division of Penguin Books Ltd)
Penguin Books Australia Ltd, 250 Camberwell Road, Camberwell, Victoria 3124,
Australia (a division of Pearson Australia Group Pty Ltd)
Penguin Books India Pvt Ltd, 11 Community Centre, Panchsheel Park,
New Delhi – 110 017, India
Penguin Group (NZ), 67 Apollo Drive, Rosedale,
North Shore 0632, New Zealand (a division of Pearson New Zealand Ltd)
Penguin Books (South Africa) (Pty) Ltd, 24 Sturdee Avenue, Rosebank,
Johannesburg 2196, South Africa

Penguin Books Ltd, Registered Offices:
80 Strand, London WC2R 0RL, England

First published in the United States of America by Portfolio,
a member of Penguin Group (USA) Inc. 2010
This paperback edition with a new preface published 2011

1   3   5   7   9   10   8   6   4   2

Figure on page 58 ("The Inflection Curve") from *Only the Paranoid Survive: How to Manage
the Crisis Points That Challenge Every Company* by Andrew S. Grove. © 1966 Doubleday.
By permission of Andrew S. Grove.

Figure on page 105 ("IBM's Market Capitalization in Comparison to the Rest of the Industry") from
Design Rules, Volume 1: The Power of Modularity by Carliss Y. Baldwin and Kim B. Clark. © 2000
Massachusetts Institute of Technology. By permission of The MIT Press.

THE LIBRARY OF CONGRESS HAS CATALOGED THE HARDCOVER EDITION AS FOLLOWS:

Tedlow, Richard S.
Denial : why business leaders fail to look facts in the face—and what to do about it / Richard S. Tedlow.
p.   cm.
Includes bibliographical references and index.
ISBN 978-1-59184-313-9 (hc.)
ISBN 978-1-59184-391-7 (pbk.)
1. Management—Psychological aspects.   2. Denial (Psychology)   3. Business failures—Case studies.
I. Title.
HD31.T426 2010
658.001'9—dc22   2009039396

Printed in the United States of America
Set in Minion
Designed by Vicky Hartman

While the author has made every effort to provide accurate telephone numbers and Internet addresses at
the time of publication, neither the publisher nor the author assumes any responsibility for errors, or for
changes that occur after publication. Further, publisher does not have any control over and does not
assume any responsibility for author or third-party Web sites or their content.

This book is dedicated to the future:

ANNA, CARLA, EMILY, GIOVANNI, JULIE,

MARY, NATALIE, WILLIAM

Nothing is easier than self-deception. For what each man wishes, that he also wishes to be true.

Demosthenes (384–322 B.C.)

There is something in the nature of CEOs—pride, vanity, a primal need for control, an obsession with success, good old-fashioned idealism—that makes many smart, well-regarded chief executives into idiots when the world turns against them.

"CEOs in Denial," *Fortune*, June 21, 1999

Contents

PART II: GETTING IT RIGHT

Preface to the Paperback Edition

As you can see from the introduction to the first edition, *Denial* is a book about "knowing but not knowing" . . . "seeing but not seeing" . . . "protective stupidity." There have, unfortunately, been innumerable examples of these deadly habits of mind since the book was first published.

At this writing, the United States continues to wallow in a state of denial about its economic problems. We —or at least those of us fortunate enough to be employed—seem to think that the economy is climbing out of the calamity of 2008. No one can predict the future. Perhaps it will. But the dangers to our extremely fragile economy are obvious to anyone who cares to look at them.

One such person who does not shy away from reality is Harvard Law School professor Elizabeth Warren, who was appointed Chair of the Congressional Oversight Panel to keep track of where the hundreds of billions of dollars in the so-called Troubled Asset Relief Program (TARP) are actually being spent. As her questioning of Secretary of the Treasury Timothy Geithner vividly illustrates, there are many unanswered questions that demand responses. Clashes between Warren and Geithner have been covered in the press and posted on YouTube. She probes for the truth, unafraid to speak bluntly to power. He responds with what we might call "word salad"—avoidance, evasion, and either feigned or genuine ignorance. Our whole economy hangs by the thread of encounters such as this.

From the heights of the macroeconomy to individual business firms, three distressing examples of denial today foul (in one sense literally) the corporate landscape.

The first to which we should turn our attention is the Gulf Oil Spill, also known as the BP Oil Spill because British Petroleum operated the Deepwater Horizon drilling rig that exploded on April 20, 2010. The immediate result of the massive explosion and fire was that eleven workers lost their lives and seventeen were injured. The long term result has been the worst oil spill and probably the worst environmental disaster in American history.

No one involved in this catastrophe has handled themselves well. BP's operations were supposedly regulated by the Minerals Management Service (MMS) of the U.S. Department of the Interior. In a report issued a year and a half prior to the blowout, staff at the MMS was charged with unethical and illegal conduct. They had had sexual relations and used drugs with industry representatives amid their "culture of ethical failure." You couldn't make this stuff up. These were the people purportedly looking out for the nation's welfare, but official reports made their many malefactions clear. The implications were simply denied.

From the moment the Deepwater Horizon blew up, BP, which had already compiled an unenviable safety record, did everything wrong. There are a few standard rules to follow in a situation such as the one BP faced on April 20, 2010. First, get the truth out immediately. The unvarnished, undeniable truth. Especially in a case like this in which the truth is bound to become visible soon enough. Second, define the crisis. Third, under promise and over deliver. Fourth, be very, very careful what you say. By that I don't mean descend into corporate-speak. That only makes things worse. I mean speak with genuine empathy for the people most affected by the disaster you created.

In a textbook example of "how not to do it," there is not one of these rules which BP followed. In fact, the company violated them all. BP's CEO Anthony "Tony" Hayward proved himself wholly inadequate to the task at hand. An early comment was, "It was a bit bumpy to get going. We made a few little mistakes early on." "The Gulf of Mexico is a very big ocean," he unhelpfully explained. "The amount of volume of oil and dispersant we are putting into it is tiny in relation to the total water volume." This does not capture how it felt to the people whose businesses were being ruined.

On June 1, Hayward was quoted as saying, "There's no one who wants this thing over more than I do, I'd like my life back." This cannot have been a comforting statement to the families and friends of the eleven workers killed on the Deepwater Horizon. And it was a declaration that has not done him any good. In the words of a *Washington Post* headline on July 26, "Tony Hayward is about to get his life back." In other words, rumors that he was about to be fired had been swirling for weeks. Those rumors were confirmed on July 27 when, following a record $17 billion quarterly loss, BP announced that Hayward would be replaced by the company's first American CEO, Robert Dudley.

Especially in the early days and weeks, BP consistently underestimated the extent of the catastrophe it had created for the residents of the Gulf Coast. Why? We do not yet know, but there are a number of possibilities, none of which make BP look good.

The first is that the company itself did not know how bad things were. In that case, they should not have been in the business of deepwater drilling at all.

Another possibility is that some people lower down in BP's organization knew—or at least suspected—the truth but they did not want to tell Hayward or chairman of the board Carl-Henric Svanberg, himself hopelessly inept before the press. After a meeting with President Obama at the White House, Svanberg declared, "We care about the small people whose lives were being ruined along the coast." The "small people" in question did not find this observation comforting. Perhaps BP was and is a macho "shoot the messenger" company.

Yet another possibility is that everyone, top to bottom, was actually aware of the volcano beneath the sea that BP had uncorked. However, the implications of the unleashed volcano were so dire that it may be that no one in the company could face them. The truth was so awful that it simply could not be true. They saw but they didn't see. They knew but they didn't know. They were protectively stupid.

I don't know which of these three possibilities is the best explanation for the BP Gulf story. But if it is the third, that is denial in its purest form.

There are two lessons—both vitally important—that business executives can derive from this sorry saga. First, sometimes events generally viewed as extremely rare are not that rare at all. This assertion admittedly depends on one's definition of "rare." Nevertheless, the fact is that oil extraction under the best of conditions is hazardous. Deep water drilling is among the worst of conditions. On June 3, 1979, for example, the Ixtoc 1 blew up off the Mexican coast in the Gulf of Mexico. An estimated 140 million gallons of oil were dumped into that "very big ocean" on that occasion. The well wasn't capped until March 23, 1980. Search "oil spills in history" on the Web. What you will find isn't pretty.

Second, people who make decisions have yet to figure out how to think about events that are in fact rare. In the words of the brilliant organizational scientist James G. March, "[T]here appears to be a tendency for human subjects to assume that extremely unlikely events will never occur...." This is a dangerous assumption indeed.

The second cautionary tale comes from Toyota. For decades, Toyota had served as the model for how a corporation should run. The company traces its roots to Sakichi Toyoda (1867–1930). Ranked by one survey as the thirteenth most influential businessperson of all time, Toyoda became obsessed at an early age with building looms for weaving cloth. When he invented the Toyoda Wooden Hand Loom in 1890, Great Britain was far and away the world leader in textile machinery production, as it had been for well over a century. The United States was beginning to make its presence felt in the field. Japan was a nonfactor. It was not on the map.

Yet with a persistence bordering on fanaticism, Toyoda kept inventing looms. His persistence was rewarded with success. In 1924, he created a loom capable of detecting errors and halting production. In 1929, what was once thought to be impossible took place. Toyoda's Automatic Loom Works sold its patents for its automatic loom to Platt Brothers of Great Britain, at the time the world's largest manufacturer of spinning and weaving machinery. Japan was selling knowledge of cloth manufacturing to the country that had given birth to the industry. It is no accident that Sakichi Toyoda became known in Japan as the "King of Inventors."

As a dying man, Toyoda said to his son: "The automatic loom business was my life's work.... You should have your own life's work. I believe in the automobile. It will become indispensable in the future. Why not make it your life's work?"

This was a crazy idea. The United States was the "automobile kingdom," the first nation to put the car within the reach of the common man. Japan was nothing. But the idea was no crazier than achieving dominance in textiles. Through persistence equally fanatical, Toyota (the name was changed for a variety of reasons) rose to leadership in the automobile industry both in terms of sales and profits.

This achievement was made possible by numerous factors, but they can be boiled down to a single word. Quality. Through its unique Toyota Production System, by the mid-1970s Toyota was producing the highest quality automobiles in the world. The Toyota Production System featured "just-in-time" inventory, respect for the workforce, quality circles, and a whole host of other innovations that were alien to its competitors not only in Japan but around the world.

Perhaps more than anything else, the symbol of the "Toyota Way" is the "andon cord." Here is how Toyota explains that device and its purpose. "Toyota team members treat the next person on the production line as their customer and will not pass a defective part on to that customer. . . . When a problem on any vehicle is spotted, any team member can pull a rope—called an andon cord—strung along the assembly line to halt production. Only when the problem is resolved is the line restarted."

The revolutionary character of the andon cord cannot be overstated. The American way was to treat the assembly line worker as a fool and troublemaker whose job was to do what he (or she) was told and to shut up. Management had control of the speed of the production line. The worker was a brainless cog in the process, an extension of the machine he tended.

The American way was based on the speed of the production line. That was the basis for mass production. An automobile assembly plant represents a very large capital investment. For that investment to pay off, the plant had to spit out as many cars as possible to keep costs down by amortizing them over a multitude of units. Stopping the line cost a fortune.

Why, then, was the andon cord and the approach it embodied such a spectacular success? Because that cord represented a focus on quality, on the full costs of producing an automobile, and on customer satisfaction.

Take the following situation. Let's say a ball bearing is misplaced on the assembly line. In the American way, that mistake, which, let us assume, may not cause anything to malfunction but does produce an annoying rattle, makes it all the way through assembly and through final testing. The car is then shipped off to the dealer. The dealer sells it to a customer.

The customer is annoyed by and worried about the persistent rattle. He brings the car, still under warranty, back to the dealer. The dealer is clueless and fiddles with the car without fixing the problem. The continuously inconvenienced and very disappointed customer becomes irate. The car winds up back at the factory where someone will or will not be able to fix the problem. Think of the full costs of this process. Think of the cost in terms of customer goodwill.

Compare this scenario to the Toyota Production System. A ball bearing is misplaced on the line. The worker who misplaced it pulls the andon cord. The line stops, and the problem is fixed then and there. Later, at a quality circle, the workers discuss the problem and decide how to prevent it from recurring.

Which of the two approaches seems better to you?

But all was not well. Toyota, already fabulously profitable, set its sights on becoming the world's largest automobile manufacturer in terms of number of units sold. This was a goal the company reached in 2009, but at a fearful price. In its rush to achieve volume, Toyota began to cut corners in its famed production system. The company denied it was making a quantity/quality tradeoff. Toyota's top people stopped being honest with one another about what was happening.

Back in 2006, Harvard Business School Professor and Toyota expert H. Kent Bowen observed that Toyota's biggest dilemma "is getting too big, too fast, which they feel would make it hard to find enough good managers, thereby jeopardizing the company's legendary quality." And that seems to be what happened.

Auto journalist Paul Ingrassia noted that one of the company's immutable rules was never to build a new product in a new factory with a new workforce. Toyota violated that principal and quality suffered commensurately. Andon cords be damned. Full speed ahead!

The evidence was there for all to see as early as 2005, when Toyota recalled a staggeringly high 2.38 million vehicles in the United States, more than it sold in the U.S. that year. When a *Wall Street Journal* reporter, Norihiku Shinorizu, began writing about Toyota production issues the following year, "some company executives," reports Ingrassia, "reacted angrily," saying the issue was being blown out of proportion. They shot the messenger rather than heeding the message. Unvarnished denial.

The problem with denial is that it may temporarily change perceptions and postpone having to face reality, but it does not change facts. Recalls continued at a remarkably high rate.

Finally, in August 2009, the rubber band snapped. A California state trooper and his family were killed driving a Lexus ES 350, one of Toyota's most expensive cars. "Minutes before the fatal crash, passengers called police to report that the . . . vehicle was accelerating out of control at speeds as high as 120 m.p.h. Witnesses reported that the car's tires were on fire, which was likely due to the driver slamming on the brakes before hitting another vehicle, falling off an embankment, rolling multiple times, and bursting into flames."

After this tragedy, it became known that Toyota had been aware of sudden acceleration issues for two and a half years. Lives had been lost because of the company's inaction and prevarication. Lawsuits, regulatory action, and congressional hearings followed. As of late March 2010, Toyota has been forced to recall more than eight million vehicles. The company's reputation for quality, so carefully nurtured since the miraculous days of the King of Inventors, Sakichi Toyoda, is in tatters.

How did this happen?

For the world outside, the company basked in what we might call the "Toyota Reputation Bubble," comparable in its own way to the recent housing and dot.com bubbles. A veritable industry developed over the years singing the praises of Toyota's magical manufacturing. This prism distorted facts. A Toyota vehicle that performed poorly was "the exception that proved the rule," an odd phrase when you think about it. Very few people until late in 2009 were saying that perhaps it was time for some revisionism concerning Toyota's putative manufacturing excellence about which we were all so endlessly lectured.

We outsiders were slow to face the facts about Toyota. I know people who won't take their recalled Toyotas back to the dealer because they still believe their cars are safe. The mystique may prove slow to shatter completely. But shatter it will. On July 23, *BusinessWeek* reported that after a decade on top, Toyota's Lexus was in danger of losing its market leadership in the luxury automobile category in the United States. In the words of the article, the Lexus

> has been marred by record recalls this year. . . . Problems including fuel leaks, engines that may stall, and vehicles at risk of rolling over during emergency driving maneuvers surfaced after Toyota had already recalled more than 8 million vehicles under its main brand for defects linked to unintended acceleration.

The most perplexing question of all is: Where was that andon cord when we really needed it? Not just the literal andon cord on the assembly line but the metaphorical andon cord in the upper reaches of management. How could the people inside Toyota have allowed these catastrophic product failures to be sold to trusting consumers? We may not have known the truth about the breakdown of the vaunted Toyota Production System and the sacrifice of quality for volume, but a not insignificant number of decision makers within the company did know. What on earth were they thinking? Did they believe that the failure of this most public of products would pass by unnoticed?

These people were in denial.

The third episode I will recount leaves one speechless. Or almost so. I will be as brief as possible.

As you will see, this book is divided into two sections: "Getting It Wrong" and "Getting It Right." A shining example of the second section is the manner in which Johnson & Johnson and its CEO James E. Burke handled the Tylenol poisonings in 1982 and 1986. There is no better example of conquering denial by finding out what the real truth is and unblinkingly looking it in the face.

For more than twenty years, a case I wrote and videotape I produced about the Tylenol tragedies of the 1980s have been used at the Harvard Business School, in corporations, and in business schools around the world to illustrate brilliant business practice in the face of terrible odds. Now, unfortunately, another case must be written to explain how Johnson & Johnson's subsidiary, McNeil, which produces Tylenol, Motrin, Benadryl, and a variety of other over-the-counter medications, fell from grace.

Since 2008, hundreds of millions of units of McNeil products have been recalled, and the company has closed its plant in Fort Washington, Pennsylvania. Strange odors emanated from some products. In other instances, particulates such as acetaminophen, cellulose, nickel, and chromium were found in liquid medication. Johnson & Johnson and McNeil have been consistently ill-informed about their own operations and tardy in responding to requests for information from regulatory authorities such as the Food and Drug Administration.

Rather than demonstrating the leadership pioneered by Johnson & Johnson CEO Jim Burke in the 1980s, J&J's executives today are missing in action. Their communications to the public read as if they were written by lawyers. The company has been consistently behind the news cycle and has stimulated a good deal of suspicion as a result. One blogger asked: "Should J&J Replace the McNeil Management Team?" He thinks so. Indeed, the team's performance has been inept. Have they denied that bad things could happen to a company with their "stellar reputation"?

The CEO of J&J is William C. Weldon. He was born in Brooklyn in 1948, the son of a Broadway stagehand and a costume designer. He graduated from Quinnipiac University in 1971, and his first job was in sales for McNeil. He has spent his whole business life at J&J. That means he was there during Jim Burke's presidency from 1976 through 1989. He saw the master at work. Yet he seemed to learn none of the lessons that he has been in such need of mastering now. Weldon's total compensation for 2009 was well over $20 million. For that kind of pay and with all that experience, the public has every reason to expect more than Weldon has delivered.

On May 7, 2010, Weldon wrote a lame letter (which was not easy to find on the corporate Web site) apologizing for past mistakes and promising to do better. It is unconvincing. Is Weldon in denial about the damage done to so many J&J flagship brands because of the company's sloppiness during his tenure? Or is this just a case of a man being promoted to a position which is beyond his capabilities? Time will tell.

Two years earlier, Weldon spoke at a Wharton Leadership Conference on "Leadership in a Decentralized Company." In a podcast that followed, he expressed concern about the responsibilities that would fall upon the shoulders of the CEO who succeeded him. The public and investors are more worried about whether he himself can handle the responsibilities that he is facing today.

▪ ▪ ▪

Since writing this book, I have received a good many e-mails about denial in various contexts. And I have learned a lesson. Denial is a disease that you have to fight every day. It is a moving target.

There is no cure.

Richard S. Tedlow
July 27, 2010

DENIAL

Introduction

This book is being written in the midst of the worst global economic crisis since the Great Depression. How, when, and indeed if the crisis will end no one knows. But whatever the future holds and the postmortems reveal about the crisis, one culprit is abundantly clear: denial.

Denial by financiers who pursued short-term gain while ignoring long-term consequences that were highly likely, if not inevitable.

Denial by the banking and real-estate industries that what goes up can come down.

Denial by homeowners and consumers that the bills for goods bought on credit will someday come due.

Denial by investors who convinced themselves, once again, that "this time, it's different."

Denial by politicians and bureaucrats of inconvenient truths that didn't fit their free-market ideology.

Denial even by swindlers whose Ponzi schemes could only end in disaster, not just for their victims but for themselves.

Denial today is all around us. Eliot Spitzer, the governor of New York (who made his name while the state's attorney general as the "watchdog of Wall Street"), was in March 2008 caught patronizing a high-priced prostitute in a fancy Washington hotel. It quickly came out that this was not his first such dalliance. Later, after he had resigned as governor because of the scandal, Spitzer was asked by a television interviewer how a well-known politician such as himself could possibly have expected to get away with such behavior. "[Being caught] crossed my mind," he replied, "but like many things in life, you ignore the obvious at a certain moment because you simply don't want to confront it."

If you're looking for a succinct expression of the essence of denial, it would be hard to do better than this. You ignore the obvious. Why? Because you simply don't want to confront it. You know the consequences, but you don't know. You see, but you don't see.

Denial is the unconscious calculus that if an unpleasant reality were true, it would be too terrible, so therefore it cannot be true. It is what Sigmund Freud described as the combination of "knowing with not knowing." It is, in George Orwell's blunt formulation, "protective stupidity."

From the young child who insists that his parents haven't separated even though his father has moved out, to the alcoholic who swears he is just a social drinker, to the president who declares "mission accomplished" when it isn't, denial permeates every facet of life. Business is no exception. In fact, denial may be the biggest and potentially most ruinous problem that businesses face, from start-ups to mature, powerful corporations.

But surely businesspeople ought to be among the most hardheaded and clear-eyed among us. Why would a sane, smart person deny a fact of critical importance to his or her business? Because, to state the obvious, he or she is human. And the impulse to avoid painful truths, just like the impulse to avoid pain itself, is a part of human nature.

I have been teaching and writing about business history for four decades, and what is striking about the dozens of companies and CEOs I have studied is the large number of them who have made mistakes that could and should have been avoided, not just with the benefit of hindsight, but on the basis of information available to decision makers right then and there, in real time. These mistakes resulted from individuals denying reality.

Denial is a pervasive problem not only historically but today. It seduces not only dreamers but the most rational people among us. Why is it seductive? Because it is soothing. It is convenient. It allows us to live in a world of our own creation—while it lasts. It permits us an "as if" existence. We live "as if" things were the way we want them to be, rather than the way they are.

But this is only part of the seduction. Denial sometimes actually works. Plenty of entrepreneurs have succeeded even though others denied they had a chance. The overwhelming majority of new businesses fail. Everyone who starts a business denies that the statistics apply in his or her case.

Even denial in the face of certain catastrophe is not necessarily irrational. The inevitability of catastrophe does not mean that we personally will suffer its consequences. Our successors or descendants may pay the price instead. *"Après moi, le déluge"* was the famous phrase attributed to Louis XV. "After me, the deluge." He did not use the preposition *pendant*, which means "during."

Anyone could increase the profits of Procter & Gamble this year by eliminating the advertising for Tide. It would be a terrible blow to the brand in the long term, but sales might not slump too badly right away. A decision like that would be so obvious that it would make news. However, the same result could be achieved in a thousand less public ways throughout the corporate world.

Even in the case of certain catastrophe, denial can be an intelligent strategy. Permit me to provide a personal illustration. As my late wife was dying of cancer, she once said to me that we should declare a forthcoming holiday a "disease-free weekend." I immediately agreed. Denial was automatic and complete. We lived "as if" she were healthy. She bought us four wonderful days in the face of the abyss.

Denial is seductive because it can work in the short term. Occasionally it works in the long term, but that is rarely true in business. In business, pretending that things are better than they are virtually ensures failure.

As we have noted, however, denial is a part of human nature. You can never avoid it completely, and its avoidance is not a matter of raw intelligence. The protagonists in the first part of this book were not stupid. If they could succumb to denial, anyone can.

Yet as the second part of the book shows, some people rise above denial and stare reality unblinkingly in the face. These exemplars of courage and clarity are remarkable and merit scrutiny. Indeed, the British sociologist Stanley Cohen suggests that denial is so common that rather than trying to fathom why we deny, we should instead focus on when and why we do not. "When do people pay attention?" he asks. "When do they recognize the significance of what they know? When will they be aroused to act, even at personal risk?"

Shedding light on these questions is the aim of this book. Discovering who got it right, who got it wrong, and why may help us to answer them and move us closer to our goal. A goal that should be no more or less than this: to confront more than we deny.

Part I

GETTING IT WRONG

1

Shooting the Messenger:
Henry Ford and the Model T

October 1, 2008, was a noteworthy date in the history of the automobile industry. It was the centennial of the sale of the first Model T Ford. The Model T, anointed the "car of the century" in 1999 by a vote of international automotive journalists, revolutionized transportation in the United States. It made the Ford Motor Company the signature firm in the world for a quarter of a century, and it made Henry Ford America's second billionaire after John D. Rockefeller.

Lately the Ford Motor Company has become a shadow of its former self, losing money by the billions, shedding employees by the tens of thousands, and ceding market share point by point to foreign-owned companies. The chairman of its Board of Directors is William Clay Ford Jr., the great-grandson of Henry Ford. He is fifty-two years of age, and there is a good chance he will live to see the Ford Motor Company disappear. The company has had near-death experiences in the past, but it has never faced the forces bearing down on it now. Some part of what made it great years ago is dragging it under today. At this writing, it is still hanging on, which is more than can be said for Chrysler and General Motors, both of which have gone through and emerged from bankruptcy.

Despite the fact that an enormous amount has been written about Henry Ford, and he has been described as "the most widely discussed man of his time," there is still a lot we don't know about him. Specifically, what generated that spark of genius that enabled him to transform America and the world?

Ford was born on July 30, 1863, and brought up in Dearborn—at the time a village composed of a couple of farms just south of Detroit. It was an unexceptional upbringing. Ford's earliest memory was of "my father taking my [younger] brother and myself to see a bird's nest under a big oak twenty rods east of our home and my birthplace." He remembered "the nest with four eggs and also the bird and hearing it sing." Tens of thousands of American youngsters had similar experiences with a parent amidst nature in what was at the time a predominantly rural country.

Ford's relationship with his father was difficult to decode, but he was close to his mother. "I never had any particular love for the farm," he later wrote. "It was the mother on the farm I loved." In 1923, at the peak of his power in the automobile industry, Ford observed, "I have tried to live my life as my mother would have wished."

Ford's mother died on March 29, 1876, at the age of thirty-seven following her eighth pregnancy. Ford was twelve years old. Later in life, he used a mechanical metaphor to describe this most emotional of events. The house, he said, became like a watch without the mainspring.

William and Mary Ford recognized their son's talents with all things mechanical. He was fascinated by watches and could, while still young, disassemble and reassemble them with ease. Four months after his mother died, Ford was in Detroit with his father when he encountered his first steam-powered road vehicle, "a sight almost as astounding to the boy as if Elijah's chariot of fire had suddenly appeared." For the remainder of his long life (he died on April 7, 1947), Ford never forgot this sight. He had found something new to love only a few months after his mother passed away. And unlike a person, a machine could not die and abandon a loved one.

Between 2:00 and 4:00 a.m. on the morning of June 4, 1896, Henry Ford completed his quadricycle, tinkered together in his spare time—of which there was not much, illustrated by the fact that he was working on it at four in the morning. But the small self-propelled motor vehicle was a beginning. Ford was in the industry, and he was there to stay.

With the enthusiasm so typical of the entrepreneur, Ford founded a company three years later. One of the people he tried to entice into joining the venture was a friend named David M. Bell. "Dave," Ford told him, "you'll grow with the business."

"What business?" Bell replied.

In this instance, Bell's reluctance served him well. Ford's first company failed. He tried another, incorporated in 1901. That failed too. Nothing daunted, Ford tried yet another, incorporated on June 16, 1903. He did not have to found a fourth. This was the Ford Motor Company.

We have to provide a little background here to place Ford's achievement in sharp relief. There were a lot of reasons to believe in 1900 that the automobile would never become a mass-marketed product. According to the president of the Carriage Builders Association, 350,000 carriages were sold in New York City, compared to 125 cars, between 1894 and 1899. The idea, he said, that the car would someday replace the horse was "a fallacy too absurd to be mentioned by intelligent men." As we will see repeatedly, incumbents often try to trash-talk a new technology away. Mark Sullivan, a journalist in 1900 writing his memoirs three decades later, observed, "That a time should come when horses would be a rare sight on city streets seemed, in 1900, one of the least credible of prophecies."

Horses in cities were not an unmixed blessing. In 1900, horses deposited 2.5 million pounds of manure and sixty thousand gallons of urine on the streets of New York City every day. Thousands of horses died each year in the city, and their putrid, swelling carcasses had to be removed by the municipal authorities.

That is not all. More than 1 million bicycles were sold in the United States in 1896. Clearly there was an underlying demand for personal, mechanical transportation. Transportation that, unlike a horse, did not eat and drink when it was in its stall.

But could this inchoate, unformed demand be transformed into effective demand? Could it be served by a mass-marketed automobile? There was a great deal of skepticism at the time. The United States in 1900 did not have improved roads. We were more than a half century away from the interstate highway system that we enjoy today. We didn't have gas stations. Indeed, we didn't have much gas. Rockefeller was refining kerosene from most of his petroleum for use as an illuminant. We did not have traffic lights or rules of the road. We did not have a network of parts-distribution and repair shops. So in the not unlikely event that your car broke down on some rural road, you either fixed it yourself or waited until someone else happened along and then found yourself dependent upon the kindness of strangers.

Automobiles were expensive in 1900. No bank would lend you money to buy one. Dealerships would not finance their purchase. There was no equivalent of GMAC. No one was writing automobile insurance. The mass-marketed automobile demands a complex and expensive financial infrastructure that did not exist in 1900. The unreliability of that infrastructure in 2008 and 2009 dealt yet another blow to the staggering automobile industry.

Let us turn our attention from what the nation was lacking in 1900 to what early automobiles did not have. The few cars that had been tinkered together by the turn of the century did not have all-weather bodies. Nor did they have headlights. The great majority of Americans lived in the northern states in 1900. Half the year, daylight was in short supply. The weather was often inclement, periodically severe.

What must be kept in mind is that most of us march backward into the future. We see what was. If we are particularly perspicacious, we can see what is. Only true visionaries, however, can imagine what might be. Think of the term *horseless carriage*. The automobile was originally named not for what it was but for what it was not. So people looking at cars in 1900 could reasonably conclude that they would never be used for commuting regularly to work. You couldn't drive when it was dark, raining, or snowing.

Cars did not have self-starters. You had to crank the engine to get it going, and this could prove dangerous. Indeed, it could be fatal. The series of events that set in motion the invention of the electric self-starter began in December of 1910, when a man named Byron T. Carter encountered a female motorist whose car had stalled. To help her, he cranked her car. Unfortunately, the motor backfired, as it often did, and the crank suddenly spun into reverse. Carter's arm was broken and so was his jaw. He died soon thereafter of pneumonia contracted in the hospital to which he was taken. Carter had a friend in the automobile industry, and word reached the great inventor Charles F. Kettering that something had to be done. In 1911, Kettering invented the self-starter. In 1900, cars were dangerous even when they were not in motion.

Many early cars, such as Ford's own quadricycle, did not have steering wheels. They had tillers instead. What other vehicle has a tiller? A boat.

People think in terms of analogy, and it was not terribly outlandish to think of a horseless carriage as a "land yacht." As a plaything for the rich.

Despite these obstacles, there were some who predicted a promising future for the automobile. In 1895, the great Edison himself said that "the horseless vehicle is the coming wonder. . . . It is only a question of time when the carriages and trucks in every large city will be run with motors." Bicycle manufacturer Albert A. Pope predicted in 1900 that within a decade there would "be more automobiles in use in the large cities of the United States than there are now horses in these cities."

Both Edison and Pope, however, were predicting that cars would be electric. Edison said this would be made possible by the development of an improved storage battery. *Motor Age* magazine dismissed this idea brusquely: "Mr. Edison's bunk has come to be somewhat of a joke—a real joke." Indeed, more than a century after he predicted it, we are still waiting for the battery Edison imagined. As for Pope, he also was betting on the battery. To him, the very idea of the internal combustion engine was ridiculous. "You can't get people to sit over an explosion," he explained.

Predictions cost nothing. But cars cost money . . . quite a lot of money. Per capita realized national income in the United States in 1900 was $480. Although the number of automobiles sold in the early years of the century was climbing fast, so was their price. In 1903, 11,235 were sold, about two thirds of them for $1,375 or less. In 1907, 43,000 were sold, but two thirds of those were for more than $1,375.

As the industry developed, the pressure to produce more expensive machines was relentless. That was the pattern in Europe. France was the world leader in automobile manufacture in 1907. The pioneering firm, Panhard and Levassor, produced short runs of expensive vehicles targeted at the high end of the market.

At first, this was also true in the United States. Entrepreneurs seeking to serve what they perceived to be a beckoning mass market were thwarted in their efforts. Some, such as Alanson P. Brush, sold cars inexpensively because they made them cheaply. Brush sold his Runabout for the attractive price of $500 from 1907 to 1912, but it was also cheaply made and unreliable. Brush kept costs down by substituting wood for metal wherever possible, resulting in the consumer lament "Wooden body, wooden axles, wooden wheels, and wooden run."

Ransom E. Olds saw the same market and began producing his "Merry Oldsmobile" in 1901. Sales were encouraging, but Olds, like many another entrepreneur, lost control of his company, which with seeming inexorability began to make bigger, heavier, pricier cars for the swanky set. This trend seemed so unstoppable that in 1906 Woodrow Wilson, at the time president of Princeton University, is said to have voiced the fear that the automobile might promote socialism because it was obviously desirable but only the rich could afford it.

After the Ford Motor Company was founded in 1903, the same relentless pressure to move upmarket asserted itself. Big, heavy cars were relatively easy to sell to wealthy, price-insensitive customers. They were easier to produce because the manufacturer could charge high margins that allowed him to pay skilled craftsmen to put the vehicle together.

But it was more than business that kept pushing automobile companies toward big, expensive cars. It was ego as well. Historian Donald F. Davis, in a clever turn of phrase, called the problem "conspicuous production." Investment for new car companies came, not surprisingly, from people who had money to invest. These people were wealthy, and they wanted to drive the automobiles that their investments had made possible. Henry Ford's principal backer was not interested in a mass-marketed automobile. He fell in love with the six-cylinder Model K.

The Ford Motor Company could have become the Olds Motor Works all over again, but it did not because Henry Ford proved to be adept at corporate maneuvering. He was the automobile entrepreneur who did not lose control of his company to his financiers. They lost it to him.

By the fall of 1907, Ford controlled the company that bore his name. This allowed him to realize his dream. "I will build a car for the common man," he declared, "constructed of the best materials by the best men to be hired after the simplest designs that modern engineering can devise . . . so low in price that no man making a good salary will be unable to own one— and enjoy with his family hours of pleasure in God's great open spaces."

This elegant, eloquent vision drove Ford from the Model A to the B to the C to the F to the K to the N to the R to the S and then, climactically, to the Model T. This was the vehicle that put America on wheels, but no one could have predicted the magnitude of its success when it debuted on that autumn day in 1908. In the nineteen years of its manufacture,

15,458,781 Model T's were sold, making it the second-highest-selling automobile ever. It is outranked, slightly, by the Toyota Corolla. But sales of the two cars are not really comparable. The automobile was a mature product when the Corolla was introduced, and the market was much larger.

The Model T created a market. It led to the conquest of rural solitude just as Ford had hoped it would. It also made Ford perhaps the most famous man in the world. To some he seemed to be elevated above mere mortal nature. Words such as *Fordism* and *Fordist*, meaning mass production of a standardized product, entered the vocabulary. *Fordismus* appeared in German.

The Model T hit the market at $850, but instead of allowing the price to float up, Ford forced it down. By 1912, you could buy one for $600, Ford's original target. By 1920, you could buy one for $440. Four years later, the car retailed for $290, or about half the price of a household refrigerator that year. In the early 1920s, the Ford Motor Company was producing more than 60 percent of all the motor vehicles in the United States and over half in the entire world.

Ford became famous because he put what was once viewed as a luxury within the reach of the masses. He became famous because of his moving assembly lines, first at the gigantic plant in Highland Park on Detroit's western border, then at the unimaginably large industrial complex astride the River Rouge just south of the city. At the peak of production, a hundred thousand workers were employed at the Rouge, up from the 125 who were employed in the rented shacks on Mack Avenue in Detroit when the firm opened its doors in 1903.

But of all the great innovations—the moving assembly line, interchangeable parts, the Model T itself, which seemed to have a personality of its own (people wrote poems to it)—the single most remarkable event of Henry Ford's career took place on January 5, 1914. He stood by a window at an office in the plant when his (then) friend and partner James Couzens read a press release to reporters from three Detroit newspapers:

> The Ford Motor Co., the greatest and most successful automobile manufacturing company in the world, will, on Jan. 12, inaugurate the greatest revolution in the matter of rewards for its workers ever known in the industrial world.
> At one stroke it will reduce the hours of labor from nine to eight,

and add to every man's pay a share of the profits of the house. The smallest amount to be received by a man 22 years old and upwards will be $5 per day. . . .

The flowery language should not be taken too seriously. This, after all, was the age of Hearst and Pulitzer. What is interesting is that this press release was issued to only three local papers. Ford apparently had no idea of the global impact of this news. Just a few months earlier, on October 1, 1913, the company had raised wages 13 percent to $2.34 a day. Now, even that level was more than doubled. Ford was paying his workers far above the all-manufacturing average.

There were operational reasons to raise wages. *Boring* does not come close to describing what it was like to work on Ford's assembly lines. *Mind-numbing* is closer. *Excruciating* perhaps hits the mark. According to one study:

> The skilled fitter in Ford's craft-production plant of 1908 had gathered all the necessary parts, obtained tools from the tool room, repaired them if necessary, performed the complex fitting and assembly job for the entire vehicle, then checked over his work before sending the completed vehicle to the shipping department. In stark contrast, the assembler on Ford's mass-production line had only one task—to put two nuts on two bolts or perhaps to attach one wheel to each car. He didn't order parts, procure his tools, repair his equipment, inspect for quality, or even understand what the workers on either side of him were doing.

Workforce turnover was a staggering 370 percent in 1913. The company had to hire 50,448 people to maintain an average labor force of 13,623. Higher wages meant that rather than fleeing from the plant, workers were trying to break in. Fire hoses had to be used to control the hordes at the plant gates the day after the announcement.

Undoubtedly labor turnover was a problem that raising wages would help solve. However, to attribute the $5 day to that motive alone is to miss the point. In railroad construction, slaughterhouses, steel mills, and coal mines, workers had been abused since the coming of big business to the American economy. If the worker didn't like it, he could be replaced, if not by a white man then by a black man, if not by a man then by a woman, if not by an American then by a contract laborer from abroad. "I have always had one rule," said an old-time Carnegie ironmaster. "When a workman sticks up his head, hit it." Think about that, and then think about the $5 day.

Ford was pioneering what he viewed as a whole new way of doing business. In an industry populated by companies scurrying toward higher prices, he kept cutting the price of the Model T. Though inexpensive like the Brush Runabout, the Model T was not cheap. It was built to be rugged and dependable. Then Ford more than doubled the wages of a docile, unorganized, and unskilled workforce. In the age of robber barons, solving a labor problem before the metaphorical—or actual—gun was pointed at your head was not how business was done.

That's not all. Unlike the post–World War II American automobile industry, Ford did not pass higher wages along to the customers in the form of higher prices. Wages, inflation, whatever—the price of the Model T kept dropping. Ford lowered the price even as demand exceeded supply.

Henry Ford showed that high quality, high wages, and low prices were not at war with one another. Service to the consumer and the community led to personal wealth for him beyond imagining. But at least in the early years, the wealth was the by-product of the service.

Unfortunately, there was a snake in the garden. Ford had always possessed certain unappealing personality traits. A nastiness expressed itself in practical jokes that were not all that funny. For instance, Ford once had a telegram sent to his production manager, Charles Sorensen, informing him that a Ford plant in Dearborn was on fire and about to burn to the ground. Sorenson, who was aboard a train when he received the telegram, tried to have the train stopped and arrange for a car to pick him up and drive him to the "disaster" before he discovered Ford's hoax.

Although his vision combined with his unquestionable mechanical abilities (he could do what no automobile executive in the world could do today—build a car by himself) lent him a charisma that attracted a lot of talent to his company, he also had a persistent problem in getting along with men.

Nobody is perfect; and Ford's virtues far outshone his shortcomings in the early years. Rarely can one pinpoint the moment that a talented man takes a wrong turn in life. Ford provides us with just such a moment. In fact, it was the moment of his great triumph, the announcement of the $5 day.

Prior to that day, Ford seemed to be well grounded. After it, he was overwhelmed by his own press notices. He came to believe the adulation, the flattery. Formerly, he had declined to comment upon matters concerning which he knew nothing. But those press notices convinced him that his was a wisdom that surpassed understanding. If a newspaperman wanted a quote on any subject from the gold standard to the theory of evolution, Ford was the man to provide it. Need a quotable quote about reincarnation? How's this flippant remark:

> When the automobile was new and one of them came down the road, a chicken would run straight for home—and usually be killed. But today, when a car comes along, a chicken will run for the nearest side of the road. That chicken has been hit in the ass in a previous life.

When you hear a business leader making public statements like this, it is not out of line to doubt his judgment.

Ford rambled on endlessly. Most of his statements were harmless enough. Some were not. He became fixated upon Jews as the enemy of mankind and became the most important anti-Semite in American history. He is the only American mentioned favorably in the American edition of Hitler's *Mein Kampf.*

Meanwhile, in spite of his anti-Semitism (or perhaps because of it), Ford's fame and popularity grew. He didn't seem like a plutocrat, nor did he act like one. He did not live amidst the Detroit wealthy in Grosse Pointe or Bloomfield Hills. He preferred his gloomy house, Fair Lane, on the River Rouge not far from where he was born and where his great industrial park was located.

Ford's wealth rained down upon him rather late in life. He was about forty when the Ford Motor Company was founded. He was plucked from obscurity to world fame a decade later with the $5 day, and it was a leap he did not make gracefully.

Ford did not seem to fully comprehend how rich he was. Upon visiting J. P. Morgan's house, he remarked, "It is very interesting to see how the rich live." Yet Ford was far richer than Morgan. Nevertheless, there was a homespun American-ness in Ford that never went away. "I still like boiled potatoes with the skins on," he remarked in explaining why he did not like having servants in his house, "and I do not want a man standing back of my chair at table laughing up his sleeve at me while I am taking the potatoes' jackets off." It is impossible to imagine J. P. Morgan making a similar statement.

Ford viewed himself as the champion of the farmer, even though he himself hated farm life. He also hated Wall Street financiers. "Did you ever see dishonest calluses on a man's hands?" he once asked rhetorically. "Hardly. When a man's hands are callused and women's hands are worn, you may be sure honesty is there." It was the "soft white hands" of financiers that could not be trusted.

While Ford was meandering through the thicket of his disconnected opinions about random subjects, the Model T kept selling and selling. It took seven years for the company to sell its millionth Model T. Only a year and a half later, it sold its two-millionth. Four million were sold by 1920. The number of units sold doubled by 1923.

During the 1920s, however, subtle trends, dangerous to the Model T's continued market dominance, began to evince themselves. "History," Ford famously declared, "is more or less bunk." But history was about to happen to him.

The United States following World War I embarked on an era of rapid change. In the wake of reconversion to a peacetime economy, there was a brief but sharp depression; and General Motors, Ford's only real competition, skirted the edge of bankruptcy. In 1921, in total disarray, it held a mere 12.7 percent of the market.

Following the depression, however, the nation's wealth began to grow at a rapid pace. Gross domestic product until the Great Depression grew at about a 5 percent compound annual rate. The nation was urbanizing. 1920 was the first year in U.S. history in which more than half the population lived in cities rather than on the farm or in a rural community. This was not good news for an unsophisticated man marketing a "farmer's car."

Working-class Americans enjoyed more leisure than ever before. International Harvester, the huge farm-machinery manufacturer, gave its labor force a two-week paid vacation in 1926. With this new leisure time, Americans were discovering new ways to occupy themselves. Hollywood was turning out motion pictures that riveted audiences. Through movies and through other aspects of popular culture, style and fashion were coming to the United States. Sporting events also captured the nation's imagination, especially Babe Ruth's sixty home runs in 1927—banged out without the help of steroids or human growth hormone.

The automobile business both stimulated and was affected by this transformation. Cars inspire passion in their owners. A car is the most expensive branded item the average consumer purchases. Historically, it has played a key role in defining status. Most of what we own, as historian Donald Davis has astutely pointed out, is not on display. No one knows your salary or your financial assets, and it is considered impolite in our culture to ask. Only people invited to your home know what it looks like and can make a guess about what it cost to furnish.

Your automobile, by contrast, is on display wherever you drive. If you pull up in front of someone's house in a high-end BMW, you are announcing without saying a word that you can afford to pay about $90,000 for an automobile. Either that or you are deeply in debt. That is one reason why Professor Davis believes a car is so important in defining status. It is visible, mobile, and communicates information that is difficult simply to tell others.

Henry Ford refused to believe that an automobile was anything more than an appliance that took its occupants from one place to another. His favorite slogan about the Model T was "It takes you there, and it brings you back." This man who had been so open to change and so flexible earlier in his life—remember that he founded two companies that failed and that once the Ford Motor Company came into existence it went through eight models before the T—became adamantine in the 1920s.

Henry Ford began his business career with a sharp focus on customer benefit. By putting America on wheels, he liberated a nation from the tyranny of distance. During the 1920s, his focus shifted from making customers happy to making more Model T's.

This is an important distinction, and we should pause to reflect on it. The physical object his factory was producing was the same as it had been for years. The way he was producing it—the moving assembly line, interchangeable parts, extreme specialization of labor—was by 1925 the same as it had been for years. His pricing strategy also remained the same.

What Ford steadfastly denied—the very essence of his denial—was that despite making the same product in the same way, his company was headed

in the wrong direction. A product in the business world is what the consumer makes of it. Indeed, as marketing professor Theodore Levitt observed, a product that does not sell is not a product at all. It is a museum
piece. Any product or service is a combination of what the business provides and what the consumer wants and expects.

The desires and expectations of consumers were changing in the 1920s.
There was—and this is a critically important point—ample evidence
of these changes plainly visible at the time. This is not a story about the
clarity of hindsight. Nor is it a story of greed. Nor is it a story of a businessman weighing options and simply making the wrong choice. It is, instead,
the story of one man denying plain, irrefutable evidence that the American
automobile industry was changing. A rational CEO in touch with reality
would act on that evidence. A CEO in denial would not. We know because
Ford's great rival, Alfred P. Sloan Jr., did act on the evidence.

Henry Ford elected to be the CEO who "knew but did not know." Ford
acted by not acting. In two decades he migrated from putting Americans
on wheels and thus liberating them from loneliness to making more Model
T's. In other words, he fell in love with his product and lost sight of his
market.

What is all this crystal-clear evidence that Ford denied?

All products have two principal qualities. One is the core function that
the product (or service) performs. "It takes you there, and it brings you
back" is the perfect expression of the core function of an automobile. The
second are those attributes of a product beyond its core function that add
value to it in the eyes of the consumer. This second set of attributes is the
"augmented" product. The sum of the core and augmented products com-
prises the total product, the total bundle of benefits the consumer realizes
from the purchase.

In 1908, the balance between core and augmented product was heavily
weighted to the former. In those days the car was a new item. Remember
that the problems with starting it rendered it dangerous before it even
moved. Almost everything about the automobile was new and exciting, but
also frightening, when the Model T was introduced, because almost every
purchaser was buying his first car. Indeed, first-time buyers were always
the heart of the Model T's market. These people wanted precisely what the
Model T provided. They wanted to be sure that this scary new contraption

was a dependable appliance that would reliably take them there and bring them back. If ever a product was "market right," it was the Model T in 1908—little augmentation, predominantly core.

Consumer Preference in an Automobile, 1908

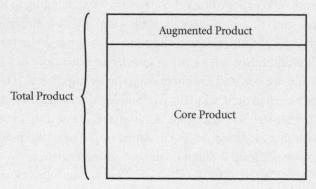

By the mid-1920s, however, consumer desires had changed. The automobile had become a status symbol for the reasons already discussed. Consumer preference could now be approximated as follows:

Consumer Preference in an Automobile, 1927

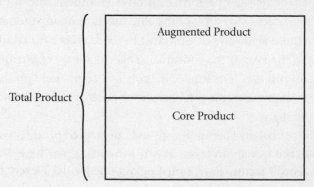

History is the story of change over time. The importance of the change in the automobile business in the two decades under discussion cannot be overemphasized.

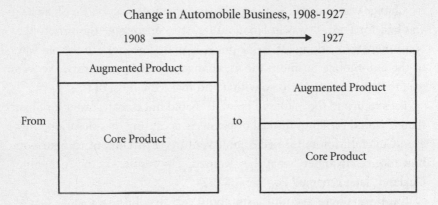

Change in Automobile Business, 1908-1927

Equally menacing, Ford's principal competitor was now under new management. General Motors had been bought out of a state approaching bankruptcy by DuPont in 1920. DuPont at the time was probably the best-managed big business in the nation. Pierre S. DuPont, who decamped from his beloved country estate, Longwood Gardens, to Detroit to straighten GM out, was an MIT-trained chemical engineer. He selected Alfred P. Sloan Jr., an electrical engineer also out of MIT, with two decades of experience in the automobile industry, to turn General Motors around. Ford had become mercurial in his management of his company. Sloan was the opposite: systematic to a fault.

Sloan well understood that Ford owned the low-priced market for first-time buyers. In his own words, it "would have been suicidal to compete with him head-on. No conceivable amount of capital short of the United States Treasury could have sustained the losses required to take volume away from him at his own game."

So Sloan decided to play a different game. Let us look, for example, at the question of color. Henry Ford wrote in 1922 that "any customer can have a car painted any color that he wants as long as it is black." This was more than merely a querulous wisecrack meant to be dismissive of the consumer. Ford's factories were turning out one Model T every forty seconds. No paint was available that would dry fast enough to keep up with that pace. Ford was not going to slow the production lines to let paint dry or store cars in some giant parking facility for that purpose. He needed people to buy black cars because the only finish available was a black enamel that could be quickly baked on.

Change was in the air in the 1920s, and that was as good for Sloan as it was bad for Ford. It was in Sloan's interest to encourage the variety that consumers were asking for. As he put it, "We had no stake in the old ways of the automobile business; for us, change meant opportunity. We were glad to bend our efforts to go with it and make the most of it."

Let's return to the matter of paint. It would not dry any faster for Sloan than it would for Ford. Instead of passively accepting that situation, however, General Motors formed a joint venture with DuPont to figure out how to give customers what they wanted. The result was the "true blue" Oakland (later renamed Pontiac) of 1924.

Car buyers were so enthusiastic about cars in color that an aftermarket developed for painting Model T's. Today, in the Henry Ford Museum in Dearborn, there is a custom-painted red Model T on display. Modern market research is exceptionally complex, an industry unto itself. But sometimes all the surveys and mathematics that go into it can be overwhelmed by common sense. Henry Ford had merely to look out the window to see that his world was changing. He could be certain about one thing concerning that red Model T (or a Model T of any color) that he may have seen driving down the road. It didn't come out of the factory that way. And every true blue Oakland he saw was something new under the sun.

Then there was the Chevrolet. It was GM's entry into the market for first-time buyers. It was more expensive than the Model T. However, Sloan believed that "better and better cars, with a bigger package beyond basic transportation . . . would be so compellingly attractive as to draw buyers away from the Model T." To make the higher price more digestible, GM established the General Motors Acceptance Corporation (GMAC) to help finance the purchase.

This strategy was not easy to execute, but it eventually proved a winner. Ford's sales in 1925 were flat compared to 1924. However, as Sloan observed, the market was growing and "Ford's share declined relatively from 54 to 45 per cent, *a sign of danger, if Mr. Ford had chosen to read it* [emphasis mine]." Sloan's words were more accurate than he himself probably realized. Share loss was dangerous. Ford chose to ignore it. Once again, this was not a case of the certainty of hindsight. All Ford had to do was look out the window. "Gee, I am seeing more Chevys than I used to." Any such suspicion would have been confirmed by published data at the time.

On top of all this, we have the remarkable chart below, published in *Motor* magazine in May of 1926. This chart is a little busy, so permit me to walk you through it. The top line ("Total Number of Families in the United

The U.S. Automobile Market in 1926

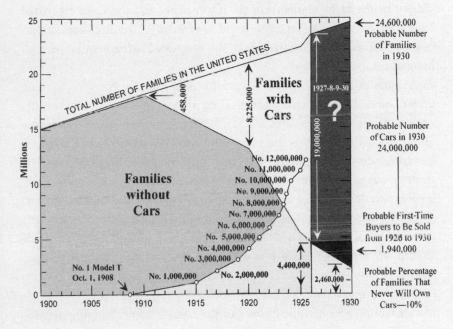

States") shows the nation's growing population. The left vertical axis shows that the number of families increased from about 15 million in 1900 to a projection of 24.6 million in 1930. The light gray portion of the chart on the left side illustrates the impact of the Model T.

Virtually no one owned a car in 1900. For the first decade of the new century, ownership crept up slowly, with fewer than half a million families owning a car. The following decade, car ownership exploded. Eight and a quarter million American families owned a car, thanks primarily to the plummeting price of the Model T, which sold its four-millionth unit in 1920. The chart shows this growth with the diagonal-black-line segment.

Note how steeply that car-owning segment grows during the Roaring Twenties. By 1927, an estimated 19 million American families, over 80 percent, would own cars. Most of these were first-time buyers, the heart of the Model T's market. Thus, as the "Families With Cars" segment grows, so does the line graph of Model T sales.

By the end of the decade, however, the chart estimates that only 1.94 million first-time buyers would remain in the nation. That number is indicated by the black segment on the right side of the chart. An estimated 10 percent of American families would never own cars either because they couldn't afford them or they lived in congested urban areas such as Manhattan.

As early as 1924, the Model T's price was so low that Ford was making only $2 on each unit he sold. More than 95 percent of the company's profits were coming from spare parts and accessories. It is no wonder that the title of the article in which this chart appeared was "What Will Ford Do Next?" The author took it for granted that Ford had to do something different. His strategy was not sustainable. Cutting prices, even if it were economically feasible, would no longer lead to an expanded market and increased sales.

One of the many problems Ford faced as the 1920s drew to a close was that the Model T was so sturdy and well built that it lasted forever. Ford had to compete for first-time buyers with an ever-growing inventory of used Model T's. My father's first car was a Model T. But he didn't buy it from Ford. He bought it from a friend for $15.

General Motors had the answer to the needs of the changing market. Not only did it differentiate its cars through colors but also through a policy designed to exploit the new meaning of the product as a status symbol. GM led the customer through a product line as he aged and as his income increased. Unlike Ford's strategy—the Model T as the "universal car"—the strategy of General Motors was captured by the famous phrase "a car for every purse and purpose." The cars in GM's line were Chevrolet, Pontiac, Oldsmobile, Buick, and Cadillac. This array was memorably characterized in *Fortune* magazine in the 1930s: "Chevrolet for the *hoi polloi*, . . . Pontiac . . . for the poor but proud, Oldsmobile for the comfortable but discreet, Buick for the striving, Cadillac for the rich."

The data, the trends, the cars driving down the nation's roads were the same for everybody. Sloan endorsed the movement of the market. Ford in the 1920s put himself on the wrong side of history.

Imagine yourself in the position of a Ford executive in, say, early 1926.

The trends were obvious. How could you get through to Henry Ford, the world-famous billionaire who owned the company and to whom the Model T was more than merely a product, it was a way of life? To him, it became ever more valuable as a repository of proper values while the world turned toward the frivolous and evanescent. "It takes you there and brings you back" wasn't just a slogan. It was an ideology.

Sloan's policy of the annual model change was anathema to Ford. The annual model change was introduced with the specific purpose of encouraging, if not forcing, the owner of a GM car to buy a new one even though the core transportation function of the one he owned was still intact. With the annual model change, driving last year's model became a comment on your status in the world. The core product may have been fine, but the augmented product was failing. This was Sloan's way of getting out of the bind illustrated by the chart above.

The sales department told Ford that the Model T was slipping and that unless the car was changed substantially it would stop selling. Ford said the car was fine—the problem was an incompetent sales department. "Most of your troubles at the present time is a question of your mental attitude," he helpfully explained to them. When Ford was shown the statistics on automobile registrations from the automotive data publisher R. L. Polk & Co., he responded that the figures were phony and that Polk was influenced by General Motors. There was not a shred of truth in this allegation. It is denial in its purest form.

You are a Ford executive. The truth is obvious for all to see. How do you get through to the boss that fundamental change is vital? Do you ask for a meeting with him to talk things over man-to-man? Do you get a couple of people together to make a presentation to him?

The man who finally decided to "bell the cat" was Ernest Kanzler, an executive in the company and the brother-in-law of Ford's only child, Edsel. Kanzler's approach was a seven-page memorandum delivered on January 26, 1926. Kanzler began by saying that his analysis was prepared for Ford

> so that I can feel I have dealt squarely with the responsibility you have given me. It hurts me to write because I am afraid it may change your feeling for me [actually, Ford didn't like Kanzler anyway, and this memorandum was unlikely to help matters], and that you may think me unsympathetic and lacking confidence in your future plans.

Please, Mr. Ford, understand that I realize fully that you have built up this whole business, that it has been your battle and your creation, and that all of the company's success day after day [is] a direct result of your conception and will really be your personal accomplishment for many years after your lifetime. [Reference to Ford's mortality may not have been strategically wise.]

Any powers I have are mostly due to the opportunities you have given me and have not created in me any exaggerated ideas about myself.

Kanzler ladled it on pretty thick about how wonderful Ford was. Such a bright shining light was Ford that his wonderfulness actually posed a problem to average folks. "It is one of the handicaps of the power of your personality which you perhaps least of all realize, but most people when with you hesitate to say what they think." Another cause and effect of denial is here illustrated. Ford cushioned himself from reality by surrounding himself with "yes men."

"It is unique in the commercial history of the world," Kanzler went on, "that one man should run away with the field as you have done in the motor industry. We have had a wonderful head start because your first designs of a car were twenty years ahead of the world, as well as your methods of production and marketing. But. . ."

"But me no buts," wrote Henry Fielding back in the eighteenth century. Should Kanzler have followed this famous advice?

But we are losing our position because the world has learned from you, and with its combined efforts, each learning from the other, it has now developed a product that is alarmingly absorbing the public's purchasing power.

The best evidence that conditions are not right is in the fact that with most of the bigger men in the organization there is a growing uneasiness. . . . They feel our position weakening and our grip slipping. We are no longer sure that when we plan increased facilities that they will be used. The buoyant spirit of confident expansion is lacking. And we know we have been defeated and licked in England. And we are being caught up in the United States. With every additional car that our competitors sell they get stronger and we get weaker.

With our competitors' volume increasing, they are rapidly approaching our formerly unique powers of producing at lowest cost.

Inwardly we are alarmed to see our advantages ebbing away, knowing
that the counter-measures to prevent it are not immediately at hand. . . .
The feeling exists not outwardly, but I will stake my reputation it exists
in every important man in the company.

Kanzler spoke truth to power. His reward was the same as for most
people who do so. He was fired.

This is the most noteworthy step on the road from denial to demise. If
Ford fired a man as well connected to his own family as Kanzler for speaking truths that were apparent not just with the benefit of hindsight and not
just to industry insiders but to the whole nation, surely he would fire anybody. The fantasy that if you get rid of the messenger, you can render the
message untrue is a powerful one. By the mid-1920s, Ford was living in a
world of his own. Anyone intruding on his idyll paid the price.

In the face of irrefutable evidence that his strategy was failing, Ford
nevertheless told *The New York Times* late in 1926, "The Ford car will continue to be made in the same way. . . . I am not governed by anybody's
figures but by my own information and observation."

"The old master had failed to master change," Alfred P. Sloan Jr. recalled
in 1963. "Don't ask me why." We can answer why. It was because of Ford's
denial of reality.

Henry Ford at last had to come to terms with the fact that the Model T
had run its course. It had won the hearts of Americans, but they were fleeing from it in droves as customers. "He could not continue losing sales and
maintain his profits," wrote Sloan, so "the Model T fell."

This marked the end of the leadership of the Ford Motor Company.
Occasionally over the next decade it would beat GM in sales. However, with
the exception of three years (1929, 1930, and 1935), Ford has trailed GM
in share of market by a wide margin for eight decades. Whether it will
continue to trail GM in the wake of the current crisis in the industry remains to be seen.

Although the question on everybody's mind was the one posed by the
journalist whose chart we used earlier—"What will Ford do next?"—the
answer came as quite a shock. "Not many observers expected as catastrophic and almost whimsical a fall," Sloan later wrote, "as Mr. Ford chose

to take when he shut down the great River Rouge plant completely and kept it shut down for nearly a year to retool, leaving the field to Chevrolet unopposed and opening it up for Mr. Chrysler's Plymouth."

"Catastrophic" is a well-chosen word. Shutting down the River Rouge for a year cost between $200 million and a quarter-of-a-billion dollars. Apparently there was never any question of bringing out a "new and improved" Model T. Nor was there a question about keeping the Model T in production while a newer automobile was introduced to the market. General Motors was selling five different nameplates. Surely, Ford could sell two. Ford had purchased the Lincoln Motor Company in 1922, but its sales were negligible. The Mercury was bought out in 1938, but it did not matter either. All Ford's efforts were focused on the Model T's replacement, the new Model A.

It is intriguing to see Sloan describe Ford's decision as "almost whimsical." *Whimsy* is not a word one expects from Sloan, and my guess is it appears nowhere else in his writings. Its use here shows that to a rational man such as Sloan, who knew the industry as well as any man living at the time, Ford's course of action was far more radical and far more destructive of the value in his firm than was remotely necessary.

Unlike the early Ford, Sloan was not in business to put America on wheels. Unlike the later Ford, Sloan was not in business to make more cars. He was, by contrast, in business to make money. "The measure of the worth of a business enterprise [is] return on the shareholders' investment," Sloan wrote, "since it is their capital that is being risked and it is in their interests first of all that the corporation is supposed to be run." By 1927, Ford could not have given anything approaching so succinct a statement of what he was doing on the River Rouge.

We do know that he remained steadfast in his denial of what the automobile market had become. After killing off the Model T, he created the Model A.

Note that this was not called the Model U, following T; nor was it given a stylish name like Cadillac. It was as if Ford would reset the clock and start all over again at the age of sixty-four. The Model A was a technical advance over its predecessor. However, although the company's car model changed, its business model did not. It planned to ride the Model A the same way it had ridden the Model T. There would be no "car for every purse and purpose," no annual model change. The Model T was finished as a product. It was not finished as an idea. That is to say, it was finished as an idea in the marketplace but not in Henry Ford's mind.

Henry Ford never changed. By the end of World War II, his company was skirting the edge of bankruptcy. It was saved by his grandson Henry Ford II, who took the company over and, with the help of the "Whiz Kids," brought it back to life. The company's rebirth is a story for another day.

2

What Denial Is,
and Is Not

In *States of Denial*, sociologist Stanley Cohen refers to a scene in Saul Bellow's novel *Mr. Sammler's Planet*. Elya, the title character's nephew, is a doctor lying in the hospital after an operation for a blood clot. Sammler says to himself, "Elya would die of a hemorrhage. Did he know this? Of course he did. He was a physician, so he must know. But he was human, so he could arrange many things for himself. Both knowing and not knowing—one of the most frequent human arrangements."

A frequent human arrangement, Cohen says, and an enigmatic one. "The ability to deny is an amazing human phenomenon," he writes, "largely unexplained and often inexplicable, a product of the sheer complexity of our emotional, linguistic, moral, and intellectual lives."

Denial *is* mysterious and complicated. Let us attempt a brief discussion of what denial is and is not, how it works, and why it exists. This will require a brief theoretical discussion, the goal of which is purely practical: to provide greater context for the examples in this book and, most importantly, to help you better understand how you can identify and overcome denial.

. . .

On April 7, 1923, in Vienna, Austria, Sigmund Freud's physician paid him a visit. Freud, an incessant cigar smoker, asked him to examine his mouth, warning his doctor to "be prepared to see something you won't like." Indeed he did. Freud had cancer of the jaw and palate. His physician told him to have the growth removed and to stop smoking. Freud did have the growth removed. But he did not stop smoking. He was sixty-six years old at the time of the diagnosis.

Freud was a physician, and he knew that cigars could cause oral cancer. But now, cancer was no longer a risk. It was not a probability. It was a cold, hard fact. Undeniable.

Freud's cancer did not recur until 1936. It eventually caused his death on September 23, 1939, when he chose assisted suicide over the continued agony of the advancing disease.

From 1923 onward, Freud was constantly plagued by precancerous growths that had to be surgically removed. He underwent more than thirty operations for this purpose. He had to be fitted for a prosthesis to separate his nasal and oral cavities. According to Peter Gay, Freud's most important biographer, the prosthesis "was a torment to put in or take out, often chafing or irritating. . . . Some measure of discomfort never left him."

The voice of this once "masterly lecturer and brilliant conversationalist . . . never really recovered in clarity and resonance." The operations eventually cost him his hearing in his right ear, and his famous analytic couch had to be moved from one side of his office to the other so he could hear his patients. Eating became difficult, and he began to avoid dining in public.

The price Freud paid for those cigars is difficult to overstate. Yet this man who conceived of himself as dedicated to the truth above all else— the truth in spite of the pain it might cause his friends, his admirers, and himself—could not stop smoking. In the words of Professor Gay, "Freud's inability to give up smoking vividly underscores the shrewdness in his observation of *an all-too-human disposition he called knowing-and-not-knowing, a state of rational apprehension that does not result in appropriate action* [emphasis mine]."

This is ironic, since it was Freud who first described denial in a psychological context. The word he used was *Verleugnung*, which is variously translated as either "denial" or "disavowal." For Freud, *Verleugnung* was an unconscious defense mechanism against external realities that threaten the ego—a basic formulation of denial that survives to this day.

Freud's key to unlocking the riddle of denial was the insight that mental processes are split into the conscious and the unconscious. Without such duality, the notion of "knowing but not knowing" would make no sense.

As Immanuel Kant wrote in 1797 in *The Metaphysics of Morals*, "To deceive oneself on purpose seems to contain a contradiction." That is, unless there is more than one being inside "oneself."

"The strange behavior of patients in being able to combine a conscious knowing with not knowing remains inexplicable by what is called normal psychology," Freud wrote in 1913. "But to psychoanalysis, which recognizes the existence of the unconscious, it presents no difficulty."

The discovery of the unconscious made it possible to conceive of the mind's becoming aware of something but protectively burying it out of conscious recognition. We have the knowledge. But we are not aware that we have it. We know, yet we don't know.

In *Vital Lies, Simple Truths*, Daniel Goleman describes a set of psychology experiments performed in the 1960s. Subjects were shown pictures, some of which contained sexual imagery, while a special camera precisely tracked their eye movements. Some of the subjects, presumably those less comfortable with sex, managed to avoid letting their gaze stray even once to the sexually provocative parts of the pictures. When asked about the pictures some days later, they recalled little or nothing suggestive about them.

"In order to avoid looking," Goleman writes, "some element of the mind must have known first what the picture contained, so that it knew what to avoid. The mind somehow grasps what is going on and rushes a protective filter into place, thus steering awareness away from what threatens."

Herbert Fingarette, a philosopher who has studied denial, asserts that this kind of self-deception "is as ordinary and familiar a kind of mental activity as one can imagine." As an example, he cites the everyday process of writing. A writer's conscious awareness is focused almost entirely on arranging his thoughts, choosing the words to express them, and similar challenges. But writing requires a myriad of other tasks that he is rarely, if ever, aware of: the physical act of gripping the pen, for example, or moving his fingers to tap the correct keys. The writer could choose to pay attention to these things if he wanted, and he does so when necessary—if his pen runs out of ink, for example. But for the most part, he chooses, effortlessly and without being aware of doing so, to direct his attention elsewhere.

Even in today's multitasking world, paying attention to *everything* is impossible, so we are constantly making unconscious choices about what to notice. This of course means that we are also always making unconscious choices about what *not* to notice. Usually the candidates for inattention are automatic or extraneous things, such as the physical act of writing or the background buzz of traffic outside our window. But sometimes they are difficult or distressing realities from which we wish to protect ourselves. This is where denial comes in.

Sometimes we divert information from awareness because it is too painful or stressful. This is denial as anesthetic. More commonly, we do so because the offending information contradicts assumptions with which we are comfortable, and it is easier to reject the information than to change our assumptions. Sometimes, this diversion is explicit. "I will look at any additional evidence to confirm the opinion to which I have already come," Lord Molson, an English politician of the last century, is said to have declared. More often, it is unconscious. As another Englishman, Sir Arthur Conan Doyle, has Sherlock Holmes explain to Dr. Watson in "A Scandal in Bohemia," "Insensibly, one begins to twist facts to suit theories, instead of theories to suit facts."

This feat can be accomplished individually, but it is often a group effort. Thus the conspiracy of silence—or conspiracy of concurrence—known as groupthink. The term was coined by journalist William H. Whyte Jr. in a 1952 article in *Fortune* magazine but more fully developed two decades later by Yale psychologist Irving L. Janis. In *Victims of Groupthink*, his psychological study of the decision-making processes that produced such foreign-policy fiascos as the Bay of Pigs and Vietnam, Janis explored how the quest for group cohesion can spawn shared illusions, rationalizations, and denial.

Janis identified several common symptoms of groupthink. Among them are:

- The illusion of invulnerability
- Rejection or rationalization of data that might cause the group to reconsider its assumptions
- The stifling of dissenting views that undermine shared illusions
- Self-censorship by group members of dissenting views

- Self-appointed "mindguards" who protect the group from adverse information that might shatter shared assumptions
- Stereotyped, demeaning views of competitors

At your next meeting, be on guard for these symptoms of what Princeton's Roland Bénabou calls "mutually assured delusion." If you encounter any of them, don't fall prey to denial. Don't let them pass by unnoticed.

• • •

If denial is so harmful, why is it so common? Some sociobiologists assert that denial evolved as the handmaiden of deceit. Believing our own lies made us more believable liars, the theory goes, and better liars were more likely to survive. Natural selection therefore favored self-deception. This is an intriguing theory but not an easy one to prove.

Another way to explain denial's persistence is that it makes us feel better. In the introduction to this book, I mentioned that denial enabled me and my dying wife to enjoy a much needed "disease-free weekend." Denial is common in cases of illness and death. It is the first step in psychiatrist Elisabeth Kübler-Ross's well-known five-stage model for dealing with grief and tragedy, which she set forth in her book *On Death and Dying*. Far from dismissing denial, Kübler-Ross embraced it as a healthy way of dealing with the most difficult of situations. "Denial functions as a buffer after unexpected shocking news," she wrote. "[It] allows the patient to collect himself and, with time, mobilize other, less radical defenses."

Consider the saying "Better a lie that heals than a truth that wounds." This is not always the case, but hope often depends on illusion. Substituting optimism for hard-nosed realism sometimes makes people happier and healthier. To someone who is dying, certainly, a vain hope may be preferable to utter despair.

But these things are only true in cases where the outcome is inevitable and no amount of fact-facing can alter it. When the ending to the story is at all in doubt, denial can be harmful, even fatal. For example, some studies have found that patients who avoid thinking about surgery ahead of time recover faster than those who obsess about the impending procedure. But the presurgical patients in these studies had nothing to gain from worrying. Now imagine a medical situation in which the patient's action or inaction *does* matter—say, a diabetic who's in denial and doesn't monitor his blood-sugar level—and you see the difference.

One of the difficulties of dealing with denial is that even when there is no more than a sliver of hope that one can affect the outcome, some measure of denial that there are great odds against your success can in some cases pay dividends. Consider the hero who, rather than weighing rational odds, rushes the machine-gun nest or tackles the hijacker. Or the baseball team that redoubles its efforts even though it is down three games to none in the championship series and no team in the long history of the sport has ever overcome such a deficit. At least some denial is at work in all of these cases. And at least some benefit, to the denier and sometimes to others, can come from that self-deception.

In business, consider the prospective entrepreneur, the dreamer whose odds of success are famously long. If there were no denial of those odds, no optimism or "protective stupidity," who in his right mind would ever start a new business? How would any new enterprise ever come into being?

When all the evidence points to long odds, denial can seemingly lead to notable triumph. "They laughed at Edison," as the saying goes. But figuring out exactly what those odds are—and whether and when denial truly comes into play—is tricky. There may be, for example, only a 10 percent chance that any new venture will succeed. But what are the odds for someone with an inordinate amount of self-confidence? Or superior education? Or family wealth? Or extensive background in the field? Or a record of success in previous ventures? These people can easily say that their venture has a good chance of being among that 10 percent . . . or 5 percent . . . or even 1 percent. Are they in denial?

It is easy for an imaginative man to talk himself out of an unappealing probability. Consider this observation attributed by Stendhal to Schiller: "Disconnected remarks and chance meetings are transformed into undeniable proofs in the eyes of a man of imagination if there is some flame burning in his heart." What does a 10 percent chance that something will happen really mean? What, for example, does a forecast of a 10 percent chance of rain mean? It means that either it will rain or it won't, which you knew before the forecast. But what is the proof? If it does rain, the forecaster has covered himself by saying it might. If it does not, he may actually have been incorrect. There might have been no chance at all that it would rain, not even 10 percent.

The denial with which this book is concerned is not the gray area of a calculated roll of the dice, however. It is the unwillingness to see or admit a truth that ought to be apparent and is in fact apparent to many others. Sometimes, the denial is literal, the assertion that the reality in question simply is not true or did not happen. This delusion is often achieved by discounting the source or shooting the messenger. We have seen this with Henry Ford when he fired Ernest Kanzler. In other instances, the denial is interpretive. One accepts the facts but denies their implications: *It doesn't apply to us. It's not a big deal. It's not our problem. It's never happened in the past. It can't happen here. There's nothing we can do about it.* And so on. We will encounter many examples of interpretive denial in the coming chapters.

Finally, a point of clarification. There are almost as many ways to go wrong in business as there are businesses. Only some of those involve denial. Those instances are what this book is about. Our focus here is *denial that is avoidable and that leads to failure.* A graphic representation may help to make the point:

Denial Flowcart

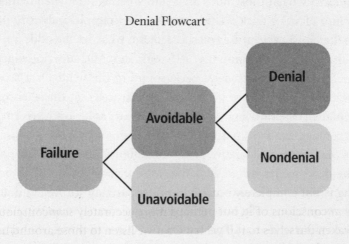

As the graphic illustrates, not all failures are avoidable. If the failure is inevitable, it is not our concern here, because no matter how squarely the facts are faced, they cannot be changed. Denial is irrelevant to the outcome. For example, let's say you were in the buggy-whip business in 1899, and you refused to believe that the automobile would ever replace the horse and carriage. This is a classic case of denial—but not relevant for our purposes, since it didn't much matter. The automobile was a bullet that could not be dodged.

Likewise, not all avoidable failures result from denial. This distinction is important. As we just mentioned, there are a million ways to blunder in business. You can make a bad bet—knowingly take a risk and lose. You can be ignorant, as opposed to *willfully* ignorant, of the facts. You can be stupid. You can miss the key point, fact, or metric amidst the static of less relevant or misleading information. You can simply make an honest mistake. You can just be wrong on an issue about which reasonable people can disagree. None of these are examples of denial.

Neither should we equate denial with what is commonly described as avoidance. One can knowingly choose to banish a hard truth from one's "selective attention" for strategic or tactical reasons. Take for example a cyclist on a long, grueling climb up a mountain. As a psychological ploy, he deliberately averts his gaze from the distant peak and focuses only on the few yards in front of his front wheel, choosing to divide the task into a series of small, achievable steps rather than see it in its intimidating whole. This is not denial. The cyclist's choice to attack the problem in this manner is just that: a choice. When you're in control, it is not denial (at least not the kind you have to worry about). When you're not, it is.

Luckily, despite its association with the unconscious mind, denial is a process over which we sometimes *can* exercise some measure of control. There are times and circumstances when we have the ability to turn our "selective attention" to what we are in danger of denying or have already denied—if we make the effort to do so. Sometimes the reality that we are denying is not completely buried, but only partially so. We are not completely *un*conscious of it, but perhaps more accurately *semi*conscious. We can awaken ourselves to it if we try. Or if we listen to those around us who see the truth and try to persuade us to see it too. As we will discover more than once later on, our willingness to heed their warnings often makes the difference between denial and awareness, failure and success.

Denial is a powerful impulse, but we are not entirely powerless to resist it. Through self-knowledge, openness to criticism, and receptivity to facts and perspectives that challenge our own, we can arm ourselves against denial. This is easier said than done, as we will see. But as Part II of this book will show, it is not impossible.

3

The Technological Chasm:
Denial in the Tire Industry

"The major tire companies have a virtually unthreatened hold on U.S. tire sales," announced *Sales Management* magazine in April 1970. The five major tire companies were Goodyear, Firestone, Uniroyal, BFGoodrich, and GenCorp; and the magazine's assessment was understandable.

Since World War II, the economy of the United States had rotated around a Detroit-Pittsburgh axis. Astride the axis is Akron, Ohio, the rubber city. Founded in 1825, Akron is the home of the Soap Box Derby. Alcoholics Anonymous was born there during the Great Depression. But for decades during the late nineteenth and twentieth centuries, Akron was most well known as the center of the nation's rubber industry.

For decades, Akron was the headquarters of the tire business in the United States. Its population tripled from roughly 70,000 to 210,000 during the 1910s, all because of tires. This looked like destiny, and it looked like it would last forever.

In the 1970s and 1980s, however, the "radial revolution" rocked the tire industry. The long-established tire firms met radials with denial. Their denial of the impact of this new technology took place in two distinct phases. At first, they refused to believe that radial tires would succeed in the American market the way they had in Europe. Second, after it became clear that radials would indeed make it in America, the tire manufacturers denied that their world would change forever. Denial, however, does not change reality. It simply makes reality tougher to deal with. Today, no tires are produced for the mass market in Akron, only a few specialty tires for high-performance vehicles.

The rubber industry preceded the rise of automobiles. Benjamin Franklin Goodrich was lured to Akron by an entrepreneurial chamber of commerce and established his rubber business there in 1870. Twelve years later, eleven companies merged to form the United States Rubber Company, the only major firm in the industry not located in Akron (it was headquartered in Naugatuck, Connecticut). Both these firms produced industrial products, such as belting and hose, and consumer goods, especially rubberized footwear and outer garments.

With the coming of the automobile, the market for tires expanded dramatically. Dozens of new firms, most of them clustered in Akron, entered the rubber industry to serve the tire market. Two of these survived the inevitable shakeout and became historically important—Goodyear, founded in 1898, and Firestone, established two years later. The last domestic tire manufacturer to enter the industry and survive over an extended period was GenCorp, founded in 1915.

It is no wonder that *Sales Management* remarked upon the market power of the five major manufacturers. In 1919, they dominated the industry, with Goodyear ranked first, followed by Uniroyal, Firestone, BFGoodrich, and GenCorp. A half a century later, the same five firms were on top, with the only difference being that Firestone and Uniroyal had switched places in market share.

The five majors were big companies in 1970. Goodyear ranked 20th on the *Fortune* 500 in terms of sales, Firestone was 37th, Uniroyal 66th, Goodrich 90th, and GenCorp 106th. These firms had long-established relationships with their suppliers. They had networks of company outlets numbering in the hundreds.

Their relations with the automobile manufacturers were equally stable and long-lived. General Motors ranked first in the *Fortune* 500 in 1970, followed by Ford (third) and Chrysler (sixth). The "Big Three" annually divided their purchases among the big five tire suppliers. The tire companies sold about 30 percent of their output to the Big Three automobile manufacturers in Detroit and the remaining 70 percent through their company-owned stores, through large chain distribution outlets such as

Sears and Atlas (owned by Esso, now known as ExxonMobil), or through any of the thousands of smaller distributors such as independent gasoline stations or auto repair shops.

In 1966, the Federal Trade Commission found that the top four tire firms accounted for 74 percent of industry shipments. (In 1919, the same four firms sold 65 percent of the nation's tires.) In 1970, if we include GenCorp, the top five firms were responsible for more than four fifths of the nation's tire sales. Despite periodic efforts, foreign manufacturers had failed to make an impact in the United States. They accounted for under 4 percent of sales in 1970.

Tires were a tough business for an outsider to break into. Industry ties had existed for generations. For instance, William Clay Ford Sr., Henry Ford's grandson, married Martha Firestone, Harvey Firestone's granddaughter, in 1947.

The rough-and-tumble world of "creative destruction" that is supposed to characterize capitalism was far removed indeed from the placid atmosphere in Akron. "On Friday and Saturday night," in the words of an old-timer, "everybody who was anybody in the tire industry drank together at the Portage Country Club." Often, executives from the four Akron-based tire companies (this leaves Uniroyal out) would form a foursome on the links. Many of these men had spent their whole business lives in the same city climbing the executive ladder rung by rung at the same company.

This was a stable, predictable world. For two decades following 1948, growth was constant. Sales of new automobiles increased from under 4 million to nearly 9 million. Replacement tire sales grew every year but one during those decades. Even though profits were never quite what one wished—for a variety of reasons they hovered around the all-manufacturing average—there was a *Mad* magazine Alfred E. Neuman "What? Me worry?" attitude in Akron. Executives recalled those days fondly. Theirs was a "no-brainer" industry where the hardest decision was where to build the next plant.

There was, alas, a cloud on the horizon. It was called the radial tire. The radial tire was no secret in 1970 when *Sales Management* wrote of the immortality of the incumbent American tire manufacturers. The quartets golfing at Portage that year knew about radials as well. But no one dreamed that the advent of radials would cause a fundamental restructuring of the industry. In just a few years, at the end of the 1980s, four of the five tire firms just mentioned had ceased to exist. Only Goodyear has survived, and just barely.

This upheaval was predictable in 1970. But no one predicted it. Reality was too terrible to face. So everyone denied it.

In 1970, the American tire manufacturers were selling "bias-ply" rather than radial tires almost exclusively. What was the difference? Bias-ply tires were made by putting down layers of rubberized fabric, or plies, finished with a rubber tread. These plies were connected at a diagonal angle, or bias, to the direction of travel. In a radial tire, in contrast, the plies ran from one bead of the wheel's rim to the other, perpendicular to the direction of travel. Radial tires also included an extra ply made from steel wire coated with rubber.

If you are not an engineer, the words just provided are not going to be particularly helpful. The point to grasp is the consumer benefit of radials over bias-ply tires. Above all, radials lasted longer.

The life expectancy of a bias-ply tire in the mid-1960s was about twelve thousand miles. Radials lasted about forty thousand miles. The purchase price of radials was 30 percent to 50 percent higher than of bias-ply, but their longevity combined with improved gas mileage meant that the radial was actually less expensive than a bias tire per mile driven.

Tires were the most obnoxious component of an automobile for many consumers. They were expensive and frequently replaced. Nevertheless— or perhaps for this very reason—automobile manufacturers did not provide a warranty for the tires they sold mounted on new cars. A flat tire is among the most annoying of driving experiences. A blowout is potentially hazardous. Longer-lived radials mitigated these problems and were thus a boon to consumers. They were, however, a menace to U.S. tire manufacturers.

To understand why, we must note that the five big tire makers could sell plenty of product without making much money. It was simply not possible for Akron to make money selling to Detroit. Firestone, for example, actually lost $1.1 million on an operating-earnings basis from 1969 to 1973 inclusive of its business with the Big Three. It was equally difficult to make money selling to the huge chains.

Professor Michael E. Porter has identified five forces that determine industry attractiveness, forces that shape how companies in a particular industry generate sales and then capture those sales as profits: bargaining power of suppliers, bargaining power of buyers, threat of new entrants, threat of substitute products, and rivalry among existing competitors.

On some of these dimensions, the tire industry looked pretty good in 1970. The bargaining power of suppliers was minimal. It was at least as difficult for a commodity chemical company to make money selling carbon black to Firestone as it was for Firestone to make a buck selling a tire to Ford.

Nor was there a threat of substitute products. According to *Value Line*, "There is no substitute for the pneumatic tire and we doubt that one is forthcoming. So long as there are automobiles, there will be demand for tires." That was true when it was written in 1990, it is true today, and it will be true for the foreseeable future.

New entrants did not pose a problem either. No company had entered the domestic industry since 1923, and that one did not last. The barriers to entry were high. It took considerable capital to build a tire plant, and patterns of doing business were long established.

There was always the potential menace that one of the big Detroit firms might backward integrate into tires. Ford actually did produce them for a couple of years in the late 1930s. But this was customarily used more as a threat to keep suppliers in line than as a real possibility. The mediocre profits in tires stood as a powerful deterrent to those looking to start new ventures.

Rivalry among competitors was on the basis of frills and fads rather than the development of fundamental competitive advantage. The tire companies spent a good deal of money on advertising and auto racing, but that was about it. They produced tires with whitewalls in a variety of widths, but that only increased costs (variety costs money) and decreased quality (variety also adds complexity).

The real problem was the bargaining power of buyers. They were the channel commanders in this business. Tire manufacturers only made money in replacement tires sold through their company-owned stores or through small, independent dealers. All the other outlets, such as mass-merchandisers or gas stations owned by major oil refiners, dwelled in the land of the giants, where the purchasers were at least as large as the tire companies themselves.

Radials were a dagger at the heart of tire profitability. Forty thousand miles was 3⅓ times more durable than Akron's standard-issue bias-ply. The tire companies were thus face-to-face with a technological chasm it was very hard to see across.

Technology casts a long shadow. Michelin had been marketing radials in commercial quantities in Europe since 1948. By 1965, they accounted for 70 percent of the French market. That year, radials began to diffuse with dramatic speed through other major nations in Western Europe.

The American firms were aware of these developments. Three of them had European subsidiaries manufacturing radials. As early as 1966, Sears, at the time the largest retailer in the United States, began to source radials from Michelin on a private label basis—the Allstate radial. In 1968, *Consumer Reports* awarded five of its top six ratings to radials even though they made up a mere 2 percent of the American market that year. In July of 1969, Michelin announced plans to build a large plant in Nova Scotia to penetrate the American market. For Michelin, which until the Sears order had not sold tires in the United States, every tire was "plus business." For the American incumbents, every Michelin radial sold meant three fewer bias-ply sales for them.

Careening toward catastrophe, what was the response? First came the telltale sign that people are scared—trash-talking. Europeans and Americans were somehow *different* from one another when it came to tires, one of the world's least style-intensive products. Akron, commented *Fortune* as late as 1974, "tended to sniff at the belted radial as a 'European' tire—okay perhaps for little doodlebugs scooting around on cobblestones, but not suited to the high-powered sofas on wheels that Americans piloted." Bias-ply construction provided flexibility in the face of bumps and potholes, the manufacturers contended, giving American drivers the sense that they were driving moving living rooms.

The radial was, in the words of a Goodyear vice president in 1974, "a sophisticated tire. If the American car owner doesn't learn to take better care of his tires, he's going to be badly disappointed with his radials. There is definitely the possibility of a disenchantment with radials a few years down the road." Americans were used to sloppily constructed tires slapped together in aging plants by disaffected workers. In the words of one engineer, "You could leave out one of the plies of a four-ply tire by mistake, and the average driver wouldn't know the difference." You could not build a radial like this and get away with it.

What can one make of all this blather when faced with cold, hard facts? Radials lasted longer. They had less rolling resistance and thus delivered better gas mileage. They held the road better, especially in wet conditions. In short, they represented every industry's nightmare—a technological development that was good for your customers but bad for you. Moreover, they constituted an invitation to foreign firms to penetrate the American market. Not only Michelin but Bridgestone, the Japanese tire giant, began exporting radials to the United States in 1971. Apparently, the Japanese scooted around on cobblestones in doodlebugs just like the Europeans.

As if all this were not trouble enough, radials could not be manufactured in plants designed to produce bias-ply tires. In the early 1970s, tire executives were estimating that it would cost between $600 million and $900 million in new plants and equipment for the domestic industry to convert to radials. The workforce would doubtless also have to be retrained. Radials required greater "accuracy and consistency" in factories that had become accustomed over decades to sloppiness.

No wonder the industry was in denial about radials. It appeared inevitable that the radial revolution would force it to spend more in order to make less.

Denial in the case of radials took two basic forms. One we have already discussed: the belief that, although radials had swept the European market, they would not cross the Atlantic and wind up over here. The second form was the belief that radials were not necessarily bad news. Or, more precisely, that they might provide an opportunity for the second-tier players in the tire business to leapfrog the leaders.

Since the 1920s, Goodyear had been the largest tire manufacturer in the world. Known as the "gorilla," Goodyear controlled a healthy share of the market year after year. From the time the firm achieved market dominance, smaller firms would often quote their prices as percentages of Goodyear's list price.

Considerably smaller than Goodyear, but still in its class when considered in the context of the industry as a whole, was Firestone. As one business magazine noted in 1972, "In the rubber industry there are two good big companies, Goodyear and Firestone, and two large also-rans, Uniroyal and BFGoodrich. (The industry's fifth large company, General Tire, is really another kind of kitty [presumably because it was so diversified])."

Both Goodrich and Uniroyal tried to innovate their way out of their secondary positions in the industry. Goodrich tried early and vigorously. The first mention of radial tires in its annual report was in 1963. In 1965, it announced the "most revolutionary automotive development by BFGoodrich since the tubeless tire ... the Silvertown Radial 990 passenger car tire. . . . This is the first American-made radial passenger car tire to be developed and offered commercially for all American-made automobiles."

Unfortunately for Goodrich, the Silvertown radial failed. The reasons for this failure provided by the trade press at the time are not altogether satisfactory. The company's "research pioneering," it was alleged, was "wasted by its marketing and management ineptness." Its radials were adjudged "a dismal flop." A Wall Street analyst called Goodrich's foray into radials "one of the major errors ever made by a manufacturer in the judging of a market."

Despite this dismal outcome, Uniroyal tried its hand at improving its market position through radials a few years later. The company's annual report for 1972 observed, "The tire industry is in a period of extensive change. Revolution, perhaps, is too strong a word [it actually was quite appropriate]. Most certainly, it is an extremely rapid technical evolution which is having a profound effect on tire production, performance, and marketing." Uniroyal's Rallye 180 tire was described as "one of the most popular radials in Europe," where three quarters of the tires sold were radials, as opposed to just under 7 percent in the United States.

Uniroyal decided to invest in radials in the American market with its Zeta 40M. This met the fate of Goodrich's Silvertown.

An important reason for the failure of Goodrich and Uniroyal to commercialize radials was Goodyear, which led the way in developing the "bias-belted" tire in the hope that this halfway measure would block the move to radials.

Bias-belted tires featured a belt of polyester fiber or fiberglass under their tread. This modification increased tire life, it was claimed, to twenty thousand miles or more. Many experts, however, including *Consumer Reports*, disputed that claim.

It was also alleged that the radial tire would demand changes to the suspension systems of the automobiles manufactured by the Big Three. How costly such changes would be or indeed if they were really necessary at all was always a matter of dispute.

At any rate, from the point of view of the tire manufacturers, the bias-belted tire did not demand any real changes in tooling or production methodology, which was a definite plus. True, twenty thousand miles was longer than twelve thousand, which meant eating into the vital replacement business. However, at the risk of stating the obvious, it was not as bad as the forty thousand miles radials promised.

But bias-belted tires were soon widely recognized as a stopgap. Goodyear and Firestone were not only the nation's two largest rubber companies, they were also the least diversified. Even though both entered the 1970s with a decade of growth behind them and strong balance sheets, both had a lot to lose unless they could somehow craft an effective response to the radial revolution.

By 1972, General Motors and Ford made it clear that they were going to equip their cars with radials. No more stopgaps. No turning back. By now it was clear that radials were going to sweep America in the 1970s just as they had Europe in the previous decade. Everyone knew it. The projections of U.S. radial penetration in the early 1970s based on the existing European data turned out to be remarkably accurate.

Few people in the industry thought through the implications of the radial revolution. Most executives thought the oligopoly would somehow continue to function. This was impossible. But it was believed because the alternative was too draconian fully to take in. People believed it because they wanted to believe it. They had to believe it.

Here, then, is how the industry looked:

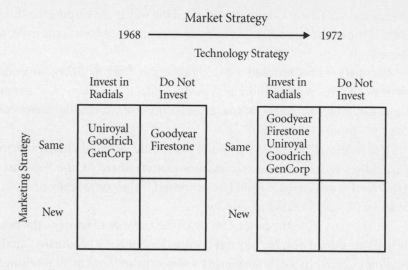

By 1968, the three smaller and more diversified tire manufacturers were at least willing to experiment with finding out what the radial revolution might mean to their companies. The two industry leaders were trying to stop the future.

As you can see, by 1972 when the Big Three made it clear that they were going radial, all five firms in what had appeared to be an immortal oligopoly had decided to manufacture and market radials. Moreover, all five were maintaining their marketing strategies. They were committed to selling to the Big Three at or even below cost, still assuming that they would somehow make their money on replacements.

The upper-left quadrant of that matrix was the one cell in which none of those companies belonged. If they were going to market a longer-lasting tire, it was simply essential that they charge enough for it to stay in business. This meant higher prices in the replacement market, which should have been sustainable because, although the consumer would be paying more per tire, he would be purchasing fewer tires. It also meant that they would have to shake off their historic vassalage to the original equipment manufacturers (OEMs) and charge higher prices for what was, after all, a better-performing tire that was more expensive to produce.

In other words, the vertical axis on the chart above simply had to change. The tire companies had to move from the old marketing strategy of making money solely from their own company stores and small dealers to a new marketing strategy that required raising prices across the board to fund the necessary added investment and to return reasonable profits to shareholders. Otherwise, they were heading toward the unprofitable graveyard of once viable companies.

The price of radials was indeed above that of bias tires. At the 1974 price points, which represented a premium of slightly more than 70 percent, the tire manufacturers were still far removed from the added value of a tire that lasted three times longer than its predecessor.

It was not going to be easy to push prices up yet further. Michelin, a privately held company more interested in long-term market share than short-term profits, was standing in the wings more than happy to sell radials to the OEMs; and the carmakers let them know that they were willing to buy. Indeed, Ford mounted Michelin radials on the Lincoln for the 1970 model year. Not everyone was thrilled with this decision. When the boss, Henry Ford II, happened to notice it, he demanded to know, "Who put those damn Frog tires on the Lincoln?" Notwithstanding this characteristic outburst, the decision to source Lincoln tires from abroad was a shot across the bow of the domestic industry.

Let us take a look at the responses of two of these companies to the industry crisis they faced. In both cases, denial played the central role in their failed attempts to extricate themselves from the collapse of their profit model. We will begin with Firestone and then turn to BFGoodrich.

Firestone decided to compete in radials. It claimed that the key to its survival was not a new marketing strategy but rather production breakthroughs. These breakthroughs would enable Firestone factories to turn out radials on bias-ply equipment.

Firestone's engineers were congratulated for this achievement in the decidedly upbeat annual report for 1973. The tone was the result not only of the money-saving news on the production front, but because of the company's finances. Sales increased more than 17 percent, the twelfth successive annual rise. Profits were up over 21 percent. Sure, there were some clouds on the horizon, but the company had "successfully faced and overcome major challenges and adverse conditions in the past." The report added, "We will continue to do so." When the company's president, Richard

A. Riley, was asked the following year about Firestone's future, he answered with a single word: "Growth." But for the rest of its existence, Firestone would never see another year like 1973.

The result of the putative production breakthroughs was the Firestone 500 Steel-Belted Radial, which quickly became the fastest-selling tire on the market. But problems surfaced just as quickly. On November 2, 1972, Firestone's director of development wrote a memorandum to the head of North American Tire Operations warning that the 500 was "badly in need of an improvement in belt separation performance, particularly at General Motors where we are in danger of being cut off by Chevrolet because of separation failures." Atlas, a division of ExxonMobil, told Firestone the following year that "it appears that Firestone is coming apart at the seams and drastic action is required." Warranty adjustments for the 500 in 1973 were 2½ times greater than for Firestone's bias tires. September of that year saw another salvo from the director of development: "We are making an inferior quality tire which will subject us to belt-edge separation at high mileage."

The evidence was everywhere apparent and everywhere ignored. Denial dominated, as *Time* magazine reported: "The company just kept churning out the 500 tires; they just kept failing; customers kept returning them. And company lawyers just kept defending lawsuits brought by accident victims—and their heirs." *Time*'s gallows humor captured in that last brief phrase was apt. Denial can lead to death. It is as blunt as that.

The Firestone Corporation was founded by Harvey Firestone back in 1900. The first tires he sold were to Ford, and Henry and Harvey liked to go camping together. Firestone sponsored high-toned television shows featuring opera soloists in the 1940s. Firestone owned rubber plantations around the world and had always been a full-line supplier. The country club it ran in Akron was open to any employee.

Firestone entered the 1970s as a fixture of the American industrial landscape. But it did not exit the decade that way.

The radial revolution and the Firestone 500 combined to kill the company. The man charged with saving what could be saved was John J. Nevin, a Harvard Business School graduate who was a veteran of Ford and Zenith and had no prior connection with Firestone or with the industry. When he took the helm, the denial that so plagued his predecessors was quite apparent to him. Only an outsider, it seems, was willing to look facts in the face.

Nevin's clear-eyed assessment was not a happy one. "The published information," he said, "didn't convey the severity of what was happening." The company was "hemorrhaging cash" at such a rapid rate that it might have led to bankruptcy. In short, Firestone "had a crisis and an organization that was not as demoralized as it should have been." That is because the organization was in denial. Nevin said his job would have been easier if the organization had been more willing to face facts.

Nevin sold off assets all over the world, reduced by almost two thirds the variety of tires the company produced, and fired people. Firestone employed 107,000 people in 1979, 80,000 in 1982, and 55,000 in 1987.

The 1980s proved a very different decade from the 1970s in the world of corporate America. The rise of a market for corporate control signaled an increased emphasis on shareholder value and concomitant limitations on the freedom of action of general managers. In 1988, Bridgestone, the giant of the Japanese tire industry, decided to buy what was left of Firestone. And in the process, Firestone's shareholders got lucky. The company's stock was selling at $31 a share in January. On February 16, 1988, Bridgestone announced its intention to buy many of Firestone's assets. With this news, the share price jumped about $15 to $47. Then, unexpectedly, the Italian tire manufacturer Pirelli offered to purchase all of Firestone's 31.7 million shares for $58 per share.

The response from Bridgestone on March 17 was even more unexpected. It countered with an offer that according to Professor W. Carl Kester of the Harvard Business School "astonished the financial community": $80 a share for all Firestone's shares. This represented "a fantastic 60% premium over pre-tender offer market prices." Bridgestone wound up purchasing Firestone for $2.56 billion. No one knows why it raised its bid to such heights. The trade press reported that the Japanese didn't like bidding wars. They certainly avoided one with this offer.

The consensus in 1988 and today is that Bridgestone paid a good deal more than Firestone was worth. When the deal was closed, Firestone's board of directors dined at an Italian restaurant—their way of symbolically thanking Pirelli for the bid that prompted Bridgestone's more-than-generous counteroffer.

There is a tragic addendum to the story of the company now known as Bridgestone/Firestone. During the 1990s, it became apparent that the new company was again producing tires that could be hazardous. The Firestone Wilderness AT tire, when mounted on the rear wheels of the Ford Explorer and driven on roads in hot climates, might result in a catastrophic failure— a blowout that would cause the Explorer to roll over with consequent danger of injury or even death.

On August 28, 2000, *The Wall Street Journal* observed, "Ford and Bridgestone/Firestone are writing the most important chapter in the history of product recalls since the Tylenol case [which we will encounter later in this book] eighteen years ago." Neither company handled itself as well as Johnson & Johnson, which owned Tylenol.

Bridgestone/Firestone's chief executive, Masatoshi Ono, at least had the good grace to apologize when he appeared before a congressional investigating committee on September 6, 2000. Ford languished in denial about its own responsibility. The first fatality resulting from a Firestone blowout on a Ford Explorer was reported to the National Highway Traffic Safety Agency way back in July 1992. By 1996 it was clear that the Ford Explorer and the Firestone Wilderness tire could be a lethal combination.

When on the lookout for denial, it is always a good idea to pay close attention to language. In August of 1999 when Ford started to replace Firestone tires sold in Saudi Arabia—remember, the problem only occurred in hot climates—it did not designate its action a recall, although that is undeniably what it was. Rather, Ford labeled its move a "customer notification enhancement action." This surely must rank with the worst examples of corporate-speak extant.

Ford's CEO, Jacques Nasser, was fired on October 29, 2001. His mishandling of the Ford/Firestone tire disaster was one of the reasons. He was replaced by William Clay Ford Jr., ironic considering one of the results of this episode is that the Ford Motor Company and Bridgestone/Firestone terminated commercial relations after almost a century of doing business together. "Billy" Ford is the great-grandson of Henry Ford and Harvey Firestone.

Another upshot of the tragedy, which by October 31, 2001, had caused an estimated 271 deaths (compared to 41 deaths attributed to the Firestone

500), was that for the first time Ford began to include tires in its standard automobile warranties.

Let us now turn our attention to the equally instructive story of BFGoodrich facing the radial. Recall that Goodrich embraced the radial early, in the hope that the change in technology would result in greater market share and profitability. Goodrich ran advertisements about the coming of the "Radial Age." But Goodyear outspent Goodrich by a factor of four in advertisements that trash-talked (perhaps one should say "trash-shouted" given the amount of money spent) radials and touted that limp stopgap, the bias-belted tire.

The late 1960s were rocky years for Goodrich. In 1969, Ben Heineman, a corporate raider of a type that would become quite familiar during the 1980s, attempted a hostile takeover of the company. CEO J. Ward Keener fended him off, but not by much.

J. Ward Keener is not well known today. The authoritative company history of BFGoodrich by Ohio State University historians Mansel G. Blackford and K. Austin Kerr treats Keener evenhandedly, but their ultimate verdict is not positive: "A man with great intelligence and a sharp analytical mind, Keener's weakness as an executive lay in more human qualities. He seemed aloof to less senior executives, a forbidding person lacking in empathy and warmth. A principled man, dedicated to his company and to his family, he simply lacked any leadership quality that could help him transcend the problem of the moment and command respect from subordinates."

Keener was not a native of Akron, as were so many other top tire-company executives in the 1960s. He was born in Alabama. However, he had a long history with Goodrich. He was an economics professor at Ohio Wesleyan in Delaware, Ohio, about one hundred miles down I-71 from Akron, when Goodrich first hired him as a consultant in 1937. Two years later, he left the groves of academe to join Goodrich. From that point on, he assumed the pattern of the Akron tire world—he worked his way to the top step by step and never worked for another company.

Although Keener's career was quite similar to that of so many other Akron big shots, he alone among his peers understood that *Sales Management*'s 1970 declaration was wrong. Following Goodrich's failed foray into the radial age and Heineman's raid, Keener realized that Goodrich could no longer continue to compete in the tire industry. The problem he now faced was, how do you exit this industry? An article in *Forbes* in 1975 asked, "Who would want to buy an ailing tire company? The bigger tire companies might be interested, but the Justice Department would almost surely block it [on antitrust grounds]. How do you liquidate a $1 billion tire company employing around 30,000 people and owning more than a few marginal plants?"

These questions seemed unanswerable. However, there *were* answers if you looked hard enough. Goodrich had brand recognition and a distribution system. Michelin had the technology and manufacturing capability but needed a key to open the American market. The two could make quite a team.

Keener arranged a secret meeting in Paris with top executives from Michelin. A joint venture was discussed. Michelin held all the high cards, but for reasons that we will never know, the Goodrich team could not accept that fact. Michelin, a proud, secretive, family-held private firm, insisted on being the senior partner in any joint venture. Goodrich could not quite take that leap. Apparently still living in the shadow of the French defeat and the American victory during World War II, the Goodrich executives simply could not deal with the truth, which was that the French were on top in this business and the Americans were second-raters. One wonders what next move the Goodrich executives could have thought possible as they flew back from Paris.

The fact is that Keener was out of ideas. He approached his board of directors with the suggestion that it recruit his successor from outside Goodrich, a remarkable proposal given that he himself had spent three decades there. The board not only agreed, it acted with unwonted dispatch— Keener was forced into retirement ahead of schedule to make room for the new CEO, O. Pendleton Thomas, an executive with the Atlantic Richfield Oil Company (ARCO).

Thomas had no ties to Akron or the tire industry. Soon Goodrich's top seven managers had been brought to the company from outside Akron, and Thomas began hiring outside consultants. He concluded that the tire industry was a loser for Goodrich and that the best way to handle the business was to milk it. That is to say, the tire division had to produce more cash than it consumed. Goodrich would put just enough money into the business to make it possible to sell itself to another company. Capacity was reduced. Goodrich was the first among the old-time oligopoly to terminate manufacture in Akron.

Goodrich continued to produce radials, but as of 1981 it stopped selling to what had been known as the Big Three. A decade previously, General Motors was Goodrich's biggest customer. Now it focused on the replacement market, where, as the 1981 annual report accurately pointed out, "returns are substantially higher." Goodrich never sold GM another tire. Once again, to benefit from "out of the box" thinking, someone had to be hired from out of the box.

1981
Technology Strategy

	Invest in Radials	Do Not Invest	
Goodyear Firestone Uniroyal GenCorp			Same
Goodrich [with radial investment at bare minimum]			New

(Marketing Strategy)

So if we return to the two-by-two matrix presented above, we can see that Goodrich was the first of the American firms to migrate out of the unsustainable cell on the upper-left quadrant.

By 1989, Bridgestone had purchased Firestone, and Uniroyal and Goodrich had spun off their tire businesses into the Uniroyal Goodrich Tire Company. The latter case proved once again that the merger of two weak companies invariably fails to produce a strong one. Uniroyal Goodrich was quickly gobbled up by Michelin. This is ironic considering that a decade earlier Goodrich had refused to become a junior partner in a joint venture with Michelin. Now Michelin was buying the whole company. In 1987, GenCorp sold its tire business to the German firm Continental. Of the "immortal oligopoly," only Goodyear remained.

At last, in 1996, Goodyear struggled to move out of the upper-left quadrant of the matrix. CEO Samir F. Gibara turned down $40 million of business from General Motors and successfully recouped it in the replacement market.

Lessons learned? A technological discontinuity as fundamental as radials is going to affect the structure of an industry. All five American companies denied that. They thrashed about trying to find half-court solutions to a full-court problem. What was needed was a clear-eyed, long-term view of the inevitable outcome of the decline in replacement tires resulting from the radial age, and of the entry into the domestic market of Michelin and also Bridgestone.

Denial is all about you—and how you view the world. Your view does not change the world, the realities of which you will inevitably have to face sooner or later.

4

"They Just Didn't Believe These Things Were Happening": Denial at the A&P

Never in the history of American business has the decline and fall of a company been more avoidable than in the case of the Great Atlantic and Pacific Tea Company, better known as the A&P. Denial, once again, was the culprit. In this case, the story of denial was internal to the company. The A&P was not undone by some new, orthogonal technology that rendered its business model obsolete. Nor was the problem foreign competition with new management methods or with privileged access to capital. What did the company deny? In this instance, that is a tough question. The best answer is that it denied the needs of the marketplace and the need to respond to the innovations of competitors. This is particularly ironic because it had managed the challenges of market leadership so well for so many years.

The company had a long run, longer than most American firms. The A&P was founded on Vesey Street in lower Manhattan by George F. Gilman in 1859. When it celebrated its centennial, it was the colossus of food distribution in the United States as well as the nation's largest retailer.

In 1950, the A&P was the third-largest corporation in the United States, behind only AT&T (which probably should not be counted because it was a government-sanctioned monopoly) and General Motors. Into the mid-1960s, it remained a force to be reckoned with. By the 1970s it was clear to everyone that it had lost its way.

In 1979, the A&P was acquired by the Tengelmann Group, a West German firm, and so ceased to be an American company. It did not take long for the acquisition to cause second thoughts. In just three years, it was being described as "Tengelmann's Vietnam," not a bad analogy. Tengelmann CEO Erivan Karl Haub said, "If we had it to do all over again, we wouldn't do it."

Doubtless to the surprise of most people reading these words, the A&P is still in business. Indeed, as of 2009, the company was operating in eight states and the District of Columbia and posting annual sales of close to $10 billion. It is, nevertheless, not much of a factor in an industry in which it was once the leader.

What went wrong? You can't point to one moment, one event, or one person. The whole set of people running the company went wrong over an extended period.

Intel CEO Andy Grove, in his classic *Only the Paranoid Survive*, introduced the phrase "strategic inflection point" into the business lexicon. The strategic inflection point is the moment at which the balance of forces shifts from the old structure, from the old ways of competing, to the new. Before the strategic inflection point, a company each year was simply more like it had always been. After the strategic inflection point, the company's situation changes fundamentally. It is a point where the curve has subtly but profoundly changed, never to change back. Hit it right, and "business goes to new heights." Hit it wrong and business declines. Here is how Grove pictures this moment:

The Inflection Curve

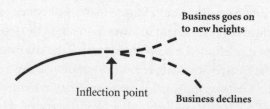

Business goes on to new heights

Inflection point

Business declines

As we shall see, the A&P experienced two strategic inflection points and navigated them both successfully. The question at hand is: Why did it fail at the third?

. . .

George Francis Gilman was born in Waterville, Maine, in 1826. When he opened up shop in New York City in 1859, he specialized in selling hides and leather goods. Soon, however, he was in the tea business and by the end of the Civil War he was running four stores in lower Manhattan. By the end of the decade, there were eleven, all in Manhattan.

Many early grocers began with tea. The United States was a predominantly rural nation throughout the nineteenth century. If food prices rose too high, consumers could grow their own. Tea, however, was a specialty item not cultivated in America, which gave the retailer a little latitude with regard to price.

Among Gilman's business acquaintances in the early years was another native of Maine, George Huntington Hartford. Details are hazy, but by 1870 Gilman and Hartford were partners. They were thinking big, naming their nascent chain the Great American Tea Company. And they had an idea. While others would mark tea up and make their money on margin, Great American would sell it for less and make its money on volume.

The company was aggressive. It increased the number of stores it owned as America urbanized, up to a hundred in 1881 and twice that many two decades later. It also diversified its product lines. "We first got into baking powder and then into extracts," recalled John A. Hartford, George Huntington Hartford's younger son, many years later. "We got into the grocery business gradually." A typical A&P store in the 1880s might carry six product categories. By 1911, an A&P store in New York City carried twenty-five product categories in a total of 270 varieties, ranging from 23 different kinds of tea to single selections of butter, cornstarch, and baking powder. At first, the company bought from independent wholesalers, but by the turn of the century it was relying to an increasing extent on its own company-owned warehouses. As its size increased, so did its vertical integration.

In 1900, the company posted sales of $5.6 million and profits of $125,000 on invested capital of $936,000. The following year, George F. Gilman died. Ownership of the company eventually passed into the hands of the Hartford family and remained there until its initial public offering in 1957. The company made the family one of the world's wealthiest.

George Huntington Hartford died in 1917, leaving an estate reportedly valued at a staggering $125 million. Well prior to his death, management of the company had passed to his two sons, George L. Hartford, or "Mr. George," who began as a cashier at the age of fifteen, and John A. Hartford, "Mr. John," who joined up in 1888 when he was sixteen. Mr. George and Mr. John ran the company into the 1950s. George was an accountant. It was John who was the real merchant, and he was to prove one of the greatest America ever produced.

In 1926, John Hartford had this to say to a meeting of A&P's top executives, "Unless we can operate in the future along economy lines, I do not believe I can put my heart in the business. . . . *I have always been a volume man* [emphasis mine] and it is hard to divert my mind to any other policy. If anybody feels this is the wrong policy, I want him to be frank and come out and say so." The room was silent. In other words, he wanted to stick to the policy of making money on volume rather than raising prices and making money on margin.

As early as World War I, John Hartford had established the power of the strategy of high volume made possible by low prices and low margins. It was his devout adherence to this policy that made it possible for A&P to make the right choice in the two strategic inflection points it handled well.

In 1900, the A&P was probably the largest food retailer in the United States. However, it did not dominate the industry. Historically, food retailing had been the stronghold of the small, local mom-and-pop shops. Freshness was critical for some products, such as baked goods, and many food stores prepared these on the premises. It was not as apparent that there were efficiencies to be captured in food retailing as it was in such manufacturing activities as steel production or oil refining, both of which were dominated by giant firms in 1900. However, such economies did indeed exist if entrepreneurs were shrewd enough to locate and exploit them.

The A&P must have been doing something right because sales tripled to $15 million in the first seven years of the new century. Some of this growth must be accounted for by a general increase in food prices. From 1900 to 1912, the price of food increased by more than a third. The much talked of "high cost of living" got a lot of attention, including government investigation.

In the midst of all this, the A&P was making increasing use of gimmicks such as premiums and trading stamps. It also provided the full range of services, such as delivery, for its customers. This cost money, and prices at the stores reflected the added expenses.

Adding services and raising prices to cover them is so common in retailing that a theory was developed to explain it. Harvard Business School professor Malcolm P. McNair called it the Wheel of Retailing. This is the most important idea ever developed in the academic world to explain the dynamics of retailing. It is worth our attention because this is precisely what, time and again, did *not* happen at the A&P.

"It seems to me," said McNair, "that there is more or less a definite cycle in American distribution. . . . The cycle frequently begins with the bold new concept, the innovation. Somebody gets a bright new idea. At the outset he is in bad odor, ridiculed, scorned, condemned as 'illegitimate.'" This is the trash-talking that we have already encountered. Be on the lookout for it. Trash-talking is usually a signal that somebody is scared.

"Bankers and investors are leery" of the upstart. "But he attracts the public on the basis of the price appeal" that his innovation facilitated. "As he goes along, he trades up, improves the quality of his merchandise, improves the appearance and standing of his store, [and] attains greater respectability." If things turn out well, he now grows rapidly, and with his rapid growth comes that respectability which had earlier eluded him. Meanwhile, capital investment and operating expenses increase.

Now the onetime upstart has entered the mature mode of retailing. His enterprise "has a larger physical plant," explained McNair, "more elaborate store fixtures and displays, and it undertakes greater promotional efforts." The dilemma posed by this maturity is that it "tends to be followed by top-heaviness, too great conservatism, a decline in the rate of return on investment, and eventually vulnerability."

Vulnerability to what? "Vulnerability to the next fellow who has a bright idea and who starts his business on a low-cost basis, slipping in under the umbrella that the old-line institutions have hoisted." It was this very dynamic from which John Hartford was determined to save the A&P. In 1912, he convinced his aging father to let him try a new kind of store. We can consider this the first inflection point that the A&P handled successfully.

John Hartford's "Economy Store" has been described as "simplicity itself." All the extras were eliminated. No credit. No delivery. No telephone orders. No stamps. No premiums. No fancy fixtures. No advertising. No high-rent locations. Not even any clerks until the volume of business demanded it. The store would be run by the manager alone; when he took his lunch hour, it would be closed. The goal was to achieve gross margins of 12 percent and keep expenses at 10 percent of sales, well under the 20 percent to 22 percent gross margins common at the standard A&P store of the time. John, the volume man, would make it all up on just that—volume.

What Hartford did deserves note because it is so rare. He had one big idea about grocery retailing: high volumes at low prices. Throughout the history of retailing, as Malcolm McNair so astutely observed, margins were allowed to float up and prices rose to cover them. This took place not because the consumer wanted it. No one gets up in the morning with the newfound desire to pay $5 for what cost $4 yesterday. Rather, prices rise because of the internal dynamics of the firm's bureaucracy and perhaps also because of the ego of the store's owner.

It is an old saying that the time to make a change is when you don't have to. Everybody knows it. Nobody would argue with it. Few abide by it. John Hartford did, and the rewards were princely. In the words of an A&P executive, "From an established, successful fifty-three-year-old chain and annual volume of $24 million, the Great Atlantic & Pacific Tea Company was literally to explode over the next fifteen years into a retailing Goliath with more than fifteen thousand stores and annual volume exceeding a billion dollars." If John Hartford had not kept prices down, he would unwittingly have been issuing an invitation for some new upstart with what McNair referred to as a "bold new concept" to enter the market and underprice him.

By 1930, the A&P was indeed a behemoth on the American corporate landscape. It owned and operated about 15,700 stores, which, when you think of it, is a fantastically high number. Today, only a handful of chains have more outlets, and most of these are franchised.

These 15,700 stores were run without the benefit of computers. The company was backward integrated, in some categories all the way to the farm. It was the largest coffee merchant in the world and owned plantations in Brazil. Its sales of $1.066 billion in 1930 made it the fifth-biggest corporation in the United States (not counting AT&T). Ahead of it were only Standard Oil, GM, Ford, and U.S. Steel. Its sales in 1929 were $173 million greater than Sears, Ward, and J. C. Penney combined. The closest competitor in food retailing was Kroger, which ran fewer than a third as many stores. A&P in 1930 accounted for slightly over 16 percent of the historically fragmented food-retailing business, while Kroger had a 4.1 percent share.

The market power of the A&P was even greater when one considers the geographic distribution of its stores, most of which were concentrated east of the Mississippi, the most densely populated part of the country. With dozens of stores in geographically small cities such as Boston, the A&P had locked up the desirable locations for food retailers. In bricks-and-mortar retailing, the existence of a store is the ultimate barrier to the entry of new competition. If I have a store at a certain address, you can't have one there as well. This is an aspect of retailing that the Internet has changed forever.

The second inflection point that the A&P successfully navigated took place during the Great Depression. In 1930, the first full year after the stock-market crash, the A&P operated two thousand more stores than its four largest competitors (Kroger, American Stores, Safeway, and First National) combined. It restricted itself largely to private-label merchandise with names such as Ann Page or Jane Parker. These brands were exclusive to the A&P. It had the most convenient locations at which to shop. It was not publicly traded, and the stock-market crash did not affect it. People have to eat, so if ever there was a depression-proof business, this was it.

The A&P, we should emphasize, was more than just a collection of stores—it was a system. Here is how *Forbes* magazine described the operation of the classic mom-and-pop shop: "The typical independent grocer who buys here, there, and everywhere is not often much of a merchandiser." Because he "scatters his buying in this way [he] buys more of some things than he should, and less of others." A clever, assertive salesman insists, "Buy this!" and too often the merchant does. "Anyhow, he 'thought he could sell it'" was the oft-heard lament.

A&P stores did not buy "here, there, and everywhere." They did not, in other words, have market relations with their suppliers. Instead, A&P stores were visited only by A&P representatives, and inventory was managed to minimize waste. Twice a week, store managers filled out order sheets. These orders were processed at a warehouse owned and managed by the company in which merchandise was arranged in the same sequence as it was listed on the sheet. A hand truck with the store's number collected each order in a highly efficient system.

There was, however, a major challenge emerging on the horizon. This was to be more than a market. It was to be a *super*market. There had been big food stores before 1930 in the United States, but they never lasted long. This time, however, supermarkets were here to stay.

Michael J. Cullen is usually viewed as the founder of the supermarket movement. The year 1930 found Cullen, forty-six years old, working for Kroger in southern Illinois. He wrote a lengthy letter, actually more of a business plan, to Kroger's president, William H. Albers, at the company's headquarters in Cincinnati. In it, he suggested a radically new kind of food store.

The most obvious difference between the supermarket and the traditional chain outlet was sheer size. Cullen wanted his supermarket to be between 5,200 and 6,400 square feet, far larger than the 1,134 square-foot outlet recommended by *Progressive Grocer* magazine. He wanted it located away from busy city street corners because he wanted to keep his rent expenses down and, of great importance, he wanted room for a large parking lot.

When John Hartford proposed the A&P Economy Store concept to his father back in 1912, there was no need to worry about parking lots because very few Americans owned cars. But as we have seen, by 1930 the United States had entered the auto-industrial age. Cars meant that consumers were no longer tied to the hub-and-spoke system of urban trolley transportation. They also meant that customers could buy heavier, bulkier items when they shopped for food because they did not have to carry their shopping bags home on public transport. And cars meant that they could travel longer distances to get to the store. "One great asset in being away from the business section," Cullen wrote Albers, "is parking space. Another is, you can generally get the kind of store you want and on your own terms."

Entrepreneurs are notorious for their optimism, and Cullen was certainly no exception. When they saw his low prices, the public, he wrote, "would break my front doors down to get in. It would be a riot. I would have to call out the police and let the public in so many at a time. I would lead the public out of the high-priced houses of bondage into the low prices of the house of the promised land. . . . I would be the 'miracle man' of the grocery business. The public would not, and could not believe their eyes. Week days would be Saturdays—rainy days would be sunny days."

Behind the mania were years of experience, financial estimates, a pricing strategy, a merchandising strategy, and a legitimate business proposition. Cullen put forward the warehouse food concept and showed how to execute it. He needed a backer, but he was so certain of his success that he was willing to put up half the funds for his first store from his own pocket. He was not a rich man, and his willingness to invest $15,000 of his own money was a statement.

The final line in Cullen's letter to Albers was "What is your verdict?" His verdict was "No." This was a verdict of which he would come to repent. Albers became the first president of the Supermarket Institute, a trade association, in 1937.

If Cullen was going to make a big career move, he decided that this was the moment. He immediately resigned. With the backing of a vice president of the Sweet Life Foods Corporation, he opened the King Kullen Grocery Company's first store in August 1930 at 171st Street and Jamaica Avenue in Queens, New York. When Cullen died in 1936, he had at least fifteen stores operating.

At first the supermarket met with the standard trash talk targeted at menacing new ideas. Large food stores had been experimented with in the past. They had always failed. The problems in running them were innumerable. For example, what do you do with your groceries while you are in the store? You only have two arms. The stores are big so you are in them for a longer period of time than otherwise. No matter how much your two arms can carry, they will tire.

This problem was not solved until an Oklahoma grocer named Sylvan Goldman invented the shopping cart. This hardly sounds like an earth-shattering innovation, but much to Goldman's surprise, shoppers were reluctant to use it. To women, it looked like the baby carriage they had spent the day pushing around. Men took it as an aspersion on their masculinity. Only after Goldman hired people of various ages and both genders to push carts around his store as if they were shoppers were they eventually adopted.

The new supermarkets were as brash as the letter from Cullen, the self-described "world's greatest price wrecker," suggests. On December 8, 1936, full-page advertisements announced that another supermarket operation, Big Bear, the "Price Crusher," "crashes into New Jersey." It was easy to dismiss this "hype" as creating a "circuslike" atmosphere that people would tire of soon.

John Hartford had led the charge to A&P's economy format back in 1912, but the world was a very different place in 1930. The father of John and George was no longer living. They themselves were eighteen years older. In 1930, John Hartford was fifty-eight years old, and for forty-two of those years he had worked for the A&P. He had seen the company explode from a small, regional chain to the nation's fifth-largest firm, and he had seen himself amass one of the greatest fortunes in the United States. Both he and his brother George viewed the A&P in family terms and had a paternalistic attitude toward the company's thousands of employees. How would John react to this particular turn of the wheel of retailing? The supermarket challenge was a genuine strategic inflection point for the A&P.

Faced with a retail format that "could profitably sell goods at prices which would be ruinous to a conventional store," A&P's initial reaction was paralysis. "We did not take it very seriously at first," Hartford recalled in 1945.

There were three hundred supermarkets in the United States in 1935 and four times that many the following year. The results were undeniable. A&P had a profitable store in Brooklyn. King Kullen and other independents invaded the trading area. "In a very short space of time," said Hartford, "they priced that Brooklyn [store] into deep red figures."

The impact may have been undeniable, but would it be denied? Mr. George and Mr. John had become, as mentioned above, paternalistic toward their people. This paternalism, reported *Fortune* in 1938, "has taken the tangible form of high wages (currently $30 a week for managers and clerks, which compares favorably with the Department of Labor figure of $22 for all retail stores). And it has left hundreds of marginal stores open when unsentimental business judgment would have closed them."

"Unsentimental business judgment" was undoubtedly called for in the face of this new competition. That would inevitably mean that loyal employees would have to be fired. In the teeth of the Great Depression, that was not a happy prospect.

Even if the undeniable facts were not denied, the A&P was faced with a host of questions. Could it pound expenses and improve its warehousing and logistical support so that it could save at least some of its present stores? Should it experiment with deep discounts? Should it close stores? If so, which ones? Should it open supermarkets? If so, would they be like the King Kullen and Big Bear operations? Specifically, should the A&P abandon its tradition of private-label merchandise and feature instead nationally known manufacturers' brands, which the supermarket competition was doing? Where should the new stores be located? Who would run them? How much money should be spent on advertising?

In a word, how on earth should the A&P enter the brave new supermarket world? By the mid-1930s wasn't it already the late mover in what was essentially a new industry? Developments external to the industry seemed to have changed the firm's position. The automobile has already been mentioned, and to it should be added a fourfold increase in surfaced roads between 1921 and 1935. There were slightly fewer than 2 million refrigerators sold in the United States prior to 1930. In the 1930s, 20 million were sold. The result was that vastly more people could stock up and store perishable goods at home. Some people felt that the retailing world had therefore changed fundamentally and forever. In the words of one business journalist, "Basically, the supermarket represents the complete antithesis of all the important factors that have been considered essential to success in retailing."

The A&P knew by 1935 that something had to be done to meet the supermarket challenge. Experiments began in earnest with the Baby Bear program, which featured stores with lower prices and more publicity. (I assume that Hartford chose the name Baby Bear for two reasons. One was the existence of Big Bear. The second is that the bear has always been used as a metaphor associated with falling prices. Thus a bear market on Wall Street means that prices are going down. The bull is associated with rising prices. This is because when a bear attacks its prey, it claws them down. When a bull attacks its prey, it throws them up on its horns.)

Results of the Baby Bear program were encouraging, but a business upturn in 1936 blunted the company's sense of urgency. George Hartford, the accountant, bemoaned the emphasis on volume rather than margins, and the divisional presidents agreed with him.

However, John Hartford was steadfast in rededicating the A&P to the strategy that had made it great. "It has always been our idea—we have been volume. We thought it was sounder business to sell two hundred pounds of butter at a cent a pound profit, than one hundred pounds at two cents. That was a theory," he later recalled. And that was the theory the A&P put into practice.

In 1938, the A&P made the decision to transform itself into a supermarket company. By then even Mr. George agreed with Mr. John that this step had to be taken. An executive wrote John Hartford, "It is easy to build up a complicated and expensive structure, but very difficult to adjust and reduce it to time and conditions."

That "very difficult" task was, however, precisely what the A&P accomplished. At the beginning of the Depression, the company ran more than fifteen thousand small stores. By the end of 1945, it ran four thousand large ones. All the tough questions posed above had been answered. For John Hartford, the A&P was not its stores. It was an idea—two hundred pounds of butter at a cent-a-pound profit rather than one hundred pounds at two cents. If competitive conditions and infrastructure transformation meant that his idea could only be realized in supermarkets rather than small stores, then supermarkets it would be.

Perhaps because of its later decline, the A&P's remarkable achievement has largely been overlooked by historians and students of management. For the second time in its history, the A&P had figured out the key success factors in its industry and had handled them as well as anyone could have hoped. The company had been a model of nondenial management.

• • •

In 1950, the A&P was in at least as strong a position as it was in 1930 and stronger than in 1912. Its sales of $3.2 billion that year were over $1 billion higher than its two closest competitors, Safeway and Kroger, combined. Its profits exceeded $32 million. Its balance sheet was debt-free. Its distribution system had proven itself both powerful and supple over the years. Its executive corps was second to none in the industry.

Mr. George once said, "We're just a couple of grocery boys trying to do an honest business." But while you didn't have to be a rocket scientist to succeed in grocery retailing, you did have to know what you were doing. John Hartford provided the simple but clear principles: high volume, low prices, low margins, high turnover. The "secret" road to profit "lies almost entirely in a rapid turnover of merchandise, and a rapid turnover simply means unceasing attention to the needs and buying habits of your customers."

This particular "secret" was not much of a secret at all. There were and are few secrets in retailing. The stores are there for all to see. Any competitor can walk in and see the merchandise assortment and price points. Indeed, this happens all the time. Competing retailers are always shopping one another's stores. That is why, of all industries, execution plays such a key role in retailing. So much of a retailer's strategy is transparent. The goal for everyone is to get the right product in the right place at the right time for the right price. Actually doing that—execution—is, however, damned difficult. No retailer was better at these tasks in 1950 than the A&P.

Mr. John and Mr. George graced the cover of *Time* magazine on November 13, 1950. John was seventy-eight and looked younger. George was eight six and looked older. Both were childless widowers who "live[d] only for the A&P." The living was good. As just noted, A&P broke the $3 billion sales barrier in 1950. It had broken the $2 billion barrier a mere four years earlier. The company had about 110,000 employees.

Mr. John lived in a mansion in Valhalla, New York, in Westchester County, and at the Plaza Hotel. Mr. George lived in Verona, New Jersey, also a suburb of New York City. "When at home, both these lonely old men spent much of their time watching television," which was yet another recent innovation in an age of innovation. George had put in seventy years with the company, John sixty-two. Nothing else in American business history compares to this fraternal longevity.

The size of the A&P made it a political issue. During the 1930s it was threatened by various pieces of federal legislation. In 1939 the National Association of Retail Grocers petitioned for a federal antitrust investigation of the company. Eventually the Antitrust Division of the Justice Department brought a criminal action under the Sherman Act. After mountains of paper and an appeal, the A&P was fined $175,000 in February 1949.

The following September, the Justice Department launched a civil action aimed at breaking up the company. The Hartford brothers were "heartsick" at this development and mounted a full-scale legal and public-relations counterattack. The case dragged on until January 19, 1954, when it ended in a consent decree favorable to the A&P. Meanwhile, however, the antitrust cases had cast a shadow over the company for more than a decade.

Even when they are resolved favorably for the corporate defendant, endless antitrust battles tend to sap the energy—and, more importantly, the aggression—from an organization. Companies become careful when their executives are told that every move they make and every document they write will be subject to the legal scrutiny of a prosecutor whose sole purpose in life is to find them guilty of something, perhaps to send them to jail, or at the least to make them look foolish. Even when you survive such withering assault, you do not do so unscathed.

In 1947, John Hartford relinquished the title of president and became chairman of the board. George was always comfortable with the title of treasurer, and that remained unchanged. The brothers agreed that the man to succeed them was executive vice president David T. Bofinger. A&P was a devoted promote-from-within company, and Bofinger certainly qualified on that dimension. He had joined in 1900 as an office boy at the age of fifteen. From there he rose to stock clerk and then to buyer. In 1922, he became vice president in charge of buying, a key position in the company and one of the most important jobs in the whole industry.

Not much is known about Bofinger. He is thought to have been an able man. He obviously knew the company as well as it could be known, having spent half a century with it. Bofinger's career is the embodiment of the organization man's. He worked for one company his whole life, climbing the ladder of success one step at a time. He apparently never attended college. A&P had no reputation for executive education, so it is a fair bet that Bofinger did not have a wide knowledge of the business world. It is worth asking whether this kind of background is ideal for leading a giant company.

We will never know the difference Bofinger might have made in A&P's

history. On December 19, 1949, he was attending a luncheon in honor of the A&P's retiring general-traffic manager at the Biltmore Hotel, just around the corner from the company's headquarters in the Graybar Building at Lexington Avenue between forty-third and forty-fourth streets. There, he suddenly and unexpectedly died, the day before his sixty-fourth birthday.

To succeed Bofinger, John Hartford chose Ralph W. Burger. The selection did not inspire a lot of enthusiasm at the Graybar Building or in the field.

Burger too was very much in the A&P mold. He had been with company forever, landing his first job at the A&P when he was eleven years old in 1901. Second, he was old. No one in a prominent position at the company was under fifty. Most were over sixty.

Burger was not and never had been a line executive. He was a staffer at the home office. This means that of those dozens of encounters with consumers that retailers experience every hour, Burger had known none. "He was considered no more than an office boy who had matured into an executive's secretary . . . a highly paid 'get me or go for' this and that," recalled an A&P executive. "Of course, such thoughts were never expressed publicly or in meetings." So much for speaking truth to power.

From his appointment to the presidency in 1949 to September 20, 1951, Burger did not really matter much in the company. After that date, however, he mattered a great deal. On that day, John Hartford strolled down from his apartment at the Plaza on Fifty-ninth Street and Fifth Avenue to the Graybar Building. "The company was prospering, it was autumn in New York, and all was right with the world." The morning was unexceptional for John—a chat with his brother George, a couple of meetings with executives, pushing some paper.

At one-thirty, John left the office for a board meeting at the Chrysler Corporation, just a short walk away. At the end of the meeting, Hartford walked to the elevator bank on the fifty-sixth floor. As he entered the elevator, in the midst of a conversation, he had a heart attack. The elevator rushed him to the lobby, and a doctor was summoned immediately. To no avail. Hartford's death was instantaneous.

Suddenly, Ralph W. Burger was a true decision maker at the center of the company. George Hartford was eighty-seven years old and had no interest in managing daily operations. Burger was not only president of the

A&P, he was also president of the John A. Hartford Foundation. When George Hartford died at the age of ninety-two, six years almost to the day after the death of his younger brother, it was learned that he had not bothered to set up a foundation in his own name or to add his name to his brother's. His whole estate, therefore, was simply deposited into the John A. Hartford Foundation, which as a result became one of the nation's largest. In December of 1958, the foundation's 7 million shares of A&P were worth $400 million.

Burger took office with becoming modesty. He consulted with many operating executives and appeared anxious to learn as much as he could. As early as the 1940s, the A&P had been known as Grandma. That is because A&P's private-label bread, introduced before World War I, was called Grandmother's bread. In the late 1920s, the company was selling 600 million loaves a year. The nickname also suggested that the company was not the place to look for innovation. Indeed, it wasn't—"just a couple of grocery boys trying to do an honest business." Burger managed the A&P in this spirit.

The seduction of denial lay in the fact that by some very important measures—sales and profits—Burger's first years looked pretty good. Sales grew at a torrid pace, topping $4 billion in 1954 and $5 billion in 1958. Think of it. The company was founded in 1859. It took seven decades for sales to reach the billion-dollar mark. It took sixteen years to hit $2 billion. Just four years later, sales reached $3 billion. A mere four years after that, the $4 billion mark was surpassed. A&P's sales in 1954 were twice what they had been in 1946. Profits increased every year from 1951 to 1958, when they exceeded $53 million. Profits set records each year from 1954 to 1958.

What more could one ask? Wherein lay the denial? In this case, denial was not as blatant as in some of the others. The company did not make a left turn in the face of a dozen road signs saying RIGHT TURN ONLY.

If you are a business executive, you might be asking yourself: What are you and your company doing right now that might be used as a case study in denial in five years? I am not talking about a wrong choice between alternatives concerning which reasonable people might disagree. I mean to ask whether you will find yourself accused of turning left in front of a bunch of right-turn signs. What can the decline of the A&P teach you about that possibility?

What the A&P executives denied is that there are, in Disraeli's famous phrase, "lies, damned lies, and statistics." A&P executives celebrated the statistics they liked. They ignored the statistics they did not like. So did everyone else.

What was the sobering information to which the A&P paid little heed? Sales were growing, but at less than half the industry average. This can always be excused by noting that it is easier to grow at a fast rate from a lower rather than a higher base.

But the lion's share of the A&P's sales increases were taking place by opening new stores. Same-store sales growth was not encouraging. And it was becoming progressively more difficult to locate new stores in promising markets. The A&P had traditionally signed short-term leases. That policy had served it well during the Depression. It enabled the company to get out of those thousands of small stores and make the move into supermarkets.

What was denied in this instance is that a policy that had worked well in one context might not work well in another. The duration of a store's lease should have been a means to an end, not an end in itself. The 1950s and especially the 1960s in the United States bore little resemblance to the Depression. The nation was growing wealthier. Many in the middle class were moving to the suburbs. Suburban developers, especially mall developers, demanded longer leases. A&P would not sign them and thus shut itself out of quickly growing markets. "Grandma," as *Fortune* observed back in 1947, "has rarely been an innovator." A new look at the duration of leases did not really demand much innovation. It did demand that the company change with the times, which is essential for any business and most especially retail.

Another market growing with gusto was California and the West Coast in general. As we have seen, the Great Atlantic and Pacific Tea Company had developed largely east of the Mississippi. For much of its history, one feels *Pacific* should have been spelled with a lower-case *p*. By 1960, the A&P did have some stores in Southern California and Washington State. Instead of widening that beachhead in a part of the country that obviously represented the future, however, the A&P abandoned the West Coast completely by 1970.

The West Coast market was indeed growing, but so was a powerful supermarket chain, Safeway. And Safeway, unlike the A&P, was not giving away all its earnings in dividends. With less than half of A&P's volume and number of stores in 1962, it invested twice as much in store development.

A&P was vertically integrated and heavily invested in private-label merchandise. In the 1950s, however, a powerful new medium of communication invaded America's homes: television. There were televisions in eight thousand American households in 1946. A decade later, that number was up to 35 million. Television put at the disposal of manufacturers a device for national advertising of unprecedented drama and immediacy. There were no remote-control devices. You watched and listened to those commercials with rapt attention, convinced they were truthful. Children were glued to the TV set. When Kellogg's told them they could buy Tony the Tiger along with their Sugar Frosted Flakes, that is what they wanted. Not Ann Page Sugar Frosted Flakes.

In an instance of candor rare on corporate websites, the A&P's history has the following observation under "1960s": "A&P's continuing emphasis of private-label marketing loses consumer support as the growth of national television advertising drives increasing customer demand for national brand products." This is apparent not only in hindsight. Everybody knew it at the time. Yet A&P stuck with—or was stuck with, depending on how you look at it—its own store labels.

The A&P had for most of its history been the low-price-grocery leader. But this is a position you can only hold if your costs are lower than your competitors. Through its steady disinvestment in its stores, through its high-priced union contracts, through its ill-advised store-site-location practices, and through a dozen other avoidable errors, the A&P lost that position. This fact it learned the hard way in 1972 when it launched a price war.

The hostilities were conducted under the banner of WEO, which was supposed to stand for "Where Economy Originates." This ugly, clumsy slogan, which sounded like "we owe," heralded a catastrophic year for the company. Sales increased but losses skyrocketed. A&P lost the price war it started, proving only that it could give away the store.

The most puzzling aspect of the price war is why A&P initiated it.

During 1971, published figures—please note once again that everyone knew this; none of it was secret—indicated that the A&P's stores were inferior to those of the four other leading chains. Sales per employee, for example, were almost 45 percent lower than at Jewel. Sales per store were almost 60 percent lower than at Food Fair.

What did A&P's stores look like in the early 1970s? Here are the recollections of an enraged top executive who started out with the company as a part-time store clerk in the summer of 1938:

> After almost twenty years of steady decline and cutbacks, a debilitating paralysis had overtaken most stores in a growing number of divisions. The symptoms were visible and similar. These stores had few customers and did little business, but were open long hours, often seven days and six nights. These stores were obviously short of help, shelves were poorly stocked. What carriages were on hand were usually out in the parking lot. Only one of six checkstands was operating, with no bagger to help shorten the checkout wait. Advertised sale features were often missing from the shelves, dairy, produce, and meat cases. Most times, and particularly at night, no employees were available to assist customers seeking a cut of meat not . . . on display, or to check backroom stock for sale items missing from shelves, or even to scale and price produce items or grind A&P's bean coffees. Cleanliness and courtesy standards, freshness and quality control standards, shelf-stocking and checkout standards, and store employee morale all deteriorated at the same grinding steady pace.

Take a good long look at that last sentence. That "same grinding steady pace." It was the steady downward slide that made it possible year after year to deny that things were getting as bad as they became. I am old enough to remember what an A&P looked like in the early 1970s. The contrast with the mid-1950s was stark. But it had gone to pieces by degrees. Moreover, many things went wrong, not one big thing. The cumulative effects of the slow collapse were easy to deny.

■ ■ ■

The sad story of denial at the A&P leaves us with a set of questions. What if Bofinger had lived? The seeds of destruction were sown during Ralph Burger's tenure, but he was not around at harvesttime. What if it had been Bofinger rather than Burger?

Perhaps it would not have made much difference. Bofinger had a lot of operating experience that Burger did not, but he was still very much part of the company's gerontocracy. What if John Hartford had had a son who was bound and determined that he could post a better record at the company than his father did? That is what happened at IBM. Thomas J. Watson Sr. had built IBM from a motley collection of cats and dogs into a uniquely powerful firm in a growing industry. His equally ambitious son pushed the company to its limits, presiding over the creation of the IBM 360 in 1964, one of the greatest new-product introductions in American business history. In that case, things would, in all probability, have been different. One person with power—the CEO—can make a key difference in even the biggest, stodgiest of bureaucratic companies.

Why did the company not look more deeply into the quality of its sales and earnings? Why didn't it think more strategically about its reinvestment policy? Why did it pay out so much money in dividends? Why didn't it devote more attention to its executive-development program? When the company went public in 1958, it put six outside directors on its board. One of these was Donald K. David, dean emeritus of the Harvard Business School. Surely he could have designed an executive-education program that could have fast-tracked young talent.

More questions could be asked. They are not easy to answer. My own view is that the closest we will get to an answer is the quotation in the title of this chapter: "They just didn't believe these things were happening." That statement, made by a former A&P executive in 1973, captures the essence of denial. You didn't have to be a genius to see "these things." Thanks to the transparency of retailing, all you had to do was to walk into a store and try to buy a steak, try to buy broccoli, watch your child scream for Tony the Tiger when all you could buy was Ann Page cereal, wait for what seemed like ages at the checkout counter, and so on.

This answer raises another question. Why didn't they "believe these things were happening"? Because, I think, they saw everything through the lens of their history of market leadership. They felt that because they had been leaders for so long, every problem was an outlier, a blip on the screen, not a harbinger of things to come.

All over the country, grocery retailers in the 1950s and 1960s were mov-ing faster and looking better than the A&P. But for a while, especially during the 1950s, the A&P was growing smartly as well. What the company collectively denied was that it is not okay merely to grow. If you grow in absolute terms but decline relative to other firms in your industry, you are going to sacrifice the sharpest, most ambitious executives you have. The less talented will hang around.

The A&P was not destroyed by fire. It rusted. This is the same process, but less dramatic, slower, and therefore easier to deny. "This is the way the world ends," T. S. Eliot wrote in "The Hollow Men," "Not with a bang but a whimper."

5

The Edifice Complex:
Denial at Sears

The Chicago Club is an exclusive downtown gathering place for the city's business and social elite. It was founded in 1869 and has since 1929 occupied its present location at 81 East Van Buren Street, a half a block from Grant Park and a short walk from Lake Michigan. It's a nice place, to put it mildly. The kind of place you wouldn't be ashamed to bring a friend.

Two of the city's top executives, CEOs of companies that had competed against each other for more than half a century, had a private lunch at the Chicago Club sometime shortly after VJ Day, September 2, 1945. One of these was Sewell Lee Avery. Avery had skillfully piloted Montgomery Ward through the Great Depression and was an able executive, if not beloved. He was known at the company, from his first two initials (S and L) and his last name (Avery), as Slavery.

Avery's luncheon companion was Robert E. Wood, CEO of Sears Roebuck. Wood and Avery were big shots. It was as if the CEOs of Coke and Pepsi sat down for lunch. Wood was a graduate of West Point who had served in the Panama Canal Zone in the early 1900s and as a colonel in the Rainbow (forty-second) Division during World War I. He retired from the army in 1919 as a brigadier general. Although this was hardly a typical background for a retailer, Wood's first job out of the service was at Montgomery Ward. He then moved on to Sears.

Wood had developed an "odd passion" for reading the *Statistical Abstract of the United States* during those long, lonely evenings in the Canal Zone. His study convinced him that America was becoming an urban nation. This suggested that Montgomery Ward, which sold only through its catalog, should open stores in cities. Ward wasn't interested, so Wood took his bright idea across town to Sears, which also sold exclusively through its catalog. The owner of Sears, Julius Rosenwald, was impressed. Wood was hired, and Sears went from catalogs alone to catalogs and counters. Ward quickly followed suit.

When Wood and Avery had lunch at the Chicago Club, Sears was selling about $3 worth of merchandise to Ward's $2. But Wood was a wary man. Back in 1938 he told his people, "I believe there still lingers in some, not all, of Sears's buying force a trace of that feeling of smugness or superiority [with regard to Ward]. . . . If you have such a feeling, get rid of it, for you don't deserve it. . . . Learn from your competition, examine yourself to see what are your weak spots, and see if you can't discover new ways in your line to make sales and profits."

He preached, "We must not fall into the fundamental error of underestimating our competition." One assumes that Wood's attitude had not changed when he sat down for lunch with Avery. Wood was sixty-six at the time. Avery seventy-two.

Avery told Wood at lunch that he believed hard economic times lay ahead: "This country's going into a tailspin within two years," he declared. "Every great war has been followed by a great depression, and our charts indicate it within twelve to twenty-four months." If Avery's charts showed him that there was a depression after every war, those charts needed to be revised. However, both he and Wood were old enough to remember what happened after World War I. Things looked great for a couple of months, and then the bottom fell out as the nation plunged into a severe depression. The only reason that downturn is not remembered today is its brevity. The spectacular demand for automobiles helped lift the economy. But the collapse had been sharp and left a lasting impression on people in positions of authority.

Despite all this, Wood looked at the picture differently from Avery. His innate optimism about America's future led him, at an age when most men if not already retired are thinking seriously about it, to take what has been called "the biggest gamble of his career" and invest $300 million in a great postwar expansion program.

Untouched by fears of a returning depression, Wood sensed the pent-up consumer demand that would be unleashed with the demobilization of the armed forces, which had grown from next to nothing to over 11 million men and women. These people wouldn't be headed toward Hoovervilles, the bread lines that had become a symbol of the Great Depression. Rather, they would be returning either to newly vibrant big cities or to suburban Levittowns. They would comprise a limitless market for the refrigerators, washers and dryers, and do-it-yourself tools that formed the heart of Sears's profit picture.

"Go west, young man, and grow with the country" is a remark famously attributed to Horace Greeley in 1851. A century later, Wood, his interest in population trends undiminished, saw the nation taking Greeley's advice. In 1945, Pennsylvania and Illinois were Sears's two biggest states. Four years later, they were Texas and California. Perhaps if Wood had been running the A&P, that company's history would have turned out differently.

Like Wood, Avery crafted a strategy consonant with his prognostications. To avoid being ground up in the kind of inventory crisis that devastated so many firms after World War I, Avery sold off Ward's inventory. During the decade following that chat at the Chicago Club, Sears increased the number of its stores by more than a hundred, and most of these were the largest size the company built. Ward, by contrast, closed stores.

Ward had no intention of expanding regionally, but Sears did. By 1959, Sears had seventeen stores in the burgeoning Los Angeles market. Ward did not have one. Ward had taken such a liquid position that it seemed close to liquidating its retail business altogether. It became known as the bank with the store attached.

Avery's strategy proved disastrous. There was a rapid rise in sales and profits at Ward up to 1948. From then, however, through 1954, the company unraveled. Sales declined by more than 25 percent. Profits were down almost 95 percent. The company was in free fall.

The climax was dramatic. Ward became the target of one of the first hostile takeover efforts in modern American business history. The man playing the part of what later came to be known as the "raider" was the aptly named Louis E. Wolfson. He staged a proxy fight at the April 1955 annual meeting. His strategy, according to one history of the company, was a cruel but clever effort "to show up Avery as weak, confused, and nearly senile, by asking [him] pointed questions and letting him hang himself." Avery babbled on incoherently for half an hour. Wolfson failed to take the company over, but Avery was finished.

The fate of Sears during the postwar decade was quite different. Sales almost tripled and profits more than tripled. There was no question about competing with Ward by the mid-1950s. In its classes of trade, which included almost every consumer item except food and automobiles, Sears led the nation.

Those of us who shopped in those stores, especially in the new big A stores (which were the largest, newest, and most well appointed) in the 1950s and 1960s, can tell you why the company was doing well. The stores were clean and well lit. The items they stocked were interesting, not like the average department store. They had tools and lawn mowers and sporting goods. They had really neat bicycles. True, the bicycles had a strange name. They were called J. C. Higgins rather than Schwinn. But for most kids that was okay.

J. C. Higgins was a private label owned by Sears. Why didn't sticking to private-label goods into the 1950s and the 1960s hurt Sears the way it did the A&P? The first answer is that it may have. In 1989, Sears opened Brand Central in its stores, and today their stores are full of manufacturers' branded products side by side with their own private-label merchandise.

But the second answer is that private label, at least through the 1960s, may have and probably did work just fine for Sears. Unlike the A&P, Sears made its name selling consumer durables—"white goods" like major kitchen appliances and also automotive accessories like tires and batteries. Tony the Tiger never sold a refrigerator. The core product mattered a great deal, and Kenmore appliances, Craftsman tools, and DieHard automobile batteries—all Sears house brands—had an enviable reputation for dependability. If one such item did not work, you could return it.

What is more, if a pedal broke off your J. C. Higgins bike in Portland, Maine, you could return it to the Sears in Portland, Oregon, if that is where you happened to be. This mattered a great deal in a nation in which, during the 1950s and 1960s, about one in five citizens moved in any given year. Sears blanketed the nation with seven hundred stores by the mid-1950s.

Is the story of the Chicago Club luncheon and the different directions taken by Sears and Ward in the succeeding ten years one of denial? Would it be fair to say that Avery failed because his strategy was based on the denial of what he should have known at the time? No. Not in the sense used in this book.

Avery can fairly be accused of having a flawed understanding of history and both the opportunities and limitations of history in charting the future of a business. He can also be found guilty of conceiving of himself as the indispensable man who must therefore pilot his company into the future indefinitely. He can be found guilty of not knowing that his once considerable powers as an executive were waning. But these are charges to which many CEOs who have achieved some success must plead guilty. Not least Wood himself, as we shall soon see.

Avery was not in denial in 1945. He was simply wrong. He proved that it is better to be right, which you doubtless knew before reading this book. His mistake was devastating to his company, but given the circumstances, it was understandable. Avery was no worse than most of us who march backward into the future. This is a story more of Wood's remarkable vision than of Avery's shortcomings.

Wood was no fashion plate. He boasted that he grabbed the suits that he wore "off the pile" at Sears. And he looked it. What you are about to read is the story of a company that literally got too big for its breeches. When Sears went into its swoon in the 1970s, no one there seemed to understand that there was a fortune to be made selling the breeches the company felt it had grown out of. Everybody with eyes could see it. All they had to do was look at Kmart and Wal-Mart. Sears chose denial instead. It was more comfortable.

Wood saw the United States in 1945 the way Alexander Hamilton saw it in 1794, as "Hercules in the cradle." *Time* magazine founder Henry Luce wrote in 1941 that this was to be the "American century." Luce and Wood probably never met, but they shared a view of the country that was quite correct.

Long before that Chicago Club lunch, Sears, Roebuck and Co. had come to be looked upon as a distinctively American institution. For years, the Sears catalog had been known as the "wish book." Often it occupied a prized place on the table in the living room of a farm family's home.

It is said—and if this story isn't true, it ought to be—that President Franklin D. Roosevelt was asked during World War II what American book he would put in the hands of every Russian should he have the opportunity to do such a thing. The capitalist West was allied with the very communist Soviet Union, unlikely bedfellows indeed. We had to pretend that we could be friends with the paranoid, murderous dictator Joseph Stalin and his henchmen. Roosevelt called Stalin "Uncle Joe" and felt he was a man with whom we could do business.

As far as the Russian people (really *Soviet* people—there was quite a difference as a later generation would learn) were concerned, they were just like us in Roosevelt's view. So when he was asked what book he would place in their hands, his response was not a biography of a great political leader such as Washington or Lincoln. Nor was it a novel by, say, Mark Twain. It was the Sears catalog. What America had to offer that the average person wanted was not literature, art, or music, never mind philosophy. It was stuff. Things. Good things. Things that worked. Things that made life easier.

Take, for example, the Sears cookstove from years gone by. In the words of a company history, "Sears guaranteed [its] cookstove to cook. It cooked. And it cooked for years and years." There were hundreds, perhaps thousands, of such products. "Sears's plows would plow, and Sears's washing machines would wash. That was what farm families wanted; and that was what they got from Sears, Roebuck."

In an intriguing phrase, journalist Donald R. Katz observed that Sears was about "the humbling of products." Products once available only to the elite Sears put within the reach of the middle class by slashing prices and mass marketing them. By humbling these products, Sears ennobled the consumer. For a profit, to be sure, but there you have it.

Sears was the creation of Richard W. Sears back in 1886. That is the same year that Coca-Cola, the only other company in history to rival Sears when it comes to "Americanness," was founded. Sears sold his company but went into business again with Alvah C. Roebuck in 1891. That is the direct ancestor of the Sears that flourished in the twentieth century.

Sears was one of those born salesmen who floated across nineteenth-century American history. Henry Goldman, a founder of Goldman Sachs, remarked that Sears "could sell a breath of air." It is said that he once replaced a watch dropped by a streetcar conductor, explaining, "We guarantee our watches not to fall out of people's pockets and break." Apocryphal or not, stories like this circulate and establish a company's reputation.

As was true of John Hartford, Sears was all for volume. "In my humble opinion," he said, "we must have volume—whether it be easy in the boat or not. Our very life *Demands Volume*—and if one hot fire doesn't get it I would build more fires." Where did that volume come from? Low prices. Early catalogs are still around, and they are interesting to look through. There were plenty of catalog merchants at the turn of the last century, but no one had the special Sears flair. The notices in his catalog, according to one of his executives, Louis E. Asher, "violated every rule of good advertising except one—the advertisements pulled! . . . They were unattractive to the eye, set in crowded five-point type that was hard to read. There was no white space. But every ad carried the magic three-word message in heavy black type: 'Send No Money.'" Asher said the whole company was built on those "three simple words." Of his advertisements, Sears himself, with pardonable pride, said, "They almost pulled the ink off the paper."

In 1895, Julius Rosenwald became a partner in the firm and Roebuck left it, never to be a factor again. Sears, who was not as interested in running a business as he was simply in selling, retired as president in 1908. Rosenwald ran the company until 1924, and he ran it well. Sears faced a dire crisis in the depression following World War I, and it survived through reliance on Rosenwald's personal fortune. Once the crisis passed, the company bounced back strongly. Rosenwald, who was born in 1862, was ready to retire and devote himself to philanthropy.

Rosenwald had three criteria for executive succession. He wanted someone young so there could be extended tenure in office, someone not yet rich so he would be ambitious, and someone—of the three characteristics this was the least to be expected—who had experience with the railroads. He thought that industry generated the best managers, and Sears, as a mail-order house, was vitally dependent on knowledge of distribution.

A man named Charles Kittle fit the bill and got the job in November 1924. A little more than three years later, however, he died of blood poisoning following an operation. Nine days after Kittle's death, Rosenwald made Robert E. Wood the president of Sears. Wood served as president until 1939, when he was named chairman, a position which he held until 1954. He was reinstated as honorary chairman in 1968, a year before he died at the age of ninety. Throughout that whole, long period, Wood bestrode the ever-widening world of Sears like the proverbial colossus. He was a great merchant, one of the greatest in American history.

During the years from Sears through Rosenwald through Wood (Kittle having been in office for too brief a time to make a lasting impression), Sears became part of the American landscape. For years, indeed for decades, Sears had consistently placed first in surveys of the nation's most trusted companies. There is no greater asset in business than trust. But how do you win it?

"Honesty is the best policy," Richard Sears used to say to Julius Rosenwald. "I know because I've tried it both ways." Looking at those early catalogs, it is not hard to find items that probably did not fulfill their promise. The "Princess Bust Developer and Bust Cream or Food" probably did not enlarge a woman's breasts. The "Electricity Liniment" probably was not "A New and Great Discovery" that was a "Certain cure for Rheumatism, Cuts, Sprains, Wounds, Old Sores, Corns, Galls, Bruises, Growing Pains, Contracted Muscles, Lame Back, Stiff Joints, Frosted Feet, Chilblains, Etc." "Dr. Barker's Blood Builder" did not cure cancer.

This kind of patent-medicine advertising was common a century ago. But even in those primitive times, there was something different, something a little better, about Sears. In 1906, for example, Louis Asher dispatched a man named J. H. Jeffries into the field to assess Ward's operations. Rather than solely undertaking field research, Jeffries took it upon himself to get a job at Ward's Kansas City mail-order processing plant and informed Asher that "things are not running very well." Asher responded, "I don't like the idea of your working for these people and reporting to me. I don't think it is high class either for you or for us. . . . I don't think you could continue in your employment without injuring your self-respect." Few people knew about this encounter. Asher did not publicize it. But it exemplified the way things were done at Sears.

Julius Rosenwald greatly strengthened the finer side of Sears. An admirable man, Rosenwald was not honest because it was the best policy. Nor had he tried it both ways. He was honest because he did not know how to be otherwise. He terminated the catalog entries for phony products. Apparently, he offered refunds to purchasers of bogus medical devices. This latter gesture lived on for decades in company lore. An executive talked about it at a dinner of the officers and directors of Sears in 1968.

Robert Wood was quite different from Rosenwald. For one thing, there was more than a whiff of anti-Semitism about him. Rosenwald was a Jew and made no secret of it. Despite this situation, the two men got along well. After Rosenwald died in 1932, however, his son, Lessing, who was chairman of the board from 1932 to 1939, broke with Wood over this prejudice in 1940.

Wood was idiosyncratic on a good day, and he made some public statements that the more dignified Rosenwald never would have. In the May 1938 issue of *Fortune*, for example, Wood observed that "a good night's sleep, a good appetite, and a sound elimination are a man's prime concern." This may well be true, but it doesn't strike one as the sort of thing a captain of industry should be saying in a widely read business magazine.

Despite the differences in personality between Sears, Rosenwald, and Wood, they all shared one belief with great intensity. Sears, Roebuck was a special place. Speaking to his troops in 1936, Wood said, "There is a deeper conflict between Sears, Roebuck and Co. and Montgomery Ward and Co. than just between two great business competitors. There is a conflict between two philosophies of life and business."

Sears was more than a company. It was a way of life. It was a womb wherein gestated executive after executive from Middle America who saw himself rise through the ranks to positions of great wealth and power. Why was Sears so trusted? Because Sears trusted its customers. It respected them. It treated them right. The company did not have an explicit mission statement, but every employee knew what its true aspiration was. To make the life of the average American better by providing him or her with the good things in life.

Trust was not a one-way street at Sears. It was reciprocal. The numbers were eloquent. In 1964, *Fortune* ran a cover story whose praise was unstinting. Commenting on an 11.1 percent jump in sales over 1963 (a sales increase equal to the total revenue of the Gimbels chain) coming on top of a decade with a compound annual rate of growth in sales of 5.6 percent, the article asked, "How did Sears do it?" Not through any "gimmick" or "bag of tricks." Rather, it was a place where "everybody . . . did the right thing, easily and naturally." Sears, the article gushed, "is number one in the U.S., and also number two, three, four, and five." This referred to the fact that Sears was divided into five territories.

Fortune was not alone. Everyone gushed about Sears. In 1954, in one of his innumerable tomes, the ultimate business guru, Peter Drucker, wrote,

"There is no better illustration of the practice of management" than Sears. Interestingly, William H. Whyte Jr. called the Sears executives "one of the most alert management groups in the country." Whyte, the journalist who coined the term "groupthink," wrote the 1956 bestseller *The Organization Man*. The book was quite critical in an astute fashion of what it viewed as the demise of a buccaneering, entrepreneurial business culture that valued risk and genius in favor of a business world that glorified mediocrity. What is odd is that Sears was coming to epitomize precisely what Whyte found so disturbing.

In 1965, Sears's sales increased another 11.3 percent. Profits were up 6.3 percent. In 1965, not the previous year as *Fortune* had asserted, Sears really became number one in American retailing. This was the year its sales surpassed those of the A&P. It had reached the pinnacle of retail in all classes of trade. Its profits of $323.4 million compared to $52.3 million for the A&P. The closest retail competitor was J. C. Penney, which made $78.9 million.

• • •

Robert Wood was unquestionably a retailing genius. Just look at the numbers. Wood became president of Sears in 1928. That year, sales and profits were $319.8 million and $26.9 million respectively. He stepped down in 1954. That year sales and profits were $2.965 billion and $158.8 million. The price of the stock behaved accordingly. If you had invested in Sears in 1928 and held on to the stock until 1954, you would have been well satisfied. Wood didn't do this all by himself, of course. Sears was a big company with a lot of smart people doing a lot of smart things. But he deserves much of the credit.

A rising stock price was particularly important in the company because its own pension fund was a buyer. In other words, retirees, of whom there were probably well over a million living in 1954, were vitally concerned that the stock's upward trajectory continue.

"I could not have this feeling of pride if Sears had simply made good profits and sales," Wood told a meeting of Sears executives in 1950. "Sears has been a clean business, an honest business, it has performed a real service to the American people, it has sincerely tried to guard the welfare of its employees, it has performed its obligations to the communities of our country. In short, it is not merely a business—it is a great institution." And it was an institution from which Wood did not want to be parted. So he faced a problem in 1939. He was sixty, the mandatory retirement age at Sears. What to do?

Wood asked then chairman Lessing Rosenwald (the break between the two did not come until the following year) whether he would be willing to retire. Rosenwald agreed, and Wood had himself elected chairman and had the board adopt a policy that, with regard to retirement, the chairman should not be considered an employee of the company. This cute little subterfuge allowed Wood to remain in control of the company until 1954, when he was seventy-five.

Goldman Sachs had been Sears's banker from the beginning. One of the investment bank's principals, Sidney Weinberg, finally prevailed upon General Wood to step down. (Weinberg was Jewish, and Goldman was a Jewish bank.) "This," James Worthy, a former employee of and expert on the company, has written, "he did with reluctance but good grace." Somehow, despite retirement rules, Wood remained a member of the board of directors (perhaps he was considered an outside member) for the next fourteen years.

No one became CEO without scrutiny by the General, which sometimes lasted for years. By the mid-1950s, the picture author Donald Katz paints is of a man like Ronald Reagan in his second term, senile yet powerful. Wood, reports Katz, wandered the headquarters like an apparition. He "drooled, ate cigarettes whole, forgot to take the wrappers off candy, and often forgot to zip his fly." These were not good signs.

Nor was it good that Wood remained the decision maker concerning who would run Sears. "As late as 1973, the men the General had personally selected from the pack toward the end of World War II were still coming up and taking their crack—sometimes for as little as two years—because the General, the arbiter of fairness, had said thirty years earlier that it was 'the fair thing to do.'" Four years after Wood had finally passed away in 1969, his dead hand reached up from the grave.

In all probability, no one reading this book can name any of Wood's successors. Some were talented men, but none were men of genius. They were true organization men, executives capable of tweaking a company that was doing well, but not capable of long-term thinking about the opportunities and threats facing Sears.

In their defense, Wood's successors did not have a lot of time to make history. In the sixty-eight years from the company's founding to 1954, the year Wood retired, Sears had three CEOs (not counting Charles Kittle, whose early death cut his tenure short). In the twenty-four years following, six different men held the top spot, averaging four years in office. Two were there for only two years. "The chief executive office," remarked James Worthy, had become "a revolving door."

The men who were pushed through this revolving door were not terribly happy about the situation. Wood's immediate successor was Theodore V. Houser, whom Worthy judges to have been a qualified man. Houser "bitterly resented" the fact that he had to endure the endless wait for Wood to retire before he would have his chance at the top spot. To make sure this did not happen again, he rescinded Wood's rule that exempted the company chairman from mandatory retirement. From now on, the chairman would have to step down at age sixty-five. One result was that Houser himself could serve for only four years.

Since Sears was a successful company, insiders chose Houser's successor and his successor's successor, all, of course, under the eye of Wood. The perverse effect was that "the candidate with the shortest time to go" before reaching sixty-five years of age tended to have a leg up.

Worthy said Wood "had trouble seeing in advance how a particular person would do when moved to a new set of duties or a higher level of responsibility." This "trouble" is no minor failing; its effects have memorably been labeled the Peter Principle. The Peter Principle holds that there is a tendency to promote people to the level of their highest incompetence. That is to say, if you are good at a job at level one, you will be promoted to level two. If you flourish there, then it is on to level three. But if at that third job you are merely mediocre, you will not get promoted; and if times are tranquil, you won't get fired, either.

Spotting talent that will grow with challenges is among the most important tasks in a business. If Wood and a compliant board failed at that, a major problem was in the works.

Worthy believes that Wood's failure may have been due to more than normal human shortcomings. He found "some indication that after moving up to the chairmanship Wood deliberately chose as his successors men who would not challenge his preeminence but instead would implement his ideas unquestioningly."

The Sears that Wood stepped down from in 1954 could probably not have produced another man like him. Wood was an outsider. He came to Sears by way of Ward. A career path that originated with a high executive position at a competing company would have been highly unlikely at Sears in the 1950s.

Furthermore, Sears had lost Ward as a viable competitor. That firm would roll along for no particular reason for years. However, it was never again a serious competitor to Sears. Never again could it poke a stick in Sears's eye. That left J. C. Penney. Penney had a lot of strengths, but it was well under a third the size of Sears and was known more for its soft goods than for the white goods and auto accessories that Sears dominated and found so profitable.

Wood preached that a company had to grow. It was "like an animal or a plant—when it ceases to grow, it begins to decay." Few would disagree with this dictum. Yet how does a leader grow? Do you "continuously improve," doing better and better in every way what you used to do? Do you enter related markets? Do you diversify into unrelated businesses? These are tough questions to answer, and Sears did not answer them correctly. No one seems to have seriously considered vigorously serving the market that made Sears great; that is, the shoppers who wanted "always the low price, always." Evidence of the vibrancy of that market was everywhere apparent by the 1960s and especially by the 1970s. It was evidence Sears chose to deny.

Theodore Houser served as CEO of Sears until 1958. He was followed by Fowler McConnell and Charles Kellstadt, who lasted two years each. During that period sales increased every year and profits increased six of eight years. In 1962, sales stood at $4.6 billion and profits at $233.2 million, a compound annual rate of growth of 5.6 percent and 6.5 percent respectively. These are handsome numbers.

Nevertheless, if we were to select a single year that marked the beginning of the end for Sears, 1962 would be a good choice. That year, the five-and-ten-cent chain Woolworth established a discount arm, WoolCo. The Midwestern department store giant Dayton-Hudson founded a discounter of its own, Target. Two more discounters were established as well. S. S. Kresge founded Kmart, and deep in the wilds of the Ozarks in the nation's second-poorest state, Sam Walton founded Wal-Mart.

Sears ignored these developments. Kmart eventually made it onto the radar screen, but only as an object of derision. As the folks at Sears would say, the market is a diamond. We want the 80 percent in the middle. The top 10 percent is the carriage trade. The bottom 10 percent we leave to Kmart and other "lesser breeds without the law."

Sears viewed itself as having no competition. We compete with ourselves, its executives would tell each other. This arrogance was pardonable when you look at the numbers. From 1962 to 1973, sales and profits increased to $12.3 billion and $679.9 million respectively. Both had increased every year at a compound annual rate of 9.4 percent and 10 percent respectively.

When one peeled back the kimono, however, one could see that all was not well. Sales and profits looked great, but a number of questions were arising. Why, for example, was return on equity dropping? Why was employee productivity not higher? Why were Sears's suppliers making more money selling to Sears than to other customers? Had Sears's own internal accounting become less than reliable? Conflict between the field and the central office was and is endemic in retailing. But had it got out of hand at Sears? Was just a touch of cynicism seeping into the company's proud, arrogant culture?

• • •

Beware the monument.

In 1818, Percy Bysshe Shelley published a poem entitled "Ozymandias":

> I met a traveler from an antique land
> Who said: Two vast and trunkless legs of stone
> Stand in the desert. Near them, on the sand,
> Half sunk, a shattered visage lies, whose frown,
> And wrinkled lip, and sneer of cold command,
> Tell that its sculptor well those passions read.
> Which yet survive, stamped on these lifeless things,

The hand that mocked them, and the heart that fed:
And on the pedestal these words appear:
"My name is Ozymandias, King of Kings:
Look on my works, ye Mighty, and despair!"
Nothing beside remains. Round the decay
Of that colossal wreck, boundless and bare
The lone and level sands stretch far away.

You've got to love a poem that, unlike much modern verse, is easy to understand. Ozymandias was a heavy hitter in days gone by. He built a huge statue of and to himself. If the meaning of the statue was not clear enough, he had inscribed on the pedestal that he was such a big shot that "ye [other] Mighty" were reduced to despairing at his magnificence.

But look! The ruins of the statue were all that survived, and it has become nothing more than a "colossal wreck." Whatever the "works" were that should have caused despair to the mighty have now disappeared into the sands of time.

Gordon Metcalf became CEO of Sears in 1967. Odds are he had never read Shelley's poem. "Being the largest retailer in the world," he said, "we thought we should have the largest headquarters in the world." So, just as cracks began to appear in the armor of Sears, Metcalf decreed that Sears would construct the world's tallest building. The 110-story Sears Tower, renamed Willis Tower in 2009, came to be known as "Gordon Metcalf's last erection," a witticism that would have been inconceivable in the days of Wood.

On the surface, Metcalf's explanation for building the Tower seems to make sense. But when you really think about it, it doesn't. The two clauses have nothing to do with one another, and the declaration cannot survive one single word: Why? Why is it that the world's largest retailer should have the world's largest headquarters?

In 1993, when Intel was experiencing its spectacular growth, Andy Grove, like the rest of the company's employees, had not an office but a cubicle. It was tiny. *Fortune*, in a clever variant of a classic retail metric, conducted a return-to-the-shareholders survey that year. It measured return to the shareholders per square foot of the CEO's office. Grove led the pack by far, as Intel returned $1.64 per square foot of his cubicle.

It was not apparent that Intel needed a giant building to celebrate how wonderful it was. Why was it so obvious at Sears?

Building monuments deserves a file drawer along with trash-talking when you are looking for companies in denial. I recall interviewing top executives in the Sears Tower in the summer of 1980. The pictures on their walls were quite beautiful. I wondered whether the average Sears customer could have afforded the frames. The furniture was plush. It didn't look like it came off the floor of a Sears store.

I remember looking out the windows. The view up Chicago's lakeshore was spectacular. And there was not a competitor in sight. The people down below looked like ants. Those ants were supposed to be Sears's customers. Of all industries, it is most important for a retailer to keep his or her ear to the ground. The Tower was a symbolic denial of that reality.

The year the Tower was dedicated, 1973, was the first year of the chairmanship of Arthur Wood. Wood was no relation to the slovenly general. Quite the contrary. Writer Donald Katz described him as "patrician," "elegant," "the consummate old-world gentleman-businessman." His opulent office included works from his private art collection by Degas and Monet.

Arthur Wood's problem was not that he was unlike the company's éminence grise, but that he was unlike Kmart's great merchant Harry Cunningham. An even bigger problem was that he was the antithesis of the incomparable Sam Walton.

Just prior to the first oil shock in 1973, retail sales in the United States began to decline in real terms. Sears's economist (this is prior to the oil shock) felt the country was looking at a severe recession the following year. A "senior officer" of the company, according to Katz, told the economist that if he publicized an official forecast to this effect, he would be fired. Sounds like Ernest Kanzler all over again, doesn't it? There appears to be a persistent belief in once-great companies that have lost their way that if you simply avoid speaking the blunt truth, all the problems will just go away. It is almost as if by telling the truth, you are endowing problems with a reality that they would not otherwise have. This brand of magical thinking leads to shooting the messenger.

Sears's sales in 1974 actually increased 7 percent, which would not have been bad if the company had not forecast a rise of 15. Profits were off almost a quarter, a dramatically steep slide. Here indeed is the essence of the problem of denial: reality is always just around the corner.

Arthur Wood "acquiesced" to firings that Katz labeled "arbitrary." "As lifelong Sears employees carried their belongings out of the plush new headquarters, it was noted, and passed along the grapevine out to the territories, that the departing members of the family had run into workmen carrying in hundreds of thousands of dollars' worth of house plants to decorate the 110-story testimonial to a company that never failed."

• • •

Sears wandered in the wilderness amid intermittent signs of life from 1973 until it was bought by Kmart owner Eddie Lampert in 2005. The company abandoned its Tower in 1992, a year in which it lost almost $4 billion, and relocated outside of Chicago to a town called Hoffman Estates. Kmart adopted Sears's name, and the combined company is at this writing called Sears Holdings.

Sears began to hire consultants in the 1970s, but they were no more helpful than the homegrown executives. Sears convinced itself that its market was "saturated." The way to grow, therefore, was to enter whole new lines of business. The company bought the real estate firm Coldwell Banker and the financial broker Dean Witter. Why the company's CEOs thought they would do better managing businesses in industries they did not understand than they would in general-merchandise retailing remains one of life's mysteries.

In fact, there was a fortune to be made during the preceding four decades in the very classes of trade in which Sears made its name. We know this—and everyone at Sears should have known it at the time—because Wal-Mart's spectacular success was no secret. It is incredible that in the six-hundred-page book that Donald Katz published in 1987 about the inside story of Sears, a work that contains many interviews with Sears executives, Wal-Mart is mentioned precisely one time. This is despite the fact that Wal-Mart's performance had been like nothing the retail world had ever seen and that, by the time Katz's book was written, Sam Walton was the richest man in the world. As we noted in the previous chapter, there are no secrets in retailing, and Wal-Mart certainly wasn't a secret in the 1980s. Sam Walton dressed in a grass skirt and did the hula on Wall Street itself in 1984 because Wal-Mart's stock had so outperformed what he had bet it would be. You had to be wallowing pretty deeply in denial to miss this.

The executives talking to Katz should have been talking about nothing else. Instead, they were playing around with the "store of the future" and telling themselves they would succeed selling "socks and stocks."

For the sake of symmetry, we should note that Walton did not pay much attention to Sears. In his autobiography, he only mentioned it once, and not very flatteringly: "One reason Sears fell so far off the pace is that they wouldn't admit for the longest time that Wal-Mart and Kmart were their real competition," he wrote. "They ignored both of us, and we both blew right by them."

It has often been observed there are no mature markets, only tired marketers. Unfortunately, nobody at Sears was making that observation, and there is no company which it described more perfectly.

More than a hundred years ago, Louis Asher sent J. H. Jeffries to conduct research on Ward. Jeffries got a job there. He should not have done that. But in the 1970s, there was a desperate need for a J. H. Jeffries at least to visit a Wal-Mart store and see the difference between that and Sears.

It was a difference there would have been no denying.

6

Success Today vs. Success Tomorrow:
Denial and the IBM PC

The world changed on April 7, 1964.

That is the date on which Thomas J. Watson Jr., chairman of the board, chief executive officer, and unquestioned ruler of the International Business Machines Company, stood at a podium in Poughkeepsie, New York, to make what he called "the most important product announcement in company history."

Watson announced the introduction of the IBM System/360, a breakthrough line of mainframe computers that would transform computing, business automation, and IBM. It stands as one of the two greatest product introductions in twentieth-century American business history (the other was the Model T). If the word *revolution* has a place in a discussion of business, System/360 qualifies.

The man making this announcement was the stereotype of the CEO of a great American corporation. Tall, erect, gray-haired, almost criminally handsome, Watson was fifty years old and at the height of his powers. His announcement was brisk, straightforward, and no-nonsense. One would never have guessed that behind this facade was a lifetime of self-doubt and family conflict, nor that the creation of the 360 was such a risky, high-pressure enterprise that it would destroy the careers of some of the people involved with it, including that of Watson's own brother. The price for creating this machine was high.

Why make this announcement in Poughkeepsie, a town about seventy miles up the Hudson from the nation's largest city? Like some other cities in the Hudson Valley, Poughkeepsie was an IBM company town, home of the plants and laboratories of the Data Systems Division. It was one of the sites that would give birth to the System/360. The event could have been staged at IBM's world headquarters, conveniently located at 590 Madison Avenue, in midtown Manhattan. But this particular announcement was sufficiently important for IBM to charter a train from Grand Central Station to Poughkeepsie for two hundred reporters to bask in Watson's reflected glory. The company also held press conferences in sixty-three other cities across the United States and in fourteen foreign countries. Tens of thousands of people around the world attended customer briefings.

The IBM System/360 has been likened to the Manhattan Project, which was the crash program to build an atomic bomb in the midst of World War II. In both cases, scientists and engineers—some of whom were true geniuses—worked at the sharp forward edge of their knowledge. In both cases, highly informed people doubted whether the goal could be achieved. In both cases—of course, in different contexts—failure was not an option. Both projects cost a fortune. And both projects were successful.

At the April 7 announcement, Watson, a World War II veteran, appeared in complete command. He radiated discipline, purpose, and confidence, but not arrogance. He gave his audience the feeling that success—which in reality was still very much up in the air—would be achieved without question.

Now fast-forward to another presentation by another IBM CEO in front of another audience. The man was John Fellows Akers, described by Paul Carroll, a *Wall Street Journal* reporter and author of the book *Big Blues*, as a man "who always had a regal aura about him." In other words, classic IBM. For decades (especially prior to the 360) the driving force behind IBM's success had been sales. Thomas J. Watson Sr., and his oldest son, Tom Jr., were by no stretch of the imagination technologists. These two men ran IBM from 1914 to 1971 and they were salesmen from head to toe. Sales and service was the beating heart of IBM.

Physical appearance was always a matter of the first importance at this company. You wore a white shirt and blue suit when you were selling. A business journalist noted in 1941 that when IBM recruited on college campuses, the two main selection criteria were "good looks and manners." Apparently the company assumed that it could teach its new hires everything else they needed to know at the IBM Schoolhouse in Endicott, New York, or after that, on the road. It was hard to teach good looks.

Akers "was a forceful speaker who had a firm voice and command of his audience. . . . Though of only average height, he had a firm jaw and sniper gray eyes." Akers had risen from a relatively modest background to graduate from Yale and serve as a naval aviator. At IBM, he came up, naturally, through sales.

At nine thirty on the morning of March 26, 1993, Akers met with reporters in the Mercury Ballroom at the Hilton Hotel in New York City. He was accompanied by James E. Burke, retired CEO of Johnson & Johnson and the leading figure on IBM's Board of Directors, and by Louis V. Gerstner, the man Burke persuaded to succeed Akers as IBM's CEO, a startling choice because he was an outsider both to the company and to the industry.

Two months earlier, Akers had announced he would be stepping down from IBM's top spot. When Akers became IBM's CEO in 1985, he "carried himself with a confidence born of total success in any job he'd ever had." But in this—the most important job of his life, a job that in 1985 was the most prestigious in corporate America—he had failed.

The March 26 meeting, so completely different from Watson's press conference in 1964, was the final nail in Akers's coffin. A "stony-faced" Akers was as gracious on that grim occasion, when the corporation appeared to be on the brink of collapse, as a defeated man could be. He said that his successor, Lou Gerstner, brought "a depth of experience, toughness, and energy that's going to be very attractive to IBM people and to the IBM institution and to our customers all around the world." He then "retired to a chair at the edge of the stage, where he slumped through Gerstner's brief talk."

What had happened? How had the company of companies in the industry of industries, employing some of the smartest people in the world, been bought to such a low estate? As you will see in the following three-act drama, much of the answer is to be found in denial.

Act I, which concerns the System/360, is a success story. Unlike many of the executives in this book, Watson did not fall prey to the illusion that just because the company succeeded in the past, it would succeed in the future. This classic strain of our disease, the denial of change itself, is all too common, particularly in successful companies. When you are fat and happy, it is tempting to rearrange your perception of reality in such a way that the conditions that got you where you are become part of the natural order of the universe. It was this denial trap that Watson was able to avoid.

In Act II, IBM does finally become a victim of its own success, with a hidebound culture and leadership. It denies the lessons of its own history, and most disastrously it denies the coming of one of the greatest technology revolutions ever: the personal computer. And finally, redemption. In Act III, our epilogue, IBM pulls itself out of its denial-induced tailspin, unflinchingly faces "the next big thing"—the Internet—as it was unable to do with the PC, and prospers, although never achieving the industry dominance it once enjoyed.

Act I: The IBM System/360

One of the biggest questions about the IBM System/360 is why the company undertook the project at all. It is not as though business was bad during the 1950s. Quite the contrary. This was a decade of dazzling growth. Sales and profits in 1950 were $266 million and $37 million. On May 8, 1956, Watson Sr., eighty-two years of age, finally turned the company over to Watson Jr. and six weeks later, on June 19, he died. Thus, 1957 was the first year that Thomas J. Watson Jr. ran the company in the absence of his hovering father. He could not have been unhappy with the results. Earnings rose by more than a quarter to $110 million. In its forty-sixth year in existence, IBM's sales topped a billion dollars for the first time. By the end of the year they hit $1.2 billion, an increase of almost 35 percent from the previous year.

Watson's fifth full year running the company without Dad around was even more impressive. Sales in 1961 topped $2.2 billion. It had taken forty-five years for IBM to become a $1 billion company. It took a mere four more years for it to become a $2 billion company. Profits soared to well over twice the 1957 figure. Productivity was increasing as well. Sales per employee rose briskly.

What a record! Is this any time to make a "bet the company" gamble? And gamble the 360 was. IBM's stock declined in April of 1964. There were a lot of skeptics on Wall Street. This is actually not an easy question to answer. The first response that leaps to mind is yes. The time to make big bets is when you have the market-power muscle to win them. Just a few years after the April 7, 1964, announcement, Sears, Roebuck was doing . . . what? We know from the previous chapter. Sears wasn't building its business in new ways. It was building a tower. Maybe it should have been building its own version of Wal-Mart instead.

The second response is that we may be giving IBM a little too much credit for this decision. The company knew (as we have already noted Wall Street knew) that in attempting to build the 360 it would tax all the corporation's resources—financial, intellectual, and, most important, human—to the limit. That is what Watson wanted from the company. Indeed, in 1960 IBM introduced the most powerful computer of its day, aptly called Stretch.

That said, no one really knew how hard the successful completion of the 360 would be when the first reports were written about it. The most important such study was the SPREAD (an acronym for Systems Programming, Research, Engineering, and Development) Report, which has become famous in the history of computing. It is probably fair to consider SPREAD, completed on December 28, 1961, as the beginning of the 360.

On January 4, 1962, the thirteen-member SPREAD team presented its findings to IBM's top fifty executives and their staffs. Many were concerned about the size of the task, but T. Vincent Learson, vice president and group executive for IBM's North American computer divisions, expressed "no real objections" and the project moved forward.

No one at the time, including Learson, thought the 360 would pose such challenges. No one, it is probably fair to say, thought it would cost $5 billion. It is difficult to overstate the magnitude of that amount for IBM in the early 1960s. IBM's revenues in 1962 were $2.59 billion. Therefore, a $5 billion expenditure over half decade for a highly speculative new product represented an amount 1.9 times greater than IBM's total income for that year. For the sake of perspective, it is as if in 2008 Google announced a $32 billion gamble to change the industry. The equivalent figure for Wal-Mart would be $720 billion.

Last but by no means least, IBM, though the leader in data processing, was arguably not secure in that position. During the 1950s, the industry was experiencing fantastic growth, and there was, therefore, plenty of room for new entrants. In 1951, according to one source, there were only four computers in the whole world. By 1957, there were about 250. It was clear that the number was destined to grow fast. The number of clerical workers almost doubled from 4.5 million in 1940 to 8 million in 1956. As the consulting firm Arthur D. Little reported in 1957, "There is a growing market for any device which will simplify or cut back on the load of accounting, record keeping, cost analysis, and all the other paper work that must inevitably accompany big business."

IBM had grounds for concern about the future. The competition included Bendix, Burroughs, Honeywell, NCR, RCA, Raytheon, and Sperry Rand. These were big companies experienced in technical products and business-to-business marketing. Some had been competing against IBM for years. Others were new to the company's competitive set. Old or new, they weren't welcome. Sales of Sperry Rand were higher than IBM's as recently as 1956, and RCA was bigger than Sperry Rand.

The other company IBM's top brass had its eye on in the late 1950s was not in the computer business. At least not yet. It was General Electric. More than four times the size of IBM in the mid-1950s, GE had all the tools for market entry, including cash, engineering expertise, and research capability.

The menace posed by the likes of GE and RCA made IBM's top executives realize that "Ever Onward" had to be not just a company anthem, but a strategic imperative. They understood that as powerful as IBM was, it was far from safe. "Below the surface," as a *Fortune* journalist noted, "IBM's organization didn't fit the changing markets any more, and there really was [as Bob Evans, one of the moving forces behind the 360, put it] a risk involved in doing nothing."

Although IBM's market was expanding, its growth rate was slowing. The company did grow 9 percent in 1960. But compared with past performance, even a number that impressive did not set the world on fire. "People began to speculate," Watson Jr. wrote, "that we'd gotten so big that naturally our growth rate had to fall."

This unheralded moment in Watson's career deserves our full attention. He refused to fall into the trap of complacency. He did not become the victim of denial. He did look facts directly in the face. If IBM was not growing as quickly as it should be, the fault, as far as he was concerned, was not in "our stars," it was in "ourselves." The future of computing seemed very good indeed. Watson found it "illogical" that a company in this industry would experience slower growth just because it was big. "I thought it was probably our own fault that we were slowing down." He was proven correct.

Why was Watson able to look facts so squarely in the face at this turning point in the history of his company and its industry? There is no easy answer. Most CEOs would have been more than satisfied with IBM's situation in 1960.

We can say with some assurance that the answer to this question did not lie in native intelligence in the academic sense nor in any particular insight into the industry. Watson's record in prep school (the Hun School, not Andover or Exeter) was poor, although he did do well in physics. Despite all Dad's influence, he could not persuade Princeton to take Junior. "Mr. Watson," Princeton's director of admissions told him, "I am looking at your son's record and he is a predetermined failure." At last Dad succeeded in using his personal connections to get his son into Brown. "He's not very good," the admissions director there said, "but we'll take him."

Things did not get any better when Junior hit IBM's sales-training school in Endicott in upstate New York in 1937. Sales trainees had to do more than admire the electromechanical accounting machines the company produced at that time. They had to acquire a thorough knowledge of how these machines worked. This involved, among other things, "programming" an accounting machine by "plugging up a board" (i.e., by connecting certain wires to the appropriate outlets). This was not uncomplicated, but it was sufficiently manageable that every member of the class except one could master the task. That one exception was the hapless T.J. Jr. "I had to be assigned a tutor," he later recalled. "I spent many nights with that guy in the deserted schoolhouse, trying to hook up those little wires."

I have gone into detail here (and more could be added) to make a point. Denial is not a matter of academic intelligence. If it were, Watson would surely have fallen prey to it. Rather, it is a matter of attitude. Watson eluded denial because he was scared.

Peter Drucker believed that one of the primary purposes of management is to banish fear from the organization. Intel's Andy Grove has taken issue with this observation. "The most important role of managers," he observed, "is to create an environment in which people are passionately dedicated to winning in the marketplace. Fear plays a major role in creating and maintaining such passion. Fear of competition, fear of bankruptcy, fear of being wrong, and fear of losing can all be powerful motivators."

"Fear of failure," Watson said, "became the most powerful force in my life" after he took the helm of IBM in 1956. In addition to the fears Grove mentioned, Watson always felt a sense of competition with his father, even after his father died. Watson knew he was not the favorite of his father's four children (his sister Jane was). He knew that from nothing his father had built a unique corporation. All this left him with a simply stated problem: could he top that? If he could, perhaps he would finally come in first not only in the industry but in the family. A constellation of emotions like these serves well to ward off denial.

Thus Watson chose not to deny that IBM was growing more slowly than it should. What was the problem? The biggest challenge the company faced in 1960 was that, in Watson's own words, it had a product line that had grown "wildly disorganized." He counted eight computers in the catalog as well as some outdated vacuum-tube machines.

A product line this varied resulted in a number of problems. For example, what do you do with your sales force? As we know, sales and service stood at the center of the firm. How do you organize your sales force when your salesmen have this many products to sell and also to service? These were complicated, unforgiving machines. You had to know an awful lot about them. How many machines should one salesman be expected to master? Should you have eight separate sales forces? How many different salesmen selling different machines would wind up seeing one customer? The potential for confusion was limitless.

But the biggest problem was that IBM's computers were incompatible. The software written for one would not work on another. Printers, disk drives, and other peripheral equipment designed for one line of computers were useless for the others. Every time a customer needed to upgrade from one machine to another with greater capabilities, he had to start from ground zero. It was almost as if he had never owned a computer in the first place. In a sense, it was even worse than that. Work you had already done had to be done again. And this for a machine that was supposed to save you time and money! You also ran the risk of losing precious data or having it corrupted in some way. No way to build goodwill.

To make matters worse, the necessity to start from scratch meant that there was no customer lock-in. If a customer needed more computing power than his present machine could deliver and wanted to trade up to a more sophisticated and expensive machine, he had no reason to stick with IBM. The company did not really have a "product line." It marketed fundamentally unrelated products that happened to share the same brand name. In the words of Bob O. Evans, who rose from engineering manager in the General Products Division in Endicott to vice president of the Data Systems Division in Poughkeepsie, and who eventually became one of the principal product champions of the System/360, "User migration from one architecture to another was usually difficult, if possible at all."

From the competitive standpoint, the problem posed by the impossibility of user migration was acute. Each time an IBM customer decided it needed more computing power, there was every reason to survey the whole industry—RCA, Sperry Rand, Honeywell, and the rest. Some of these offerings were quite the equal of IBM's products from a technical point of view. Remember, IBM's strength had always been in sales and service rather than technology. Therefore, incompatibility amounted to an invitation for your customer to comparison shop, the very last invitation you would want to issue.

The solution to this problem was conceptually simple. Develop a compatible product line. But as simple as the concept may have been, its execution taxed the company to its limit. "Building this new line," Tom Watson Jr. remarked, "meant putting IBM through tremendous upheavals. Careers were made and broken, and the mistakes we made along the way changed a lot of lives, including Dick's [Watson's brother] and my own."

The problems giving birth to the System/360 began as early as 1962, and they were more severe than anyone had anticipated. Speaking in retrospect about what can rightly be called his creation, T. Vincent Learson said, "We made two miscalculations. We were off on our assessment of 360's potential reception, and we were off on our assessment of IBM's production capability to meet the demand. And programming System/360 presented a particularly formidable challenge." When you think about it, that pretty much covers the waterfront. Wrong on supply. Wrong on demand.

The pressures involved in creating the 360 are hard to convey. Thousands of people writing millions of lines of code. Three quarters of a billion dollars spent on engineering. A staggering $4.5 billion spent on factories. Five major new manufacturing facilities. More than sixty thousand new employees. Somehow, all of this had to be coordinated. "It was the biggest privately financed commercial project ever undertaken," Watson observed. And it could have failed. IBM's whole product line prior to the first deliveries of the System/360 had become obsolete. If the System/360 failed to live up to expectations, IBM would have nothing to sell. The history of the computer industry and computers as a technology would have been different. The world would have been different.

But it didn't fail. The 360 was a triumph. The magnitude of the success startled the company. Here is Watson's recollection: "My anxiety was misplaced. We got immense numbers of orders—far more than expected—and even more kept pouring in."

The following chart shows the results of that triumph. You would have done far better investing in IBM at the beginning of the 1960s than in its seven competitors or in the stock market as a whole.

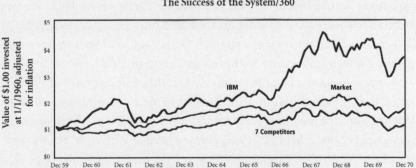

The Success of the System/360

Act II: IBM and the PC

How could a company that had grown so great sink as low as it did by the time that a thoroughly humbled John F. Akers appeared on the stage of the

Mercury Ballroom at the New York Hilton in 1993? Books have been written on the subject, and there are as many opinions as there are authors. But if you had to reduce all the opinions to one idea, it would be that IBM denied the lessons of its own history.

In the years following the 360, IBM's dominance of the world of data processing and the computer grew. So did the special place the company assumed in the business world.

Everyone did business with IBM, and IBM was everywhere. By the late 1970s, more than half the chief information officers at Fortune 500 companies had worked at IBM. More than sixty of those companies had an executive from IBM on their board. In Stanley Kubrick's 1968 motion picture, *2001: A Space Odyssey*, the computer that controls everything is named HAL. Lore has it that HAL was meant to refer to IBM. Each letter of HAL's name is one closer to the beginning of the alphabet than the letters of IBM. For the record, director Kubrick and author Arthur C. Clarke always denied the connection and chalked it up to alphabetic coincidence.

IBM was a clean company that made clean machines that were operated in clean rooms by men wearing clean clothes. The machines were quiet, mysterious, and magical. The company was full of smart people, including Nobel Prize winners. In a world in which it was expected that rich business executives would belong to the Republican Party—even Dick Watson joined a few years after his older brother fired him during the height of the 360 crisis—Tom Watson was a staunch Democrat, who became President Jimmy Carter's ambassador to the Soviet Union in 1979.

Fortune magazine became positively breathless in its praise of Watson. In 1976, it inducted him into the Hall of Fame for Business Leadership, labeling him "the most successful capitalist who ever lived." This hyperbolic nonsense became a habit. In 1987, *Fortune* invited Watson to tell its readers of the "controlled explosion that was IBM under his leadership." The title of the article was a slight variation on the previous theme: "The Greatest Capitalist in History."

But for Watson himself, despite this mountain of adulation, there was doubt, insecurity, and dissatisfaction. He concludes his discussion of the 360 on a distinctly somber note. "Objectively," Watson wrote in his autobiography, "it was the greatest triumph of my business career." Then he added, "But whenever I look back on it, I think about the brother I injured, and the dream of my father's that I could never make come right."

So there was travail amidst the triumph. Watson's brother declined into alcoholism after his failure with the 360. His father's dream to which Watson was referring was that Dick Watson, though only five years Watson's junior, would succeed him as CEO of IBM. Instead, never again would a member of the Watson family run the company.

The 360 was such a monumental success that for years IBM coasted uphill. Some big projects that were subsequently attempted failed, such as Future Systems, a would-be breakthrough on the order of the 360 that was pursued and abandoned in the early 1970s. The endless antitrust problems to which the company's success subjected it further contributed to a conservatism that suffused IBM's ever-expanding bureaucracy.

The company denied that it had been fundamentally transformed by the trauma of giving birth to the 360, and its culture was unable to adjust to this transformation. Tens of thousands of new employees were hired and put to work in a pressure-cooker atmosphere. The company went into mass-production of microelectronics and other critical components that it had previously used in such small quantities that it could purchase them from independent vendors. In a brief time the company had to develop state-of-the-art expertise in a bewildering variety of specialties, each one of which was vital to the construction of a commercial artifact that had to function flawlessly.

The glue that had held the company together for decades was beginning to crack. From 1914 to 1956, Thomas J. Watson Sr. ran the company, and he positioned himself as the man with the answers. Nothing better indicates this than the lyrics to the songs that IBM's minions endlessly sang. You can listen to them on the Web. Most well known is "Ever Onward." Here is its first verse:

> There's a thrill in store for all,
> For we're about to toast
> The corporation in every land.
> We're here to cheer each pioneer
> And also proudly boast

Of that "man of men," our friend and guiding hand.
The name of T. J. Watson means a courage none can stem;
And we feel honored to be here to toast the "IBM."

Lyrics on IBM public Website with no ©, permissions note, etc.

Taken out of the context of its time, this song seems ridiculous. There probably isn't a CEO in the nation who would countenance such adulation today ("The name of T. J. Watson means a courage none can stem") or a workforce that would put up with it.

Even in the business world of a century ago, when song singing was not uncommon, this specimen is a little over-the-top. It was not at all exceptional at IBM, however. There were dozens of songs like it. These songs made a statement. You don't have them unless you yourself plan on staying at the corporation for a long time, as Watson Sr. did. He ran IBM for almost half a century. Furthermore, you were constructing yourself as the man with all the answers, the solution to all the problems. Although the paternalism was hard to take, it was also comforting. Watson took care of you.

Watson Jr. dragged the company's culture into the twentieth century, but the residue of Dad's approach was not hard to find. Watson Jr. was a celebrity CEO. Not only did *Fortune* praise him without bounds, *Life* magazine ran a photo essay on him and his handsome family. He was on the cover of *Time* and *Sports Illustrated* (the family liked to ski). He was a friend of the Kennedys when they were at the height of their glamour. Lyndon Johnson awarded him the Presidential Medal of Freedom in 1964. He was totally devoted to IBM. No intention of leaving. The man with the answers. "Father knows best."

The best illustration of Watson's fealty to the sales-and-service religion that was Dad's IBM came during Watson's tenure as Jimmy Carter's ambassador to the Soviet Union from October of 1979 to January of 1981. This was a time of acute tension. Just after Christmas in 1979, the Soviet Union invaded Afghanistan. Here are Watson's observations:

> The president called me back to Washington, and I joined the White House consultations about how the United States should respond. Carter was determined to make the Soviets pay for their aggression.... The

> White House and State Department made up a long list of anti-Soviet moves—my own embassy contributed a number of suggestions—and in the end the president decided to accept almost every one. This meant taking apart practically all the cooperative arrangements we had with the Russians under détente, from art exhibitions to new sales of grain.

Thus far, Watson's comments are reportage and make sense. But now, listen to this: "There wasn't much I could add to the discussion; the only time I spoke up was to object to particular trade sanctions that went too far."

What might such trade sanctions be?

"For example, American companies had delivered manufacturing equipment to Russia, and now they weren't even going to be allowed to send spare parts to fix equipment that was still under warranty."

And now, a sentence that only a man steeped in IBM culture could write: "I told the president if you want to declare war or have a boycott, fine . . ."

Now think about this clause for a moment. "If you want to declare war . . . fine . . ." We are talking about World War III! Mutually Assured Destruction! Turning the planet into a smoldering ruin! Watson continues: ". . . but breaking a commitment to a customer is always wrong."

No other passage so succinctly captures IBM during the Watson years, the glory years. But what about the years after Watson and after the triumph of the 360?

IBM's "ever onward" sense of mission was slowly, inexorably transformed into momentum. "IBM has been built on problems," Vin Learson said. True. This company had transformed itself from a purveyor of meat slicers and butcher scales to one of electromechanical gears and ubiquitous punch cards. It then transformed itself to fully electronic devices, culminating in the System/360. What next?

A lot of unintended consequences flowed from the 360 that did not serve IBM well in the era to come. The company's great and successful gamble seemed to make it less daring. The 360 wore Watson out, and it exhausted the company as well. One problem was that there was no Watson or Watson-like figure to whip and drive the company forward.

IBM denied the necessity, given its culture and history, to have a "man of men" at the helm. Name the company's CEOs from Watson to the company's transformation under Lou Gerstner in the 1990s. You can't. They seem like faceless bureaucrats presiding over a company suffering from ever more severe cases of "bureaupathology."

The signs were everywhere. Ritualistic behavior replaced substance. It is not easy to capture the slow degeneration of a culture. Here is one example from journalist Paul Carroll:

> With competitors seemingly vanquished, the only way for those inside IBM to measure their success was to see how high they could rise within the company. Like civil servants, they referred to themselves and each other by their salary levels: "I'm a fifty-seven but she just became a sixty-one." People learned that the way to get ahead wasn't necessarily to have good ideas. That took too long to become apparent. The best way to get ahead was to make good presentations. People would say of comers: "He's good with foils," referring to the overhead transparencies that began to dominate IBM meetings. People began spending days or weeks preparing foils for routine meetings. They not only made the few foils they actually planned to use but made a huge library of backup foils, just in case someone had a question. Presentations became so important that it was no longer acceptable to be stumped by a question, to say, "I'll get back to you." Foils—sometimes referred to as "slideware"—began innocently enough. They stemmed from Tom Watson Senior's habit of keeping a roll of butcher paper by his desk so he could jot down thoughts. But they became such a part of the culture that senior executives began having projectors built into their beautiful rosewood desks.

This vignette contains the core of IBM's version of denial. The company denied that there was a difference between form and substance. Think about the kind of person who is going to put up with life in what might be called this "virtual" world within the real world. Gamesmen will be attracted, but anyone with an entrepreneurial bent would not join and certainly would not stay. Can you imagine Bill Gates or Steve Jobs devoting his career to a company like this?

I can't resist one further example of form's triumph over substance at IBM. IBM executives and especially its salespeople were known for dressing in uniform. Blue suit. White shirt. And that's not all. Former IBM executive Sam Albert recalled in 1996 that on his first day at the company "a gentleman said to me as we were entering the building, 'Are you an IBMer,' and I said yes ... and he said, 'Could you just lift your pants leg please.' I said,

'What?' And before I knew it, he had lifted my pants leg, and he said, 'You're not wearing any garters.' I said, 'What?!' He said, 'Your socks, they're not pulled tight to the top, you need garters.' And sure enough I had to go get garters."

Where did these customs come from? They were another legacy of Tom Watson Sr. From his early experience as a traveling salesman, Watson knew that too often the potentially demoralizing task of selling could eat away at a man's self-esteem. Many salesmen reacted by dressing flamboyantly or sloppily, talking too much, or drinking excessively. Watson wanted his salesmen to call attention to their products, not themselves. He wanted them to dress like their customers.

At the time and in that context, Watson's rules made a lot of sense. IBM's dilemma by the 1980s was that the rule—the conservative outfit—remained despite the fact that no one could remember the reason for it. IBM salesmen were wearing suits when their clients, especially in California, were coming to work far more informally.

Precisely the same custom—wearing suits when you visit clients—came to produce the opposite result from what was originally intended. Instead of uniting the salesman with his customer, it separated the two, making one or both feel self-conscious and ill at ease, if not comic. IBM's dress code became so famous that when Lou Gerstner abolished it in 1995, the gesture made the *New York Times*.

This cultural conservatism and insularity affected more than attire. It helps to explain how IBM failed to capitalize on the PC revolution. IBM had convinced itself that it defined an industry. It was unthinkable that the computer could migrate from massive air-conditioned rooms where the priesthood tended IBM mainframes to the humble desks of the hoi polloi. The democratization of consumption is a central theme of American history. But it was unimaginable that the two Steves—Jobs and Wozniak—might be doing that very thing to the computer.

Thus it was that IBM—the company with a history of making big bets, the company that had successfully crossed the chasm from gears to chips and led the world into the electronic age, the company that had launched the industry-transforming System/360—became known as the company from which products were not launched. They escaped.

One of the difficulties of discussing the cause and the price of denial at

IBM is that you cannot point to one person, one decision, or one incident as the culprit. This story is very different from that of Henry Ford and his Model T. It is the story of the slow degeneration of a whole culture from one girded by a profound, unseen environment of trust to a nightmarish bureaucratic maze, in part because the stern whip of necessity, competitive pressure from other companies, was not perceived to exist.

The clearest illustration of this degeneration is the creation of the IBM PC. IBM had been making some stabs at producing a PC for years, but nothing ever came of those attempts. At length, goaded by all the publicity Apple was getting, IBM was unable to deny that it had to make a statement in what, as of 1980, it still conceived of as a small niche business. It decided to market a PC.

Indicative of how encased in concrete the company had become was that the IBM PC was to be developed not at any major facility but at an off-site "skunkworks" a million miles from anywhere in Boca Raton, Florida. IBM did not pose its challenge this way (it never would have), but its goal was to produce a quick and dirty PC. To take the shine off Apple and to silence its critics quickly, IBM decided to buy the components of its PC from outside vendors and assemble them. This was precisely the opposite approach the company took to the 360. But the decision did not seem to worry anybody.

The IBM PC debuted in 1981 and, to the surprise of almost everybody, took the world by storm. The results were simply beyond belief. Revenues from the IBM PC alone exceeded $4 billion in 1984, meaning that if it were an independent company, it would have ranked seventy-fourth on the Fortune 500. From 1981 to 1984, sales for IBM as a whole were launched into the stratosphere, from $29 billion to $46 billion. Profits doubled from $3.3 billion to $6.6 billion, making 1984 at IBM the most profitable year that any company in any industry in any country anywhere in the whole world had ever experienced. IBM also became the most valuable company in the world, with a market capitalization of about $72 billion. IBM's market capitalization rose almost 50 percent to $106 billion on August 20, 1987.

People in the know understood that IBM was in trouble by 1987, but Wall Street played its usual role of lagging indicator by overvaluing the company. Six years later, on August 16, 1993, IBM's market capitalization was $23 billion. About $83 billion in wealth (not adjusting for inflation) had simply vanished.

What happened? Surely it would have been churlish in the extreme to complain of IBM's performance when one considers the financials during the 1980s.

Not really, though. Not if one thinks of denial.

Earlier in this chapter, I remarked that the most basic denial of which IBM was guilty was its own history. Now let me be specific. The first thing you learn in any business school is to ask, am I doing today what will enable me to succeed tomorrow? For decades—especially under the relentless, demanding cheerleading of Thomas J. Watson Sr.—the answer to that question was yes. Time and again Watson told his troops that IBM was not just another company; it was an institution, and it was immortal. That vision dominated his decision making.

But that vision was denied in the 1970s and 1980s. The IBM PC was the perfect example. The company did today what enabled it to succeed today and guaranteed its failure in the future. By purchasing the components of its PC from outside vendors, it enormously enriched Intel, which won the contract to supply the IBM PC's microprocessor, and virtually created Microsoft, which programmed the operating system.

Moreover, by allowing Intel and Microsoft to sell to others in the PC market, IBM guaranteed the creation of competition. And these new competitors had nothing like the grotesquely bloated staff and overhead structure that weighed down Big Blue.

Denial bought IBM short-term success at the price of long-term failure. Eventually, it was forced to exit the PC business.

"Why would computer executives who had proven themselves to be brilliant and entrepreneurial managers throughout their careers have such a hard time facing the reality of [the transformation of their industry by the personal computer]?" asked Andy Grove in his discussion of the IBM PC debacle in *Only the Paranoid Survive*.

> Was it because they were sheltered from news from the periphery? Or was it because they had such enormous confidence that the skills that had helped them succeed in the past would help them succeed in the face of whatever the new technology should bring? Or was it because the objectively calculable consequence of facing up to the new

world of computing, like the monumental cutbacks in staff that would
be necessary, were so painful as to be inconceivable? It's hard to know
but the reaction is all too common. I think all these factors played a
part, but the last one—the resistance to facing a painful new world—
was the most important.

Act III: IBM's Comeback

F. Scott Fitzgerald said, "There are no second acts in American lives." IBM
proved there can be three. The IBM of today is not recognizable when
compared to the IBM that denied its way through the PC revolution in the
1980s. While it is not my purpose to present complete corporate histories
of the companies in this book, some discussion of how IBM was able to
turn itself around might be in order.

One of the most significant factors in IBM's rebirth was a renewed
awareness of reality that was driven by desperation. When Lou Gerstner
took the helm, there was simply no denying that the company's financial
situation was dire. "Only a handful of people," he has written, "understand
how precariously close IBM came to running out of cash in 1993." Unlike
Ford, which was a private company throughout the 1920s, 1930s, and 1940s
and could thus deny the financial straits it was in, IBM was a publicly held
company and did not have that luxury.

Outside the company, conditions were conducive to a turnaround. Not
only was the general economic climate favorable through most of the
1990s—this was the last American decade in what will probably be the last
American century—but a transformative new technology, the Internet, was
emerging that an executive team with vision could turn to its advantage,
which IBM's leadership did.

IBM reinvented itself as less of a hardware company and more of an
e-business and Web services provider. By 2004, IBM's services unit alone
had higher revenues than any freestanding technology company other than
Hewlett-Packard. Gerstner and his team took advantage of profound shifts
in their industry in the same way that GM's Alfred P. Sloan Jr. and his team
had exploited new developments in theirs.

They were helped by the fact that service was part of IBM's DNA. Recall
Tom Watson Jr.'s assertion that global conflagration is one thing, breaking

a commitment to a customer quite another. "I think that you have to have more than just a machine," Watson said in 1993. "Other people could build the hardware. . . . But that idea of service was so ingrained in every one of us that there wasn't any of us who wouldn't jump out of bed to go try and pacify a customer."

Another key factor in IBM's revival was its decision to hire an outsider as CEO. In more ways than just relaxing the dress code, Lou Gerstner, without the accumulated baggage of years at IBM, was able to reimagine and reshape what had become the calcified corporate culture of the later Watson years. Sociologist Georg Simmel described this phenomenon in 1908. A stranger coming into an organization, Simmel observed, "is freer, practically and theoretically; he surveys conditions with less prejudice . . . he is not tied down in his action by habit, piety, and precedent."

Sometimes it is possible for insiders to metamorphose psychologically into outsiders by adopting novel points of view. We will witness such a transformation in chapter 10, when we encounter Intel's resurrection from its own near-death experience. The ability to step outside of oneself and one's assumptions temporarily is an effective prophylactic against denial. Unfortunately, it is also difficult and rare. When companies are mired in self-delusion, they are often able to extricate themselves only with the help of an outsider, such as was the case with John J. Nevin, the tire-industry outsider who was brought in to save what was salvageable of Firestone. This is the role that Gerstner played at IBM. When Gerstner left the company in 2002, he turned it back over to an IBM old-timer, Sam Palmisano, who had joined the firm in 1973.

IBM today is once again a big and important company. Its market capitalization at this writing is more than $165 billion. Few people in the early 1990s would have thought this was possible. IBM will never again be the corporate icon that it once was. But it did survive a closer brush with death than most people realize. And the major reason that it did was that the facts on the ground were awful, and an outside CEO didn't deny them.

7

Coke's New Formula for Denial

On January 30, 2009, the Coca-Cola Company removed the word *Classic* from its flagship brand. Thus came to a conclusion one of the most noteworthy episodes in the history of marketing.

About a quarter of a century previously, Coca-Cola changed its formula. This turned out to be a mistake of monumental proportions. The mistake was not merely the formula change but also the manner in which the change was managed.

When New Coke was introduced and Old Coke was discontinued in April 1985, the company swore up and down that it had made a move that couldn't miss. The very thought of keeping the "old" formula was repeatedly dismissed out of hand. According to journalist and author Thomas Oliver, "When asked if there was any possibility of bringing back the old Coke, spokesmen unequivocally said, 'Never.'"

"Never" lasted seventy-nine days. On July 11, 1985, Coca-Cola reintroduced the original formula with a slightly amended name: Coca-Cola Classic. Eventually renamed Coke II, New Coke languished until being discontinued in 2002. On January 30, 2009, *Classic* was finally removed from the last bottles of original Coke. We know today that it is New Coke that is dead and buried. When will it be reintroduced? We can confidently respond, "Never."

. . .

This is the story of how some of the brightest business executives backed up by the best research you could buy introduced a new product that will forever be to the beverage business what the Edsel is to the automobile business.

This is the story of New Coke.

How could such smart executives pool their energies only to humiliate their company and themselves? You will not be surprised to learn that denial was the culprit. In the case of New Coke, denial took a number of forms. The executives denied the depth of the meaning of the Coca-Cola tradition. They denied the aggressiveness of Pepsi-Cola. Perhaps most important of all, they denied the power of simply telling the truth. Because of their denial, these executives put themselves in a position in which they were constantly forced to be untruthful and were constantly getting caught. Nowhere to run. Nowhere to hide.

The most dramatic demonstration of the mess these men made for themselves was provided by the launch of New Coke, a high-profile event at the Vivian Beaumont Theater in New York's Lincoln Center at 11:00 a.m. on Tuesday, April 23, 1985.

The two key men making the announcement of New Coke that day were Roberto C. Goizueta, CEO, and his right-hand man, Donald R. Keough. Smart, shrewd, successful, yes. But stuck in an unenviable situation.

The flagship product of the Coca-Cola Company is, unsurprisingly, Coca-Cola. New Coke was being introduced because traditional Coca-Cola had been losing share to Pepsi-Cola for years. An increasing number of consumers, especially younger consumers, preferred the sweeter taste of Pepsi to Coke. The situation was clear and simple, yet Goizueta, Keough, and all the other top executives of Coca-Cola had convinced themselves that they could say anything and everything except this simple truth.

At seven thirty on the morning of the big press conference where the formula change was to be announced, Goizueta and Keough had a run-through. According to the reporting of Thomas Oliver, "They were understandably anxious about what lay before them." Why? Was it because they had convinced themselves that they would have to respond to questions with untruths? Or, to take the matter one step further, with outright lies?

Those were probably not the reasons. When Benjamin Disraeli became prime minister of Great Britain after years of angling for the position, he observed, "I have climbed to the top of the greasy pole." The pole is no less greasy at the top of corporate America. Many people who reach the top have told a fib more than once.

People in the public eye must develop a sense of which untruths are acceptable and which are not. Richard Nixon never did, which is among the reasons that he was forced from office in 1974. His lies were too transparent, too demeaning, too obvious. Goizueta and Keough must have sensed during that practice session that the story they were about to tell was painfully not credible. They were nevertheless determined to bull their way through it.

"Since they couldn't offer a candid picture," explains Oliver, Goizueta and Keough "employed two tactics: They inundated the press with statistics and data, while bragging their way through, joking and sidestepping the questions."

As the crowd filtered into the hall, it was greeted with a medley of all-American songs and symbols so shameless that it would have embarrassed anyone who had not put it together. "No political candidate," comments Oliver, "would have gotten away with such patrioteering without howls of protests." In fact, the big announcement was not as big as was originally planned because news of the formula change had leaked out on the previous Friday.

Goizueta strode to the podium to begin the proceedings. A consummate inside operator, he was, unfortunately, not wholly in his element before a large crowd. He was ill at ease. The message he was charged to deliver did not make him any less uncomfortable. "The best," he announced, "has been made even better. . . . Some may call [the formula change] the boldest single move in the history of the packaged-goods business. We simply call it the surest move ever made because the new taste of Coke was shaped by the taste of the consumer."

Goizueta then told the tale of how the new formula was created. And quite a tall tale it was. In the process of creating Diet Coke, an outstanding success introduced in August 1982, the company's flavor chemists had stumbled across a new formula for Coca-Cola. Research revealed that consumers preferred this to the current formula, Goizueta explained, giving the company no choice but to switch recipes and making this switch "one of the easiest [decisions] ever made."

Nothing about this story was true. But that was not the heart of the problem Goizueta and Keough faced. The heart of the problem was that the story the company was asking the press to believe was not only false, it was grossly implausible. To reiterate, the problem was not that it was a lie; the problem was that it was not a clever lie. There was nothing inviting about this tall tale, nothing to encourage the press to "play along." The proprietor of the most valuable brand in the world stumbled across a better formula by accident and decided to switch? Really?

When a company comes to a pivotal moment such as this, the press quickly decides whether to become an ally or an adversary. The decision the press reached is clear from the Q-and-A session that followed the company's presentation. The session lasted an hour, and it wasn't pretty.

Q: Are you a hundred percent certain that this won't bomb?
Goizueta: As I said, it is the surest move ever because consumers made it.
Keough: We know we have a winner.
Q: What's the difference between the new and the old?
Goizueta: When you describe flavor, it is a matter better left to the poets or copywriters or members of the press. Why don't you try it and you yourself make the judgment?

It is not often that reporters have the opportunity to grill corporate big shots in a setting uncontrolled by their PR and legal handlers. They had that opportunity now and, prepared by useful suggestions from Pepsi-Cola executives, followed up on incomplete answers. Thus, after Goizueta's answer, the next question was "Put it in your own words."

Goizueta had had a very successful half decade at Coca-Cola. He may have been a little taken aback by the bluntness of this inquisition. A follow-up question was apparently not in his briefing book. "I would say that it is smoother, uh, uh, rounder, yet, uh, bolder. . . . It has a more harmonious flavor." The reporters, Oliver observed, "began to snicker." "I think the taste kind of surrounds you," Keough chimed in.

That may have helped a little, but the questions were becoming progressively more difficult. "To what extent are you introducing this product to meet the Pepsi Challenge?" Everyone knew about the Pepsi Challenge, an ad campaign in which a majority of real consumers chose Pepsi over Coke in blind taste tests. Everyone knew that Pepsi was breathing down Coke's neck in terms of market share. However, Goizueta and his executive team felt that this simple truth could not be acknowledged. "Oh, gosh, no," said Goizueta. "That's, uh . . . the Pepsi Challenge? When did that happen?" This is a good example of the impermissible lie. Every sentient being on the planet knew about the Pepsi Challenge. Goizueta's response was disingenuous to the point of being an insult.

Thus the next question: "Are you saying that Pepsi-Cola had no more to do with this than Heinz baked beans or Hershey's Kisses?" This was more an accusation than a question. "Well, I don't know," Goizueta responded. "You can certainly handle the English language better than I can, so I'm not going to get into it with you. I can say that the consumer had everything to do with it."

It was all downhill from there. The press conference was a fiasco. Roger Enrico, CEO of Pepsi-Cola, learned along with everyone else on the Friday prior to the press conference what Coca-Cola was up to. "They're actually going to do it!" Enrico exclaimed feverishly to a colleague. "They aren't introducing a new product—they're pulling Coke off the market!"

"Driving to the office," Enrico recalled, "I can't help but notice everything along the way—adrenaline is shooting through my veins; my senses are at a peak. It's a fantastically beautiful spring morning along the Merritt Parkway [in suburban Connecticut]. I can feel the leaves budding on the ancient oak trees . . . see the grass greening . . . smell the azaleas flowering."

Brash and aggressive, Enrico knew that an opportunity such as Coke was providing did not come around twice, and he had no intention of letting this golden moment slip by. But timing was everything. It was Friday. Pepsi's response had to be ready to go on Tuesday. Wednesday would be too late.

Enrico rocketed into his office, and a letter seemed to type itself:

To All Pepsi Bottlers and Pepsi-Cola Company Personnel:

It gives me great pleasure to offer each of you my heartiest congratulations. After eighty-seven years of going at it eyeball to eyeball, the other guy just blinked.

Coca-Cola is withdrawing their product from the marketplace, and is reformulating brand Coke to be "more like Pepsi." . . . Too bad Ripley's not around . . . he could have had a field day with this one.

There is no question the long-term market success of Pepsi has forced this move.

Everybody knows that when something is right it doesn't need changing. Maybe they finally realized what most of us have known for years . . . Pepsi tastes better than Coke.

Well, people in trouble tend to do desperate things . . . and we'll have to keep our eye on them.

But for now, I say victory is sweet, and we have earned a celebration. We're going to declare a holiday on Friday.

Enjoy!

Best regards,

Roger Enrico

President, Chief Executive Officer

Pepsi-Cola USA

Enrico really stuck in the stiletto. He bought space in newspapers all over the country for Tuesday. He didn't stop there. His public relations director suggested that Pepsi put on a party at Columbus Circle, just a few blocks south of Lincoln Center. After all the bobbing and weaving at the Beaumont Theater, the reporters would get free samples of "the *real*, real thing," Pepsi, before writing up their stories back at their offices.

"Look at it this way," Enrico explained to his people:

Pepsi's early history was a rocky road—we've come back from bankruptcy twice. From the beginning, Coke's been king of the castle. Thirty years ago they outsold us . . . what? Three to one? Just look how far we've come. Now they're taking their product off the market. If that's not a victory worth celebrating, I don't know what is. It is a *human* victory—all the hundreds of thousands of company and bottler employees who worked so hard over the years to make Pepsi what it is today deserve to be recognized. Let's let our people celebrate all of that by taking a day off.

The net result of all this activity was that April 23, 1985, was a triumph for Pepsi. It was a disaster for Coke.

. . .

Roberto Goizueta, top man at Coke, was among the greatest CEOs in twentieth-century American business history. His story is also among the least likely. Goizueta was born and raised in Cuba, yet he became the chief executive of an iconic American company. He was a chemical engineer who, against all the odds you can imagine, became the leader of a company that produced an inexpensive, all-American consumer product, Coca-Cola.

Goizueta became president of the Coca-Cola Company in 1980 and chairman of its board in 1981. At the time, the firm's market capitalization hovered around $4.5 billion. When death terminated his career in 1997, Coca-Cola's market capitalization was about $180 billion. This was achieved even though carbonated soft drinks are among the lowest of low-tech products. No new, world-transforming invention made it possible for this company, which was founded in 1886 and is among the nation's oldest, to put up these kinds of numbers. Coca-Cola's performance during these years was the result of many factors. Goizueta did not do all this by himself. Nevertheless, his vision for the company and his leadership in getting it to go where he wanted it to go deserve a lot of the credit.

Coca-Cola's boss, its great man, from his accession to the presidency in 1923 to his death in 1985 at the age of ninety-five, was Robert Winship Woodruff. Born into a rich and powerful family, Woodruff epitomized what novelist E. L. Doctorow described as "that classic American hero, a man born to extreme wealth who by dint of hard work and ruthlessness multiplies the family fortune till it is out of sight."

Both Woodruff the man and his philosophy dominated Coca-Cola even after he relinquished his formal position in the firm. A few of his principles merit our special attention. First, with regard to product policy, Coca-Cola's was simplicity itself. It didn't change. This was quite exceptional because change in products was a law of life in twentieth-century America. This law was obeyed in numberless product categories. Its necessity was nowhere more vividly illustrated than in the automobile industry, at the center of the economy, when General Motors overtook the seemingly invincible Ford in the 1920s. But at Coca-Cola, as *Fortune* correctly observed in 1945, "Unlike the auto or refrigerator or electrical-goods maker, Bob [Woodruff] would be properly horrified at changing his [product]."

You could depend on Coca-Cola. It was more than mere sugared, flavored water. It was more than a mere thirst quencher. Coca-Cola was your friend.

Another of Robert Woodruff's principles was to stand well with the government. He was one of the most important citizens of Coca-Cola's hometown, Atlanta, and of the state of Georgia. He was not unknown in Washington, where his intimate connections with the government helped him transform Coca-Cola into a truly global brand. This achievement was captured in a *Time* magazine cover story entitled "World & Friend." The cover portrayed a smiling anthropomorphic circular emblem of Coca-Cola embracing a smiling anthropomorphic planet Earth and feeding the planet the traditional six-and-a-half-ounce hobble-skirted bottle of Coca-Cola. The caption reads, "Love that piaster, that lira, that tickey, and that American way of life." Advertising dollars can't buy such matchless publicity.

During the 1970s, Coca-Cola continued to project its special, uniquely American image. It conceived of itself as the brand beyond competition. When you actually looked past the hype, however, the cold, hard numbers were not all that happy. In the first quarter of 1975, for example, worldwide sales hit an all-time high, but domestic sales were actually below those of 1974. Even more worrisome, as Coke was thrashing about with internal squabbles, Pepsi, that feisty competitor that simply refused to go away, was gaining on it in the U.S. market.

Coca-Cola's CEO during the 1960s and 1970s was J. Paul Austin. But while Woodruff lived, no CEO could have a free hand. "The relationship between Woodruff and Austin," in the view of author Mark Pendergast, "had always been a peculiar love-hate affair. 'One minute they were as close as son and father,' an associate recalls. 'The next, they were spitting at each other like two cats.'"

The company could not seem to free itself from the myriad internal issues—conflicts with bottlers, conflicts between personalities, and so forth—which, while gripping to those immediately involved, did nothing for the brand. The consumer, especially in the American market, was being actively and cleverly wooed by an ever more aggressive Pepsi-Cola. Coke's domestic growth was slow. The company was treading water.

The two men Coca-Cola relied upon for leadership proved progressively less able to provide it. Woodruff suffered two strokes in 1972, and although he recovered, his health deteriorated as he aged. He was eighty-five years old in 1975, and the years were taking their toll.

Austin was two decades younger than Woodruff, but unfortunately he was not untouched by health issues himself. As early as 1975, people began to notice that he was becoming forgetful. "I knew Paul was drinking a little," observed a colleague, "and I just put it down to that. We all did." But it wasn't that. "At the age of fifty-nine, Paul Austin had begun the slow, terrifying descent into Alzheimer's disease." He and Woodruff would die the same year, 1985.

What did Coca-Cola do while chasing its tail in the mid-1970s? We have seen it before. Beware the edifice complex! The company built a new twenty-six-story headquarters, the tallest building in its Atlanta neighborhood. To pay for this monument, Coca-Cola borrowed a hundred million dollars. This further alienated Austin from the aging Woodruff, who had rescued an ailing Coca-Cola from debt back in the 1920s.

Austin was a powerhouse when he became CEO, and in the two decades of his regime, from 1962 to 1981, great things did happen at Coca-Cola. If he had retired in 1972, he would be remembered as an outstanding executive. However, perhaps principally because of his dreadful illness, the 1970s were years of drift rather than mastery at the firm.

Meanwhile, Pepsi, not suffocating as was Coke under the wet blanket of a legacy, was willing to try anything. In a speech to Coca-Cola bottlers in 1979, Bryan Dyson, who had just been imported from South America to run U.S. domestic operations, lamented that Coca-Cola's market share had grown a mere three tenths of a percent in a decade. In sharp contrast, he announced, "Pepsi's corporate share has grown from 21.4 percent to 24.2 percent." Dyson's observation was met by a gasp from the audience. The gasp was generated not so much by the data—devastating in a market in which a share point was worth millions—as by the fact that he actually said "Pepsi." That word was never to be used at Coca-Cola. Yet another stark example of denial.

The attitude of PepsiCo toward its flagship brand could hardly have differed more from Coca-Cola's. Pepsi-Cola was originally created by a druggist in New Bern, North Carolina, in the 1890s. Like Coca-Cola, Pepsi straddled the fence between medicine and refreshment. Here, by way of illustration, is part of the text of a Coca-Cola advertisement in 1905: "Coca-

Cola is a delightful, palatable, healthful beverage. It relieves fatigue and is indispensable for business and professional men . . . and is the favorite drink for ladies when thirsty, weary, despondent." And here is a 1915 advertisement for Pepsi. "Pepsi-Cola aids digestion. It relieves many stomach troubles. . . . It never injures the stomach no matter how much you drink of it. Children relish Pepsi-Cola and it makes them fat."

Pepsi-Cola went bankrupt in 1923. It was bought out of bankruptcy in 1931 and reformulated and repackaged. Unlike the literally thousands of Coke wannabes, Pepsi refused to go away. In the 1960s, creative, aggressive marketers invented the Pepsi Generation. The goal was to use one of Coke's greatest brand appeals against it. In essence, Coca-Cola told the world, "We are traditional America." Pepsi said, "You are old. We are new. 'Comin' at ya. Goin' strong.'"

Pepsi was second in the domestic market and a far distant second globally. The company's motto could have been "Anything goes." Advertising, product policy, distribution—everything in the business was always in play. For example, when Pepsi brought out a diet version, it was named Diet Pepsi. When Coke, two years after Pepsi, brought out a diet version, the name was Tab. Everything that could be played with at Pepsi was sacrosanct at Coke. The idea of leveraging the hallowed brand name of Coca-Cola by using it for another beverage was heresy.

■ ■ ■

The causes for the formula change dated back a decade before the 1985 announcement. In 1975, Pepsi executive Larry Smith was dispatched to Texas to do something about the brand's miserable performance there. "Texas was a disaster," Smith said, and there is no reason to disagree with him. At one chain in Dallas, for example, Coca-Cola had 35 percent of the market and Pepsi only 6. Pepsi was being clobbered by regional favorite Dr Pepper, with a quarter of the market.

Out of this slough of despond, Smith conceived of blind taste tests. As were others, Smith was convinced that Pepsi's taste was more popular with Coke drinkers than they realized. "We had a joke," Smith said, that "if you put Coke in a Pepsi bottle, you'd starve to death, but if you put Pepsi in a Coke bottle, you'd get rich quick. . . . We were convinced people were drinking the trademark."

Smith, with nothing to lose (what were the chances that his 6 percent share would drop to 5?), staged a series of blind taste tests in Dallas. Pepsi won. Consumers preferred its sweeter taste. This was the Pepsi Challenge. "Let Your Taste Decide."

The top people at Coca-Cola were shocked. Difficult as it may be to believe, Coca-Cola had never actually tested the taste of its crown-jewel product against any competitor. "It wasn't allowed," Keough said.

Why on earth not? A couple of reasons. First, Coca-Cola had always competed more on augmented than on core product characteristics. Coca-Cola wanted to teach the world to sing, not merely to quench your thirst as if it were nothing more than water. Second, the people of Coca-Cola—executives, independent bottlers, shareholders—fell prey to their own propaganda, which was so vividly on display at the Lincoln Center formula-change announcement. Way back in 1938, William Allan White, a Kansas newspaper editor well known at the time, described Coca-Cola as the "sublimated essence of all that America stands for, a decent thing, honestly made, universally distributed." Even to suggest that Coca-Cola was anything but the best was akin to suggesting that Russia was better than America.

Self-delusion like this is comforting and calming. Robert Woodruff loved White's description of Coke, and it was not an accident that the reformulation was carried out under the code name Project Kansas. The dangers of self-congratulation and insularity were obvious—but only to those outside the Coca-Cola cocoon.

The Pepsi Challenge was an unwelcome slap in the face. It was also a genuine threat, not only to the loyalty of the average supermarket shopper but to Coke's big contracts with fast-food chains like McDonald's. Could McDonald's sell exclusively to its own customers the cola that the world was being told tasted second best?

It is ironic that facing one set of facts led Coca-Cola's leadership to deny another set. The fact Coke was able to face was that Pepsi was gaining on it. Permission to discuss what this meant was bestowed on the company by Goizueta once he took command. The key moment was his speech at a conclave of top executives in late March 1981 in Palm Springs, California. There, he announced that the whole company was going to be reborn as a lean, mean fighting machine. There would be "no sacred cows."

This new approach brought Cherry Coke, the spectacularly successful Diet Coke, and the purchase of Columbia Pictures. It brought fabulous returns to Coke's shareholders. Things were going so well that Goizueta himself was publicly quoted in 1984 expressing concern that the company could fall into the trap of believing it was invulnerable, that it could do no wrong. Yet with the formula change, that is precisely what happened.

Coke had research and research on research proving conclusively that the formula change was the thing to do. What the company failed to understand was the nature of a brand that is an icon.

Consider the following true story. During World War II, a private in the American army fighting the Japanese in Burma wrote the following letter home to his aunt:

> To my mind, I am in this damn mess as much to help keep the custom of drinking Cokes as I am to help preserve the million other benefits our country blesses its citizens with. . . . May we all toast victory soon with a Coke—if flavored with a little rum, I am sure no one will object.

Think about this letter for a moment. Here is an American soldier in Burma, one of the more forgotten, godforsaken theaters of World War II. Why is he there in "this damn mess"? For democracy? For the Constitution? For the Declaration of Independence? No. He's there for "the custom of drinking Cokes."

Here is a guy off in the middle of nowhere willing to take a bullet for your brand. That is real brand loyalty—not something to be tampered with lightly. (The soldier's reference to rum is not surprising. "Rum and Coca-Cola" was a runaway hit song in 1945.)

There are only a handful of megabrands in the whole world. They operate with their own rules. The most important of these is the most difficult to quantify.

Great brands are cocreated. The company that places the advertising may know what it is saying, but it does not know what the consumer is hearing and feeling. To a lot of Americans, changing the hallowed formula was an insult from someone you thought was your friend.

Interestingly, three of the top four people involved in this decision— Bryan Dyson, Sergio Zyman, and Roberto Goizueta—were not born in the

United States. Only the fourth, Keough, was. He sometimes referred to himself as the token American. Goizueta, at one point, thought the announcement of the formula change would be greeted by a mere "yawn." It wasn't.

Was there a way out for Goizueta and his team other than producing the uproar they did and having to apologize to the world? Admittedly, they were in a difficult position. They were managing a brand with a declining share, but the share it did have possessed a loyalty few other products could claim.

The executives could have adopted a different approach. They could have told the truth. They could have said we have a great product, and we're not going to change it. However, some consumers want a sweeter cola so we are going to introduce an additional brand to satisfy them.

What they could not do is take old Coke off the market. There were, it is true, problems with introducing a new Coke while continuing to sell the old one. But those problems paled by comparison to the uproar created by what they did.

The problem was not only what they did, but how they did it. Not only did they discontinue an iconic brand without the permission of the people willing to take a bullet for it in the jungles of Burma. They did it in such a way that they were forced into a lie that insulted the intelligence of anyone paying attention, which meant almost everybody in the country.

What did they learn? That the consumer owned a piece of the brand. It was not theirs to do with as they pleased. And they learned firsthand and not without pain about what a tangled web we weave when first we practice to deceive loyal customers. They learned that there was no denying the power of the simple truth and the toxicity of the convoluted lie.

8

The Madness of Crowds:
Delivering Denial at Webvan

"What experience and history teaches us is that people and governments have never learned anything from history, or acted on principles deduced from it." That was the view of the German philosopher Georg Wilhelm Friedrich Hegel—a proposition with which reasonable people can disagree. But if you wanted to support it, you need look no further than the pricing of assets in the United States and the behavior of the stock market specifically. Nowhere else is the irrationality of the masses more vividly illustrated. Nowhere else do we see the same mistakes repeated time and again.

The 1990s were the era of the dot-com bubble. Scores of intelligent, experienced people threw away great career opportunities to sign on with dot-coms. An equally large number of people invested hundreds of millions of dollars in business propositions where success was so wildly improbable that they would have had a better chance in a casino. Entrepreneurs and investors bet their careers on businesses that, had they been considered in "normal" times, would not have reached first base.

Why? Do "normal" times ever exist? What did we learn from the dot-com boom and bust? Nothing whatever. This we know because it was followed immediately by a housing bubble. At this writing, we are living with the consequences of the bursting of that bubble. The implications of Hegel's observation are great indeed.

Failing to learn from history is a form of denial. Without such denial, speculative bubbles would be impossible. Bubbles require ahistorical wishful thinking, namely that long-standing rules of human and economic behavior no longer apply.

The past may be an imperfect guide to the future, but it is all we have. Do we know with absolute certainty that the sun will come up tomorrow? No. But because it has risen every day in the past, we can say with a high degree of confidence that it will do so in the future. To act as if it will not would be to deny the lessons of both history and science.

When enough people collectively declare that the sun will not come up tomorrow, however, their assertion, denial though it may be, is likely to take on a life and credibility of its own—especially when the prognosticators' ranks include putative "experts." This chapter is about just such an occurrence. The denial that fed the dot-com bubble was self-delusion on a massive, mutually reinforcing scale—a phenomenon for which nineteenth-century Scottish author Charles Mackay coined the term "the madness of crowds." We will see how this global groupthink applied to investors as a whole, as well as to the principals of one particular start-up whose story is emblematic of the era's widespread denial.

Many analysts believe that speculative bubbles originate in the discovery of new technologies. It is true that new technology can create great fortunes. Look at the United States in the past century and a half. The railroads, the steel industry, the automobile industry, oil refining, dynamite, nylon, photography, television—each of these industries was based on new technology. Each created fortunes, sometimes dozens of family fortunes, that are with us today. The Rockefeller and DuPont family fortunes date from new technologies in the nineteenth century.

A look at American universities provides a nice guide to the wealth new technology can generate. Carnegie Mellon in Pittsburgh (steel); Vanderbilt in Nashville and Stanford in Palo Alto (railroads); the Eastman School of Music (photography); Rockefeller University in New York, the University of Chicago, and Spelman College in Atlanta (oil refining); and so on.

However, plenty of speculative bubbles have had their origins in old industries. Real estate is one example. Prices have fluctuated wildly, and cycles of boom and bust are so common they are (or at least should be) commonplace in our minds. The tulip was not a new technology, yet tulipmania in seventeenth-century Holland is viewed by many as the first speculative bubble.

"New" technology is rarely new at all. The Internet had been around for decades when the dot-com boom took off. But that special combination of circumstances that makes a bubble possible took time to gel. One needs infrastructure, in this case the rapid diffusion of personal computers and high-speed Internet connections. One needs publicists, true believers (or at least effective propagandists) explaining to a skeptical public that this time it really is different. The Internet, we were told in the 1990s, ranked with the steam engine . . . no, with the wheel . . . no, with fire!!! . . . as a change agent in the way we lived. Perhaps most of all, one needs an example—a shining, shocking, startling example of what this new world portended.

That magic moment came on August 24, 1995, the day Netscape went public in one of the most successful initial public offerings (IPOs) of the time. Here is how a business journalist recalled the event a decade later:

> It was the spark that touched off the Internet boom. . . . A sixteen-month-old Silicon Valley startup called Netscape tried to go public, but demand for the shares was so high that for almost two hours that morning, trading couldn't open.

Finally trading did, at $28. The shares quickly rocketed to $75 before closing at $58. Suddenly, Netscape's chairman, Jim Clark, was worth $565 million. Others who got in on the ground floor did fabulously well also. "Netscape mesmerized investors and captured America's imagination. More than any other company, it set the technological, social, and financial tone of the Internet Age."

Netscape was traded on the NASDAQ exchange, which closed that day at 1,005.10, up from 997.12 the day previous. On March 10, 2000, the NASDAQ would peak at the dizzying height of 5,046.62. On November 27, 2009 (that is, at this writing), the NASDAQ closed at 2,138.44. Trillions of dollars were made and lost during these years. This period saw some of the craziest business ideas backed by putatively shrewd men and women convinced that this time "it really is different."

Certainly, the Internet bade fair to change the nature of commerce. But a lot of the wild speculation occurred because, unlike real estate or railroads, this new technology was invisible and mysterious. It was no better understood than was radio in 1920. The potential seemed limitless. New opportunities beckoned. The old rules no longer applied.

The Internet made it possible to do unimaginable things, like send a message halfway around the world in the blink of an eye. It revolutionized the way people got their news, listened to music, communicated, even socialized.

But the Internet did not change the rules of business. It did not enable companies with higher costs than revenues to succeed. It did not make it possible to satisfy investors without providing them a return. Technology upends some rules, but not all. This was a fact about which a great many people in the late 1990s were in denial.

That denial was amplified because in 1995 not many Americans knew what went on inside a computer. Much of what the mass-marketed computer could do had only recently been developed.

Here is a brief anecdote from the life of a self-made Texas billionaire named Sam Wyly. In 1967, he recalls, software "was barely a word." There were very few independent software vendors at the time. "I was walking down the hallway of a company in California one morning and spotted a sign on a door that said, SOFTWARE PRODUCTS. I remember stopping and staring at it and thinking to myself, how can software be a product? To me, as it was then to most people in the computing business, software was a set of instructions that you wrote to tell a computer what to do."

In the not too distant future, this nonproduct product called software would make Bill Gates the richest man in the world. His software dominated the computer industry by the time of the Netscape IPO. Microsoft possessed a beautiful business model. It shipped off master disks to computer manufacturers. They loaded the software on the disk onto each individual computer they shipped and paid Microsoft a generous royalty for the right to do so. Gates had a genuine "asset light" business.

In such a world, what was impossible? This sense of infinite possibility was another key element in the dot-com bubble. Anything goes. And anything seemed able to attract financial backing. For half a decade, people threw money at businesses that had no track record and that no sane person could believe would succeed. But a bubble is a depression in reverse. Herd behavior dominates both. The only difference is that the herd is spending in a bubble and not spending in a depression. Philip J. Kaplan in his book *F'd Companies* provides brief, acerbic comments about Pets.com, Kozmo.com, and dozens of companies that filled no need and could not possibly have succeeded. Yet an awful lot of them attracted money and effort.

Another noteworthy characteristic of bubbles is the relationship between vision and execution. In a word, vision is everything. Execution in a bubble is assumed to take care of itself.

Bubbles also engender a sense of urgency. You have to move fast or the door to opportunity will slam shut, the train will leave the station. You have to get your firm going quickly because in the new freethinking business environment, someone else will soon steal your idea. Furthermore, once you get going, you have to "get big fast." Despite the infinite possibilities that the Internet supposedly placed before entrepreneurs, there was only one best way to tackle a business challenge: grow fast, and grow big, because even if you had a great idea, someone else would copy it and try to overtake you.

Next, people have to believe that there is a very tight connection between technology and behavior. There has to be no daylight between "could" and "would." What you can do, you will do. If in the world of the Internet you could buy anything from cars to cat food online, you would.

Finally, there have to be a wide variety of "enablers," of people holding positions that the public endowed with trust, people thought to be truthful and disinterested, who promoted a "new" economy in which the old metrics didn't matter. Author John Cassidy described this set of people as "self-promoting technology 'gurus,' credulous journalists, wily investment bankers, ambitious entrepreneurs, and gullible investors."

This is a good list but not quite complete. Business school professors and economists would have to be added. So would myopic government officials. Moreover, some of Cassidy's adjectives could be profitably amended. A number of journalists were not merely "credulous," they were self-dealing, touting companies in which they themselves were investors.

But no group was more blameworthy than investment bankers. They were relied upon to provide objective analysis of businesses to investors.

They were also responsible for engineering initial public offerings for companies and syndicating their securities. The supposed "Chinese wall" between these two functions was more like a sieve.

Put all of this together and the demand for Internet stocks by the late 1990s was intense. As Cassidy points out, where once the business system used financial markets to create companies, now it was using companies to create stocks from which financiers could profit.

I remember those days vividly. Some of my colleagues at the Harvard Business School were among the most avid boosters of the "new" economy. People were throwing money at students to start companies on the basis of business plans that in another environment would not have gotten a second look, much less financial support. There were rumors of students leaving school before earning their degrees because the pressure from peers, recent graduates, and financiers to start your dot-com now before someone else exploited the idea was so great.

I plead guilty. I "invested" in the new economy also. I am very conservative when it comes to this sort of thing, and I held off longer than most. But, "just in time," I put $40,000 into two companies. I did not really know anything more about their businesses than that I liked their CEOs. Soon after my investment, the money vaporized. In retrospect, I was lucky. I now had forty-thousand reasons to agree with Warren Buffett that it is not a good idea to invest in businesses you don't understand.

What is my excuse for being so cavalier? None, really. I fell prey to the classic groupthink trap that if everybody seems to agree that something is true, then it must be true. All I can say is that you had to be there, in that hothouse environment. Everything was going up, the Dow Jones Industrial Average as well as the NASDAQ. The bears, those churlish naysayers, were consistently proven wrong. The Internet was here. The Cold War was over. It was awfully easy to make money. Everyone else was. What a fool I would be to allow the parade to pass by.

A friend of mine has run a small private equity firm for two decades, in the course of which he has made a fortune for himself and his investors. Yet he did not invest in the dot-com craziness. I interviewed him in 1999 and asked him why not. He replied that he had a screen, a set of rules, that companies had to satisfy before he would put money into them. The dot-coms he was seeing did not satisfy those rules, so he did not invest. He used fixed filters to reinforce his own common sense, which combined to enable him to avoid denial even when groupthink was going against him.

Surely, I said to him, the people whose money he was managing must be asking why he was so conservative. He became quite serious. He said he was fortunate in that he invested "patient money." He was keeping a close eye on the new-economy phenomenon, but as yet he was not buying. He never did. His investors are everlastingly grateful.

Recently, this individual (who will remain nameless—he likes to come in under the radar) told me that there was one moment when he thought his analysis and instincts might have been playing him false. That was when he heard about the would-be online grocery king Webvan.

Webvan was one of the best financed and most hyped Internet retailers of its time. With an ambitious business plan and A-list backing, it soared to an $8.7 billion market valuation on its first day of trading in November 1999. But things did not work out as Webvan's executives and investors hoped. The result was a classic example of dot-com era denial—a case study, according to the *Financial Times*, "in the illusions of the dot-com boom and the wishful thinking of Wall Street."

What most forcefully impressed my friend about Webvan was that George T. Shaheen had accepted the position of CEO in September of 1999. Shaheen was no starry-eyed, wet-behind-the-ears, recently minted MBA. He was fifty-five years old in 1999 and the CEO of Andersen Consulting, where he had spent his entire career. He had become CEO in 1989 and held that position until his leap to Webvan a decade later. Andersen, with sixty-five-thousand employees in fifty countries, was an established, old-economy firm. Shaheen was making a fortune at this $9 billion company and, according to Cassidy, "gave up a retirement package worth tens of millions of dollars" there. This package "would have kicked in just ten months" after his departure, according to a journalist. (There was also the potential for more, as Shaheen must have known. Andersen Consulting changed its name to Accenture in 2001 and had its own IPO. He would have made millions from that too.) For a big shot like Shaheen, with so much going for him, to make the move to Webvan seemed to my friend and to a lot of other people to be a powerful endorsement of the new economy.

Shaheen granted *Forbes* an interview on October 18, 1999, explaining his career move. Webvan was "all about leveraging technology and reinventing the grocery business, just as Andersen had reinvented consulting. [Webvan would] set the rules for the largest consumer sector in the country." (Interestingly, the Webvan IPO was delayed by the SEC because Shaheen was speaking publicly during the mandated "quiet period" prior to a company's going public. This was an odd mistake for a man of Shaheen's experience to have made. A harbinger of things to come.)

Webvan had to move quickly, asserted Shaheen, because competitors would soon be forced to copy his company's logistics. "This is not going to be a free ride," Shaheen explained. "I'm going to be working very hard." He was, it should be noted, not going to be doing all this hard work just for the fun of it. He was granted options to buy 15 million shares of Webvan at $8. This is less than two thirds of the $12.69 that Softbank Holdings and Goldman Sachs paid to invest in Webvan just a few months previously. If Webvan went public at $20, Shaheen "would be sitting on a paper profit of $180 million." This might help us to understand his career move.

On November 5, 1999, Goldman Sachs issued 25 million shares of Webvan at $15. At the end of that day, the stock was selling at 24 . George Shaheen was a very rich man.

"Of all the follies of the Internet boom," in Cassidy's view, "Webvan was arguably (but not indisputably) the grandest." It certainly did not seem so at the time to a lot of smart people. Should they have known better? Was their self-confidence the result of the denial of a couple of things you or I could have told them at the time? The answer comes in three letters: yes.

Before we get to the denial of reality that made this venture an impossibility from the start, let us take a look at the case in favor of Webvan's success. The company was the brainchild of Louis Borders, who was also the first chairman of its board. Borders was a successful entrepreneur already, having founded the chain of bookstores with his name on it.

Despite his success in brick-and-mortar retailing, Borders saw e-tailing, that is, retailing over the Internet, as the future. The reasons were twofold. First, in a society increasingly characterized by two-income households, making time for shopping was a heavy burden. Second, with e-tailing, you could eliminate stores. A huge warehouse, completely automated through state-of-the-art technology and located far from high-rent districts, would save a fortune on real estate charges. Orders would be received via the Web.

A fleet of vans would deliver those orders within a specified thirty-minute time frame.

In its IPO filing, Webvan promised a broad selection of goods, no membership fees, and no delivery fees for orders over $50. It also promised prices "that are generally at or below" what you would find in your local supermarket. All this sounded terrific.

First-class people were backing Webvan. There was, of course, Louis Borders. George Shaheen was betting his career on it. The board of directors included Michael J. Moritz, a general partner of Sequoia Capital, and David M. Beirne, a managing member of Benchmark Capital Management, who predicted that Webvan "could be the biggest company to come out of Silicon Valley." These high-profile venture capitalists of the Valley were bestowing their blessing and their funding on the enterprise and expecting to benefit mightily as a result.

Many analysts were on board, as well. Henry Blodget, an equity analyst whose well-chronicled rise and fall mirrored that of the dot-com bubble, rated Webvan a "buy." Enthused one Robertson Stephens analyst, "We view Webvan as one of the few true e-tailing enablers   leveraging Web technology to allow customers to shop in a way that was impossible without the Internet."

Despite constantly proclaiming that it was all about the future, Webvan certainly featured some interesting similarities to a previous revolution in grocery retailing. In 1930 when Michael "King" Cullen launched the first modern supermarket, he too located it out of the high-rent district. He was able to do so because a new technology, the automobile, freed the consumer from the hub-and-spoke transportation arrangement that characterized big cities.

Cullen's stores were far larger than those of the competition because of those low real estate expenses. Because the stores were so big, he could stock more food items than traditional markets. Another part of his business plan was self-selection. In the traditional food store, there was a clerk and a counter between you and what you wanted to buy. It was a people-intensive operation. In Cullen's supermarket, the shopper assembled her own market basket (or shopping cart), requiring fewer personnel per shopper than a traditional market.

But the similarities screeched to a halt in what came to be known in the 1990s as the last mile. In the diffusion of the Internet, *the last mile* referred to wiring millions of individual houses and apartments with the cable necessary for high-speed access. In retailing, it meant the logistical problem of delivering the goods purchased to the home of the purchaser.

Like today's supermarkets, Cullen's operation was strictly self-service. You drove to his store. You walked the aisles to select what you wanted to buy. You took your purchases home. In the case of Webvan, the customer visited the company's webpage, made product selections, specified the time of delivery, and paid. Webvan promised to assemble the order and make the delivery within thirty minutes of the time specified.

Webvan carried fifty thousand different items. To construct a distribution center capable of performing automatically all the tasks that a shopper could perform personally with ease was a technical problem of monumental proportions. Then to load dozens of vans and plan routes for them in such a way as to navigate the impossible traffic of first San Francisco and then other target cities presented a challenge that was far from trivial.

Ask a retailer to describe the ideal store. He or she will tell you that it is one gigantic warehouse located in the middle of nowhere to which price-insensitive customers trek, purchase more than they had planned, and take it all home themselves. Webvan got part of this formula right but missed on the rest. They located their warehouse in a low-rent district. But then they assembled the merchandise and delivered it at no extra cost.

Home delivery of groceries was nothing new by the 1990s. Kroger had been doing it for a century, prior even to the advent of the internal combustion engine (although it was hardly the heart of its business). Peapod had been at it for a decade and was still struggling. Home delivery of groceries is to food retailing what voice recognition is to software. Doing it profitably has consistently turned into a more difficult proposition than it seems it should.

That last mile is long indeed. But food is even trickier than cable. Some grocery items are perishable, so time is of the essence. The variety is mind-boggling. Food delivery must be almost continuous; the average family visits a food store 2.4 times a week. And there is a built-in adverse-selection problem that determines who your customers will be—those who live near a food store are less likely to want home delivery than those who live farther away.

This is all a mere taste of the problems facing Webvan. Success depended upon a complex and unproven business system. Webvan had not been in business long at the time of its IPO in 1999, and its results so far were not encouraging. It had attracted an insufficient number of customers and orders, and its sales and cash flow were too weak to make it an appealing business.

The company was not just putting a toe in the water, it was starting off with a big splash—a large distribution center that was going to demand a lot of capital.

The obstacles were legion: Webvan's business model was new. It was unproven and potentially incapable of operating at the volume necessary for high-capacity utilization of its fixed assets. It was, because of its complexity, bound to encounter operational difficulties. It might not be possible to roll the business out nationally even if it did, against substantial odds, succeed in San Francisco. Grocery retailing was intensely competitive. It is thus no wonder that Webvan's own banker, Goldman Sachs, expected it to lose half a billion dollars in its first three years as a public company.

"I believe they were doomed from the start because their business model was one that was predicated on reinventing the entire system rather than using any of the existing structure," Robert Mittelstaedt, vice dean of executive education at the Wharton School, told the *Financial Times* after Webvan's demise. Webvan's ambitions, he added, "defied economic sense in a low-margin business."

Were such appraisals available only in hindsight? Hardly. Like many skeptical analysts and journalists, technology writer Connie Guglielmo expressed her doubts long before the company's fall. "It's hard to understand why Wall Street analysts love [Webvan]," Guglielmo wrote in a January 2000 story in *Inter@ctive Week*.

> In a wired economy where yesterday's ambitious scheme is today's multibillion-dollar company, Webvan's simple plan to deliver anything to anybody any day of the week seems the most grandiose to come down the information superhighway. To succeed, it must [use] conve-

nience and quality-of-service to cut a slice of at least $1 billion out of
the $650 billion grocery, prepared foods, and drugstore markets over
the next three years. It must raise $1 billion just to build the home de-
livery network that will allow it to reach its $1-billion-per-year sales
goal. And it must become more efficient at warehousing and same-day
delivery than any company in either field—almost from the get-go.

As if that were not enough, Webvan also faces the daunting task of
changing decades-old consumer shopping behavior. For most consumers, tomatoes need to be picked personally. . . . Most [consumers] aren't
ready to leave the actual shopping to someone else. Eliminating the
retail store is no easy task.

In fact, all of the information that one needed to evaluate Webvan real-
istically was contained right in the IPO prospectus that the company filed
with the SEC. Firms are required to be blunt about the risks involved in
their business in these documents. So blunt, in fact, that it has been said
that you would never buy anything if you read a prospectus for it. In this
instance, however, the prospectus may have understated the difficulties
Webvan faced.

The assumptions were piled upon one another. According to the prospectus, customers would find Webvan's website user-friendly, customers
would place orders sufficiently large to make delivery economical, the totally automated warehouse would function flawlessly, as would the sched-
uling and managing of dozens of vans and their drivers. The returns of
purchases would not prove a problem, and the IT infrastructure would
work fine, first time out. These claims were only as strong as their weakest
link. Peapod, Streamline, and other home-delivery grocery operations had
been around for years. None of them had achieved anything like the volume or efficiency that Webvan demanded.

A detailed analysis of the challenges this firm faced would fill a library
shelf. For example, Webvan's vast Oakland warehouse, with its five miles of
conveyor belts, forty-one motorized carousels, and $3 million of electrical
wiring, struck John Cassidy as "something out of a Fritz Lang movie." But
despite the futuristic gadgetry—or maybe because of it—Webvan quickly
encountered serious logistical problems. "The cold temperatures necessary to preserve fresh produce made the conveyor belts malfunction,"
Cassidy writes. "The celery didn't fit into the produce bags; the soft cheeses
got crushed; and the delivery vans got stuck in the San Francisco traffic."

This disaster-waiting-to-happen was the most generously funded venture of 1999. It closed its doors in 2001, the victim of long-known problems that it simply denied existed in its case.

Even amidst their boosterism, Webvan's leaders gave hints of knowing-but-not-knowing the reality they faced. "Maybe we have one of the great flameouts in history going here," George Shaheen joked to a symposium at Northwestern's Kellogg School of Management in February 2000. I wonder how his investors felt about his joke. In 1999, Louis Borders admitted, "When I talk to my old friends in the book business about this, they think I'm nuts." Asked how he responded to such skepticism, he answered, "Some days, I agree with them completely." All the way back in 1997, when a Benchmark Capital partner remarked to Borders that he was creating a billion-dollar company, Borders replied, "Naw. It's going to be ten billion. Or zero."

It was zero.

Of course, some products of the dot-com bubble did prosper. Amazon, eBay, and Google are now established members of the corporate elite. Who's to say that even now there aren't new dot-coms being born that will eventually defy the odds to become household names of their own? Or that there aren't whole new technologies being hatched in some garage that will have an Internet-like impact on the world? We have seen how easy it is to overestimate the difference a technology, company, or way of doing business will make. It is possible to underestimate these things, as well.

That said, it is safe to say that when (not if) new game-changing technologies and ventures do emerge, they will have to play by the fundamental rules of economics and commerce. Of course, that won't stop some people, perhaps lots of them, from once again proclaiming, "This time, it's different." And Hegel will be proven right once again.

Part II

GETTING IT RIGHT

9

Strategy, Structure, and Facing Facts at DuPont

Pierre Samuel du Pont de Nemours was born in Paris on December 14, 1739. In the half century that followed, he became quite well known as an economist. To be well known in that field in 1789 was dangerous. He was at first a friend of the Revolution, but by 1793 the Revolution was no friend of his. He was jailed and was one day away from the guillotine when he was saved by Robespierre's execution that day, buying him a new lease on life.

Unlike his most important descendant, Pierre Samuel du Pont couldn't keep his mouth shut. In 1797 he was back in La Force prison in Paris. This time he was slated not for the guillotine but rather for relocation to a newly established penal colony on an island off the coast of French Guiana in northeastern South America. This penal colony was not a nice place. It was not called Devil's Island for nothing. But du Pont dodged this bullet too. In 1799, he and his family were headed for the newly independent United States of America. There he dreamed of founding a utopia, to be called Pontiana, where French refugees could build a paradise on earth based upon the economic philosophy that he had been espousing for decades.

Pontiana never became a reality. But he wound up with the next best thing—Delaware.

DuPont today remains Delaware's largest corporation. Most people know it as a chemical company, associating its famed oval logo and long-time slogan "Better Things for Better Living . . . Through Chemistry" with test-tube creations such as nylon, Teflon, Corian, Kevlar, Tyvek, and Lycra.

What most people don't know about DuPont is that the company made its name and its fortune as a purveyor of gunpowder and explosives. That its pioneering transformation to a modern, diversified chemical corporation at the beginning of the last century stands as one of the most remarkable success stories in the history of American enterprise. And that the unprecedented organizational revolution required to achieve this transformation provides one of the best examples of how leaders at even a large, venerable firm with a proud history can face and adjust to new realities, rather than pretend those realities either don't exist or don't apply. This chapter is the story of how those leaders actually listened to a bunch of junior executives telling them they had gotten the fundamental structure of the company all wrong. Listened, and took their words to heart. This wasn't easy. Avoiding denial never is.

But first, back to Delaware. On the banks of the Brandywine Creek, which runs north and west from Wilmington, Pierre Samuel du Pont's son, Éleuthère Irénée, established E. I. du Pont de Nemours and Company in 1802, which today is probably the oldest continuously operating large firm in the country.

DuPont began as a gunpowder manufacturer, and the company could not have chosen a better site for that purpose. The Brandywine is only sixty miles long, originating in southeastern Pennsylvania and emptying into the Delaware River below Wilmington, thence flowing to the open ocean. The creek meanders gently until reaching the Delaware-Pennsylvania border, when it suddenly falls 120 feet in less than four miles before resuming its stately pace. What historian Joseph Frazier Wall has called "this felicitous union of fall-line power and tidewater transportation" in such a brief distance made it an ideal place for mills, which, before the age of steam, depended upon water power. An added benefit for DuPont was that the area was sparsely populated. The manufacture of gunpowder was dangerous and therefore inadvisable for urban areas.

The du Pont family built their homes on the banks of the Brandywine, which came to be known as "château country." For a century, in the midst of a nation undergoing changes of staggering proportions, the du Pont family and company were notable for the stability, almost the timelessness, in which they seemed to dwell. The head of the firm was the *de facto* head of the family, and throughout the nineteenth century the firm had only four chief executives. E. I. du Pont was succeeded at his death in 1834 by his son, Alfred Victor. Alfred was succeeded at his death in 1856 by his brother Henry, the legendary "Boss Henry," who ran the firm until his death in 1889. His successor was his nephew Eugene du Pont, who died suddenly in 1902. The company was not incorporated until 1899. Up to then it had been a private partnership. At Eugene's death, there were only five stockholders, all members of the du Pont family.

According to company historians, "There had developed a tradition of what might be called 'family communism.' The firm owned most of the land and the houses in which the du Ponts lived, and accommodations were assigned by Boss Henry [while that formidable man was in charge]. The firm maintained and improved the properties and charged no rent." It was idyllic. But it couldn't last forever.

When Eugene du Pont died unexpectedly after a one-week bout with pneumonia in 1902, the family offered no obvious successor. Four of the five stockholders were elderly and frail. They were not interested in running the business, and the family did not appear to have anyone else qualified for the task. The suggestion was made that they sell out to their "ancient and friendly competitor," Laflin & Rand.

But the fifth stockholder, Alfred I. du Pont, was horrified at the idea of alienating the family "birthright." He believed that if he could secure the support of his cousin T. (for Thomas) Coleman du Pont, with whom he had roomed at MIT, he would be able to buy the company. Coleman said he was interested if they could persuade a third cousin, Pierre S. du Pont, to join them and "handle the finances." Coleman phoned Pierre. "The conversation was brief—very brief," Pierre recalled. "Would I do it? Yes.—Time less than three minutes."

The purchase price was $12 million, and the deal was formalized with remarkable speed. The final contract was dated March 1, 1902. Eugene had died on January 28. The speed was all the more remarkable because the three young cousins—Coleman was thirty-nine, Alfred thirty-seven, and Pierre thirty-two—did not really know what they had bought. For a hundred years, DuPont had not been professionally managed. No reliable valuation existed for the mills and other assets the company possessed. As Pierre said, "I think there is going to be some tall hustling to get everything reorganized. We have not the slightest idea of what we are buying, but we are probably not at a disadvantage as I think the old company had a very slim idea of the property they possess."

Pierre used the word "reorganized," but he probably could have saved himself the prefix *re*. The truth is the "old company" was hardly organized at all. Unlike his garrulous namesake, Pierre was a man of few words—"the less said, the sooner mended" was a phrase by which he lived. Luckily for the company, he turned out to be a man of action, a master of corporate strategy, structure, and, not least important, politics. It was he who whipped the company into shape.

By 1915, DuPont had been transformed from a motley collection of cats and dogs into a centralized corporation with vice presidents for manufacturing and marketing and a chief executive officer, Pierre, with a staff that could really make things happen. The company had been composed of numerous production facilities haphazardly located and sales forces that duplicated each other's efforts or left gaps in the selling program.

Now, all that was rationalized. The company's three important product lines were black powder, smokeless powder, and dynamite. The last was the newest and most dangerous to use. Salesmen had to understand its properties and educate their customers to prevent disastrous accidents. In Pierre's words, "At the time we made the purchase of the properties, we realized that if a good investment was to be made for us, it would necessitate a complete reorganization [there is that word again—it appears often in Pierre's writing] of the method of doing business; that the administrative end would have to be reorganized, numerous selling organizations or administrative organizations done away with, and we would have to establish a system of costs in order that an economical manufacture could be installed throughout the business."

In the days of Boss Henry, DuPont had tried to control markets through agreements with its "friendly competitors." Now it would control them through efficiency and scale economies. This meant building modern facilities, shutting down old ones, and keeping careful track of the performance of executives. An accounting technique, still after a century referred to as the "DuPont formula," was created by a newly hired engineer named F. Donaldson Brown to determine the return on investment generated by DuPont's capital.

Boss Henry ran the company from one room. That was all that was necessary to carry on a correspondence about prices and output. With the centralized efficiency that Pierre was instituting, however, a large headquarters was needed for the staff that would establish policies and monitor their effectiveness. As a result, DuPont built an office building for itself in downtown Wilmington.

This dramatic change in the operation of DuPont should not be allowed to appear too clinical. The accents of human passion were clearly at work. The three young cousins had started off on their great adventure as friends. Those friendships could not survive the lust for power and money involved in building the centralized DuPont. First to go was Alfred. To be sure, he was not as skilled an executive as either of his cousins, and as the foremost expert on the company's history, Alfred D. Chandler Jr. observes, Alfred's "failure as an administrator was the basic reason for his removal [as general manager and as vice president in charge of the black powder department and as a member of the Executive Committee]. He was highly competent in personally supervising work in the mills, but he had shown little talent for broader coordination, appraising, and goal setting."

Chandler also observes that "increasing deafness had hindered Alfred's effectiveness. His divorce and remarriage created intense personal and family tension." Alfred was not out altogether. He remained as a vice president presumably without portfolio and as a member of the Finance Committee of the Board of Directors. As a major stockholder, he would be heard from again.

A raft of personnel changes followed Alfred's removal, as did DuPont's loss of a federal antitrust suit. All this apparently proved excessively stressful for Pierre, whose health "broke," resulting in an extensive leave of absence from his responsibilities as president.

By early 1914, however, Pierre had returned to work, and this was to prove a tumultuous era in the struggle for control of the company. Because of a demand for funds brought about by sundry real estate operations in New York City, Coleman du Pont found himself in need of cash. On December 14, 1914, he unexpectedly approached Pierre with an offer to sell twenty thousand shares of his stock to the company for $160 per share. Two days before Christmas, the Finance Committee, consisting of Pierre, Alfred, and another cousin, William, voted two to one against purchasing the stock at that price. Alfred allowed himself to entertain the impression that Pierre—who was the one committee member who had voted in favor of the purchase—would continue to bargain with Coleman on behalf of the company to purchase the stock at a better price.

This impression was quite mistaken. Pierre and Coleman did continue to bargain, but the purchaser was to be Pierre personally, not the firm. On February 20, 1915, Pierre, with the help of a $10 million loan from J. P. Morgan & Co., bought all of Coleman's stock for himself. From that day forward until his death on April 4, 1954, Pierre controlled DuPont. Unlike the founding father of the family and his namesake, *this* Pierre Samuel du Pont knew when to be silent. He never breathed a word of these negotiations to his cousin Alfred, who only learned of the consummation of the transaction when he read about it in Sunday's Wilmington *Star* on February 28, despite the fact that the two men had offices next door to one another.

The following day Alfred demanded that Pierre turn what had been Coleman's stock over to the firm. Pierre refused. Alfred, along with some other members of the du Pont extended family, had Pierre served with papers by an officer of the U.S. Court for the District of Delaware on December 9, 1915. *Du Pont vs. du Pont* had begun. Before it was over, Pierre, in the eyes of a federal judge, "had been branded deceitful," according to Joseph Frazier Wall, "one who out of avarice had wrongfully seized for himself that which belonged to the company he was entrusted to represent." But this was a momentary setback. Pierre won in the end. DuPont was his. And when DuPont bought a controlling interest in General Motors in December of 1917, that was his too. It was his branch of the family that was to be in charge. The next two presidents of DuPont, Irénée and Lammot, were his brothers.

By 1914, DuPont was strictly centralized. Major decisions were made at the top. It was rationally organized and probably as well structured a firm as existed anywhere. That structure was soon to be put to the test.

World War I broke out in August 1914, and suddenly DuPont experienced a spike in demand such as has been seen by few companies. Demand was predominantly for smokeless powder, a propellant, rather than for high explosives, which had previously been the company's highest volume product. In 1914, DuPont had three smokeless powder plants producing at a rate of 8.4 million pounds a year. In 1915, those same three plants increased their combined production capacity to 200 million pounds a year. By April 1917, the month the United States entered the war, capacity was 450 million pounds a year. Rapid expansion occurred in the production of all the company's other products as well, including other propellants and explosives such as TNT.

On every dimension, the increase in the size of the company beggared the imagination. DuPont internalized many new operations. It was, for example, essential that the supply of raw materials for its greatly enlarged operations be secured, so the company vertically integrated, producing vast quantities of acids and other chemicals that it had formerly purchased from outside vendors.

Employment skyrocketed along with the spectacular increase in property, plant, and equipment. From the beginning of the war in 1914 to the armistice in the fall of 1918, the number of employees increased from 5,300 to more than 85,000. The number of managers, defined as individuals earning annual salaries of $4,200 or more, increased from 94 to 259. Gross capital employed rose from $83.5 million in 1915 to $309 million at the end of 1918.

Profits grew commensurately. As a result, this expansion was internally financed. No need for bankers. DuPont's net income rose from $5,871,000 in 1912 to $82,107,000 in 1916, the year before the United States entered the war. This was more than the total combined earnings from 1902, when the cousins took over the company, to 1915. "Coleman's shares," historian Joseph Frazier Wall has written, "which Alfred had wanted the company to buy in December 1914 for $125 a share and for which Coleman received $200 in February 1915, were worth $900 a share by October. The dividend paid on each share rose from $8 in 1914 to $82 in 1915.... Coleman's stock, which he had eagerly sold for $13.8 million, was ... worth $58.1 million six months later.... Poor Coleman. In dashing off to New York to find a faster track, he had foolishly abandoned what had become America's real speedway, right where he had been in little old, provincial Wilmington."

We should pause at this point to consider the achievements of the company. Less than two decades previously, it had almost disappeared. From 1902 to the war, while enduring federal antitrust prosecution and gut-clutching interpersonal conflict, Pierre had fashioned a highly centralized structure that enabled the company to flourish. The company was organized by function. Marketing and manufacturing were the most important of these functions, and each had its own general manager. These are the two principal activities of any industrial firm, and it is vital that they work together. If manufacturing produces more than marketing can sell, inventory piles up. If it produces too little, sales are lost in the short term, and customers may be lost in the long term. Other functions were also controlled by top executives.

The remarkable fact is that the fantastic expansion of the company—5,300 employees to 85,000 in less than half a decade!—was achieved without any significant change in DuPont's structure. The Unitary (or U form) of organization "proved admirably suited to meet the needs of the resulting phenomenal growth." One could not ask for more eloquent testimony to the robust character of this corporation's structure.

At the end of the war, DuPont was one of the world's most valuable companies. As Chandler writes, "By the summer of 1919, the DuPont Company was ready to meet the postwar world with a new but experienced and seasoned set of top managers and a simplified management structure. Few more rationally planned and thoroughly tested designs existed for coordinating, appraising, and planning the activities of a great vertically integrated industrial enterprise."

. . .

From 1902 onward, DuPont had always been concerned about excess capacity. The demand for gunpowder and explosives was cyclical. Building plants that could capture scale economies meant high fixed costs. With full and steady product, those costs were amortized over a lot of output. The result was lower total costs per unit. In other words, if you build a big plant and keep it busy making products, your total costs drop and you have the potential to make a lot of money.

Unfortunately, the leverage also operates in the opposite direction. If your plant is not fully utilized, the fixed costs that it embodies increase the cost of your product. Your capital will not be employed as intensively as you want. Your return on investment will decline.

What to do?

Well before World War I, DuPont began looking for an answer to this question through diversifying its product line. If you have a factory that produces only snowblowers, the factory is going to be closed half the year. But if it produces lawn mowers too, it can operate year-round. DuPont was in the hunt for products that would serve the purpose of balancing what it produced. Irénée du Pont was the designated hunter, put in charge of the development department and placed on the Executive Committee in 1906, when he was thirty-two. Things worked out well for him. In 1957, *Fortune* estimated that he was among the twenty richest people in America.

Trained at MIT, Irénée was at home among technical matters. He focused his search on products with a nitrocellulose base. The company had a lot of experience with nitrocellulose because this highly flammable material is the principal ingredient in gunpowder. After examining a number of options, Irénée settled on artificial leather as a promising path for the company. DuPont was then faced with the classic choice for a diversifying company: make or buy. Should DuPont produce its own artificial leather from the plants it currently operated or buy a company in the business? It opted for the latter, and DuPont's first important acquisition, the Fabrikoid Company of Newburgh, New York, up the Hudson from New York City, was consummated in 1910 for $1,195,000.

In 1913, the company was in the hunt again. This time it chose to enter the pyroxylin business. Pyroxylin is another nitrocellulose compound, used to make plastic products such as combs and also lacquers and photographic film. This time the company decided to make its own rather than buy a going concern.

Despite these early activities, explosives and propellants still accounted for 97 percent of DuPont's output at the start of World War I. It is indicative of Pierre's shrewdness that he resisted the temptation to allow the sudden burst of prosperity to cloud his understanding of the long-term outlook. "We must be careful," he wrote as the great expansion began, "that our point of view is not entirely warped out of line by the temporary situation" produced by the war. Expansion was occurring "beyond our wildest dreams." Early in 1914 the secretary of the Executive Committee wrote Pierre that the newly formed Excess Plant Utilization Division needed to find new uses for the enlarged capacity because "only a portion of the present equipment will be useful after the European Wars are settled." Thought was never given to shrinking the company back to its prewar size. It had grown big. Now it would grow bigger.

DuPont embarked on exhaustive studies of various industries in which its excess plant might be utilized to the full. During the course of these detailed deliberations, the company broadened its outlook. The development department, which was tasked with these investigations, began to conceive of its assignment not merely as employing plants that would otherwise lie idle, but as exploiting the full range of the company's organizational capabilities, including its laboratories, salesmen (they were all men at this time), capacity to manage large numbers of employees, and extensive staff well versed in the challenges of nitrocellulose technology. The company, in other words, was moving in the direction that defined big business in the United States in the twentieth century. It was looking at its ability to do a lot of related things well as an asset worth growing.

The industry on which DuPont eventually decided to focus its efforts in diversification was paint and varnish. The choice seemed inviting. First, these products would employ the knowledge of nitrocellulose which DuPont possessed. As we have just seen, by 1917 the company was redefining itself from "DuPont, the powder company" to "DuPont, the nitrocellulose company." Second, in a growing country the market for paint seemed limitless and obviously not dependent on the stimulus of an armed conflict. Third, with the single exception of Sherwin-Williams, the industry was populated by small, local firms. Fourth, there were no patents or secret processes preventing DuPont from entering this business.

In other words, the paint industry in 1917 looked to DuPont's analysts a lot like the powder industry looked to the three cousins back in 1902. There existed the same "opportunity for consolidation and economy." Paint seemed like a nineteenth-century industry ripe for modernization. Just as in powder, the "advantages of careful business management on a large scale would be fully realized" in paint. There were no barriers to the entry of a modern company like DuPont. It was fruit ripe for the picking.

As expected, war orders ceased when the armistice was signed. What was not expected was that after an initial burst of economic activity, the nation would be walloped in 1920 by a severe economic contraction. Even less expected was DuPont's performance in paint.

In 1917, DuPont's paint business lost more than $108,000 on sales of $1.2 million. The next year sales more than doubled to almost $3 million. Unfortunately, losses almost tripled to more than $320,000. In 1919, when the small paint companies that DuPont looked down upon were having a good year, DuPont's sales once again rose substantially, up over 35 percent to more than $4 million. Unfortunately, losses more than kept pace, up over 50 percent to about $490,000. "The more paint and varnish we sold," in the words of one report, "the more money we lost." DuPont's idea had been, in modern parlance, to use its business model in a different but related industry and reap the rewards of economies of scale and speed of throughput. But things were not turning out that way. Why not?

The company had suddenly and unexpectedly become far more difficult to manage. Administrative problems had been handled expeditiously during the remarkable wartime increase in business. Yet paint, which even in 1919 was but a $4 million business, was making life difficult for DuPont's top management. Given the scale and swiftness of efficient growth during the war, this really was a puzzle.

The problem seemed to reside in sales. The sales vice president, Frederick W. Pickard, pointed out that while, from a manufacturing point of view, the move into paint was indeed related diversification, that was not the case from a marketing point of view. Pickard explained that there was all the difference in the world between "tonnage distribution" and "merchandising." Those two categories—what today we would call business-to business versus consumer marketing—demanded "entirely different methods of selling."

Pickard offered three solutions to the sales problem. Neither he nor anyone else liked any of them. Pickard asked the company's Executive Committee to empower a blue-ribbon group to study the problem and find an answer. It complied. A subcommittee of the Executive Committee was formed in September 1919 made up of Pickard himself, representing sales; the treasurer, F. Donaldson Brown (inventor of the "DuPont formula"); Walter S. Carpenter Jr., the head of the Development Department; and A. Felix du Pont, who managed Explosives Manufacturing.

These men all found themselves too busy to devote the necessary time to the assignment, so they appointed a sub-subcommittee to carry out the investigation, composed of a representative of each department plus an assistant to the president.

In 1919, the presidency changed hands. Pierre stepped down. Instead of going into the retirement he desired, he became the CEO of General

Motors. DuPont's massive investment in that company was in jeopardy because of its many problems, so Pierre decamped to Detroit to straighten things out. His brother Irénée became DuPont's president. Pierre remained on the Finance Committee of DuPont's board to keep an eye on things in Wilmington. Nothing major would happen there without his permission, but issues would reach him through his brother.

At first glance, DuPont's decision-making process regarding the paint problem looks like a parody of bureaucratic buck passing. A top executive presents a pressing dilemma to the Executive Committee of the board. The Executive Committee appoints a blue-ribbon subcommittee. Pleading other responsibilities, the blue-ribbon subcommittee appoints a sub-subcommittee of talented but junior people to craft a report. Were the executives really too busy to deal with a matter this important? Or did their political instincts tell them that this was a good issue from which to keep one's distance?

Oddly enough and apparently by chance, the company had stumbled upon an excellent method to investigate the situation. The sub-subcommittee members were young and probably less averse to change than their elders. Whatever problems the company had could not be laid at their doorstep. They were relatively objective and disinterested. If there was an elephant in the room, they were freer to say so.

The members of the sub-subcommittee devoted a lot of time to interviewing executives at other companies and to analyzing data from within DuPont. The result was a report that proposed far more sweeping changes than any of the senior people who had delegated this responsibility had contemplated.

The problem, the sub-subcommittee concluded, did not reside with the sales function, even though that is where it first presented itself. The success of other companies using essentially similar sales approaches to DuPont's ruled that out. The real problem was not with the company's approach to the customer but rather resided "entirely within ourselves." That problem was organizational.

DuPont's functions, not only manufacturing but selling as well, were fine. The difficulty lay in the fact that no one was responsible for coordinating them. No other company selling paint and varnish (and sundry other products that DuPont now produced) was organized as DuPont was. In the words of the report, "In no case do they have a divided control, and in all cases a central control. Are we prepared therefore to say that our method of organization is suitable to these businesses?" The question answered itself—obviously not.

Thus, the move to make was to restructure the company rather than tinker with sales. The reason no one was satisfied with Pickard's original proposed alternatives was that they were trying to solve the wrong problem. The sub-subcommittee insisted that the problem was structural. In the seminal conceptualization of Alfred Chandler, DuPont had embarked upon a new strategy. After the war, it was to be a multiproduct company. That new strategy was being stymied by the old structure, a structure designed for a single-product company.

The answer therefore was to make the product, rather than the function, the center of the organization. Instead of having a single vice president in charge of marketing, manufacturing, and so on for the whole company, create new positions at the top of which would be a vice president for the paint business, for example, to whom executives in charge of manufacturing and marketing paint would report. This newly created vice president would have P&L responsibility. That is, he would be responsible for whether or not his business made money. For him to discharge that responsibility, he would need to control the elements that made profit possible. He would be the CEO of his own domain—a product-centered division—and he would report to the company's CEO.

The sub-subcommittee presented its findings to the subcommittee on March 16, 1920, six months after it was originally constituted. From the surviving record, especially the notes written on the typed report, the subcommittee was intensely displeased with what it received. If this intense displeasure is obvious from their notes, it is fair to assume that what they actually felt must have been even more extreme. They must have been enraged.

Here are some of the penciled objections. The new structure violated "the theory of our present organization," which was based on functional rather than product-based specialization. The report, it was charged, "cites the agency for solving ills (namely, change in organization)," but failed to link this solution to the problems at hand. Precisely "where is the benefit of the reorganization?" The problem wasn't structural, it was a lack of timely information, which was not all that surprising given that there would always be a shakedown cruise when new businesses are started before the ship is entirely seaworthy. The subcommittee was supposed to look for ways to get shipshape more quickly. The sub-subcommittee had proposed a new navy.

An obvious indication of the subcommittee's displeasure was that it did not pass on to the Executive Committee of the board any of the recommendations of the sub-subcommittee regarding changes in DuPont's structure. What we do not know is how the sub-subcommittee reacted to the rejection of their ideas by their superiors. Were they angry about having half a year's effort eviscerated and their most creative solution ignored? Were they frightened because they had offended people who could derail their careers? How could the sub-subcommittee have veered so far off course? Were there no interim reports or even informal discussions with their superiors? Had there been, surely they would have been warned about the direction in which they were taking their work.

One thing we do know. The sub-subcommittee members did not suffer the same fate as did Ernest Kanzler when he told Ford something Ford did not want to hear. None of them was fired. Thus DuPont showed that shooting the messenger was not part of its corporate culture. To act otherwise is to invite denial.

In fact, the deleted suggestions of the sub-subcommittee did not disappear. They were discussed informally among the company's top executives. Yet another subcommittee was created by the Executive Committee. This one was composed of the manufacturing vice president, William C. Spruance; Pickard from sales, and the treasurer, F. Donaldson Brown. Somewhat surprisingly, they came to the same conclusion as had the junior people on the sub-subcommittee. On July 8, 1920, they formally recommended organization by product rather than function for all product lines in which DuPont was involved. This came to be known as the Multidivisional (or simply M) form of organization, in contrast to the U form.

Irénée du Pont did not like this proposal, despite the fact that it came from his top people—seasoned executives all. It violated the "principle of specialization," which had served DuPont so well. Irénée was still wedded to the idea of functional rather than product specialization. He returned the report, to the committee asking for further study. In November, the committee delivered yet another report, which contained essentially the same ideas. Irénée, who must have been getting a little tired of this, rejected it on November 19.

Middle management—the men closest to the problems and seeking practical solutions for them—felt one way. Top management—which had created the modern DuPont company and seen that creation grow to unimagined wealth and size—felt another. In 1920, top management not only made the big decisions, its name was on the door. Irénée's two brothers, Pierre and Lammot, agreed with him.

This was a turning point in the history of DuPont almost as important as the 1902 consolidation by the cousins. Everyone agreed that the performance of the paint initiative was unsatisfactory. But as far as the solution to this problem was concerned, the company had split into two factions. Top management repeatedly held to the principles by which the company was run. Middle managers had to confront the daily reality that the principles of the past were not serving the corporation well as it tried to transform itself for the future.

This disagreement had to be resolved, and as this narrative is illustrating, its resolution was tortuous. However, one important lesson had been learned by the end of 1920. You could disagree with the boss and persist in that disagreement without putting your job or your future at the company at risk. The arguments were about policies, not about the people who were proposing those policies. That freedom to disagree meant that you did not have to deny your beliefs. You did not have to "go along to get along." This was the beginning of wisdom.

The men whose proposals had been rejected did not give up. However, something had to be done to resolve the stalemate.

The middle managers moved first. One representative each from development, manufacturing, and marketing decided to meet as an informal "council" (they chose the name themselves) to coordinate the paint business. With remarkable speed, the Executive Committee agreed that this was a good idea.

"Informal" did not mean secret. These moves were all made with everyone's full knowledge. The Executive Committee quickly agreed that the paint council should be made formal. On December 10, the council submitted an eight-page report to Pickard, who forwarded it to the Executive Committee.

This report showed that DuPont's middle managers had learned some valuable lessons from experience. To begin with, there is the title: "A Plan to Make 10% on Our Paint and Varnish Net Sales." Previous reports had been criticized for talking about corporate structure when the assignment was to figure out how to make money. Of course, to the reports' authors, these two were intimately intertwined. But the connection was not at all clear to the higher-ups who read them.

This report, therefore, positioned itself as directly addressing the problem at hand the way the top men conceived of it. The report was as full of quantitative calculations as anyone could have wished. Organizational matters were there, lurking in the background, but certainly not featured. Thus when the "control [of] the business by means of a council" is mentioned, it is third on a list of five items. The first phrase of this entry is "Without in any way passing an opinion on the present method of carrying on the business . . ." Thus, the authors buried what they felt was vital because, one infers, they knew if they featured it, the readers would see nothing else. They had learned that to be persuasive, they had to look at the world through the eyes of others.

Instead of leaping from U form to M form, it began to look like DuPont was going to get there by taking baby steps. Not only the paint business but others as well were beginning to look more product- and less function-centered as 1920 moved into 1921.

Appearances proved deceiving, however, because of the events of 1921. Specifically, the September review of results for the first half of 1921 revealed such bad performance that the word "crisis" might not have been inappropriate. As the economic depression in the nation as a whole deepened, DuPont's numbers deteriorated apace. The company lost almost two-and-a-half million dollars during this period. All lines but one posted losses.

A move to councils was insufficient. People started talking about "dictators" with "absolute jurisdiction over personnel" and any other resources necessary to get the job done. "What is needed," according to one executive, was "decision and action and that you get from an individual and not from an organization of talent such as is seated around this table." And from another: "The trouble with the Company is right here in Wilmington, and the failure is the failure of administration for which we, as Directors, are responsible."

The point is not merely that this executive was right. When basically solid companies in growing markets fail, the fault usually lies with top decision makers. The point is that he said what he said and that his statement was so clear and unambiguous. If you can communicate in this way without getting your head chopped off, you can solve problems.

DuPont's problems at length were solved. In September 1921, with the concurrence of Pierre, who had come down from Detroit where he was deeply involved in trying to dig General Motors out of the hole in which it was wallowing (we could use him to do the same thing today), and with the rather grudging acquiescence of Irénée, who still remained a skeptic, DuPont became the first major industrial corporation in the United States to create a product-centered multidivisional structure. The M form was born. The company had at last aligned its structure with its new strategy—an alignment that in Chandler's estimation served DuPont well in both the short and long terms. "Losses soon converted into profits," following the restructuring, Chandler writes. "And never again—not even in the middle of the depression of the 1930s—did the company face a crisis as severe as that of 1921."

Meanwhile, the M form became the dominant organizational model for large corporations and remains so to this day. According to business historian Charles W. Cheape, the innovation was a "major watershed" not only for DuPont, but for American business in general, allowing "the economies of scope that made the large, diversified firm possible."

· · ·

Times change. Institutions resist change.

These two simple observations go far toward explaining why so many once-powerful companies have come to grief. It is extraordinarily difficult to bring about change in a big company. Leadership, it has been said, consists of using minimum problems to create maximum positive change. By that standard, DuPont did well, but it could have done better. Only when the firm was on the brink of disaster, in the midst of a crisis produced by one of the worst years in its history, was it able to reconcile itself to the fact that yesterday's structure was acting as a barrier against rather than an avenue toward tomorrow's strategy.

Most remarkable is the absence of denial, the omnipresence of an engineering quest for facts, and the willingness to look those facts in the face even when they weren't pleasant. Top management understood that middle managers had standing and that it was essential they at least be heard if not always agreed with. Top managers may have had a longer view, but that was a weakness as well as a strength. The middle managers were having to cope with dysfunctional operations on a daily basis.

Each group had a role to play. Each played it well. Most of all, it was simply vital for everyone to understand that facing an unpleasant truth was of inestimable value, and that a pleasant lie was a snare and a delusion, the price of faith in which could be the company's future.

10

"Why Shouldn't You and I Walk Out the Door . . . ?": A New Perspective at Intel

Andy Grove is a man who beat the odds. He was born András István Gróf in Budapest, Hungary, on September 2, 1936. His parents were nonobservant Jews. To be a Jew—observant or not—in Hungary from Grove's birth until the Nazis were driven out of the country in 1945 was to live in the valley of the shadow of death. Hungary had its share of homegrown fascism and anti-Semitism, but this was nothing compared to the frenzied loathing of Jews that characterized Germany from the time that Hitler became chancellor on January 30, 1933.

For most of World War II, it appeared as though Hungarian Jews might escape the Holocaust. That hope came to an end in 1944 when Hitler dispatched Adolf Eichmann to Hungary to make it as *Judenrein* (free of Jews) as the rest of occupied Europe. Eichmann was all too effective. Estimates vary, but it appears that more than 550,000 Jews living in Hungary, over two thirds of the Hungarian Jewish population, perished during the Holocaust. Auschwitz is the largest Hungarian cemetery in the world. Some of Grove's extended family were killed. He and his mother went into hiding and escaped. His father was drafted into a work battalion associated with the Hungarian army and came close to losing his life on the Eastern Front.

After the Soviet conquest, life remained dangerous in a random way. Grove's mother was raped by one of the "liberating" Red Army soldiers in January 1945. Hungary was firmly attached to the Soviets and became a part of the upside-down world created by the Soviet Union. In Grove's words, "Living under a Communist regime and being told what to think and what to see and what to read and what not to think and on and on and on was pretty bad." It was the era of the "primacy of politics," of denunciations which left the people attacked (Andy's father among them) no recourse.

It was the time of one of the more bizarre features of Soviet communism, the "show trial." In this staged drama, one saw the opposite of denial. Someone innocent of a charge pled guilty to it. Thus László Rajk, a lifelong communist and Hungary's foreign minister in 1949, was thrown into jail not long after the May Day parade of that year and told to "confess" to crimes he did not commit. He did confess and was executed in the fall.

Rajk's fate made no sense to young Andy. Like everyone else, he was "glued to [the] radio set" during the broadcast of the Rajk trial. "I listened to Rajk's examination," Grove later wrote, "with morbid fascination. I couldn't understand how a man who fought against the Germans and was a member of the underground could turn against his cause and his country. But there it was: He had confessed it himself." So many occurrences under this regime simply didn't add up.

The lie was enshrined. The truth had no standing. Life was a charade. Andy in his midteens liked writing articles for a local newspaper. They were regularly published until one day when suddenly each new article was rejected. He asked the editor for a reason but received no satisfactory answer. Then he asked his mother. Grove learned that his uncle had recently been jailed, creating a cloud of official suspicion over his family. A "career in journalism suddenly lost its appeal," he wrote many years later. He began to devote more attention to chemistry, being "eager to cultivate an interest in a new profession that was less prone to subjectivity."

From the day of his birth until his escape from Hungary during the abortive revolt of 1956, Grove lived in a world in which people spoke in code. Trust was missing in action. Grove captured this absence of trust in a story he remembered making the rounds in the early 1950s:

> Two men are ogling a spanking new Western car. One of them says, "Isn't this car a wonderful testimony to the technological capabilities of our friendly Soviet Union?" The other man looks at him scornfully. "Don't you know anything about cars?" The first man replies, "I know about cars. I don't know about you."

On October 23, 1956, a revolt broke out in Budapest against the Soviet occupation. The causes of the revolt were numerous. One contribution, ironically enough, was the postmortem rehabilitation of László Rajk and his reburial on October 6. The Soviets evacuated Budapest. Radio Free Europe and the Voice of America, routinely jammed by the authorities, could now be clearly received on the radio. The countryside was up in arms also. For a brief shining moment, one could dream that Hungary might become part of the free world in the West.

A dream is all it was. The Soviets came roaring back into the capital on November 4. The thoroughness of their brutality was on full display. Hungarian lives were cheap to the occupation forces. Rumors were flying around the city. "I had never seen such devastation," wrote Andy, "not even from the bombing during the war" when Budapest had undergone a hundred-day siege.

Grove had just begun his first year at the University of Budapest, and he liked it there. But the university was now closed and stories were circulating about Soviets picking up student agitators.

The buzz in the air was about the possibility of escape to Austria. Andy and his parents discussed it often. Should he go or should he stay? If he tried to go, how would he do it? How risky was it? Was life in Budapest really so bad that the risks were worth taking? On the other hand, would Budapest become intolerable now that a rebellion had been attempted? But while rumor had it that some people were making it across the border to Austria, others were simply disappearing. To disappear was a very bad thing to have happen to you.

The person who tipped the scales in favor of making a run for it was Andy's aunt Manci. Andy trusted her judgment. "She was an Auschwitz survivor and had seen the worst that could be," he wrote. "She was not a hysterical woman and had absolutely no reason to exaggerate." Early in December, Manci came to the Grove apartment on Kiraly Street on the Pest side of Budapest with a blunt message. "Andris [the diminutive for András], you must go. You must go, and you must go immediately." Young people were being rounded up by Budapest's occupiers. Suddenly, it seemed as if it might be as dangerous to stay as to go.

Andy and his family were unfailingly decisive at moments like this. They had had all too much practice for them. Mother, father, and son agreed that Andy should try to escape. There was never a question of Andy's parents making the dash to the border with him. They were neither old nor infirm, but the chances of making an escape were vastly decreased if you tried as a family group.

Andy spent one more night in the apartment on Kiraly Street, the only home he had ever known. The next morning, he and his parents parted on a street corner. They had to feign offhandedness. Making a big deal out of the farewell might have drawn attention to them, which was a risk no one wanted to run. They knew, however, that they might never see each other again.

Andy headed for the railroad station to catch a train to a town fifteen miles from the Austrian border. From there, he would have to proceed on foot. The escape was harrowing. His account of it in his memoir *Swimming Across* sounds like something out of a Hollywood movie, complete with safe houses, mysterious guides, and whispered instructions in the dark. Finally he heard a stranger say, "Relax, you're in Austria." He had made it.

• • •

Few American CEOs lived the first two decades of their life like this. Grove spent his first twenty years in a world in which lying was a matter of course and in which questioning the lie was potentially lethal. No one could be depended upon except the closest human relations. The Hungary of Grove's youth was an Orwellian dystopia. The truth was deep in hiding. But if you did not discover it, a resulting misstep could cost you your life. Facts were precious commodities. Facing them square on, and acting accordingly, was not only advisable, but essential. Denial could be fatal.

Grove has never lost his sense of urgency about the truth. To him, it has always been about more than a point or two of market share. As an engineer and an executive he would question his colleagues with a persistence that could be maddening. He has tried to live a life the opposite of his experience in Hungary. Groupthink was bad. Doubt was good. Indeed, to use a word he has often employed, "chaos" was good, to a point. You had to "let chaos reign and then rein in chaos." These traits were to serve him well.

Grove successfully escaped to Austria in 1956, but that wasn't far enough. He wanted to go to the land of movie stars and Hershey's bars. The following year found him in the United States, where he scraped together enough money to cover his living expenses while pursuing a degree in chemical engineering at the tuition-free City College of New York. He didn't like the weather in New York, so he and his bride, Eva, moved to the San Francisco Bay Area. He has never forgotten his sense of gratitude to CCNY for giving him a chance. Engineers-in-training there now study at the Grove School of Engineering.

Grove earned his Ph.D. in chemical engineering at tuition-free Berkeley. Obviously a talented technologist, he received a number of job offers upon graduation in 1963. It is notable that both his parents were present at his graduation. He had managed to get them out of Hungary during the height of the Cold War. Grove was a survivor, and he helped those closest to him survive as well.

After graduation, Grove's choice of employers came down to Bell Labs and Fairchild Semiconductor. For most people, this choice would not have been difficult. Bell Labs was the research arm of American Telephone & Telegraph, which monopolized the telephone business at the time in the United States. It was a storied institution, the birthplace of, among other things, the transistor in 1947; and by the early 1960s it was the place to be in solid-state physics or chemistry. The Bell Labs people came out to Berkeley to see Grove, and they were in full "selling mode."

On the Fairchild side of the ledger, however, was Gordon Earle Moore. Bell's recruiter was a nice guy, but he was no Gordon Moore. Moore "asked me about my thesis, all on his own, and listened, and got it!" Grove liked Moore immediately. "He's really a smart guy—very personable, no airs. Gordon was a *big* selling factor, helping me to see what I wanted to be."

It was a close call. In the end, Moore's attraction for Grove and the fact that Grove loved northern California and could not stand East Coast weather (Bell Labs was located in Morristown, New Jersey) combined to tip the balance. Grove took the job at Fairchild and within one week proved his dissertation sponsor correct in describing him as a "truly outstanding technical person."

Fairchild Semiconductor was a highflier in the 1960s, the Google of its time. Moore was thirty-four and Grove twenty-seven when they met. Moore was already well established and wealthy. The man whom Moore viewed as his partner was Robert N. Noyce. Handsome and charismatic,

Noyce was the coinventor of the integrated circuit and widely regarded as a golden boy from the time he arrived in Silicon Valley at the invitation of William B. Shockley. Noyce led the so-called "traitorous eight" from Shockley Semiconductor to Fairchild. Grove's relationship with Noyce was a good deal less congenial than with Moore. Grove was one of the few people not smitten by Noyce's charm, although he had a healthy respect for Noyce's talent.

In 1968, Moore decided to leave Fairchild and found a semiconductor company of his own. Without hesitating for a second, Grove blurted out, "I'm coming too." Moore then told him that Bob Noyce was his partner. Grove was not happy to hear this, and he was probably the only person in the industry who would have been unhappy about it. Noyce was, after all, Noyce. The new company was his initiative. He was literally money in the bank because there was not a venture he could have dreamt of for which venture capitalist Arthur Rock would not have found the funding. Grove had to reconcile himself to news that would have thrilled anybody else.

The new firm, Intel, was incorporated on July 16, 1968. The name was said to stand for "integrated electronics." Some thought it was simply short for "intelligence." Arthur Rock raised the necessary funding with ease. The reputations of Noyce and Moore were such that talented engineers sent their résumés as soon as they heard about the new firm.

Semiconductor firms were born and died seemingly by the dozens in Silicon Valley in the 1960s. Noyce was supremely confident about Intel's chances, and Moore retained a sense of equanimity about his decision to leave Fairchild. "Changing jobs in our industry is fairly common," he observed, "and I was fairly sure if this didn't work out, I could find something else to do, so I didn't consider it much of a risk."

It is not surprising that Moore and Noyce founded Intel with the expectation of success. They had already participated in two successful start-ups, and in their midthirties they were both wealthy, although not nearly as rich as they were soon to become.

To be an American technologist in the 1960s—even in the tumultuous year of 1968, the year of domestic assassinations and global political uproar—was to be a man expecting success. Noyce was born and raised in Iowa and earned his Ph.D. in physics at MIT. Moore is a native Californian and earned Ph.D.s in both chemistry and physics at Cal Tech. One has the feeling from reading about Noyce (who died of a heart attack at sixty-two) and talking to Moore (eighty at this writing and a billionaire because of Intel's success) that failure never entered either man's mind. They were smart, and the world was just. If they applied themselves, they would succeed.

Andy Grove, Intel employee #3, hailed from quite a different background. Hard work and ability could pay off, but you could be certain of nothing. When it came to Intel, Andy's "imagination of disaster," to use a phrase from Henry James, was fully engaged. He had no illusions. As in Hungary, he did not deny the risks. He acknowledged them, even though doing so was emotionally punishing. As he put it:

> I was scared to death. I left a very secure job where I knew what I was doing and started running R&D for a brand-new venture in untried territory. It was terrifying. I literally had nightmares. I was supposed to be director of engineering, but there were so few of us that they made me director of operations. My first assignment was to get a post office box so we could get literature describing the equipment we couldn't afford to buy.

Andy had already made his share of transitions. "I went from chemistry to chemical engineering, to applied physics, to solid-state physics, to manufacturing" in a little more than a decade. He had started life with an interest in journalism. His flexibility was to serve him well.

Grove was frustrated at Fairchild because nothing ever got done the way it should have. As director of operations at Intel, he was responsible not only for technical issues but for getting product out the door. This required not only technical expertise, but also managing people. Silicon Valley in 1960 was overflowing with engineering talent, but the engineers were notoriously undisciplined. They shared trade secrets with competitors. They were sloppy in their work habits, coming to work late and not respecting the degree of precision that was required to produce semiconductors. This had to change, and it was not going to be easy to change. Andy was going to have to change it because neither Noyce nor Moore had any interest in the actual practice of management, and both avoided interpersonal conflict.

Arthur Rock once said that Intel needed Noyce, Moore, and Grove, and it needed them in that order. Grove himself sensed the same thing. He read Peter Drucker's *The Practice of Management*, in which the ideal chief executive was a combination of three people, whom Grove characterized as "an outside man, a man of thought, and a man of action." That does indeed characterize the roles Noyce, Moore, and Grove played at Intel.

For such a highly touted and ambitious venture, Intel got off to a shaky start. Moore, the "man of thought," wanted to target a new market for semiconductors, magnetic core memory in mainframe computers. It was an inviting prospect if Intel could crack the market, but the first two products the company turned out were inadequate.

The firm was bedeviled by difficulties, some big and some maddeningly small. For Grove—who all his life has been hard on the people with whom he worked but harder on himself—the difficulties of Intel's first few years bordered on the intolerable. He had convinced himself that Fairchild's problem was a dysfunctional organization, and he was certain that with those organizational problems solved at Intel, great products would result. But the plethora of dilemmas with these early devices tormented him. Self-doubt, a painful emotion for everyone but more so for the normally self-confident Grove, crept into his life. "If at Intel we can't make it," he asked himself, "how could I look myself in the mirror?" Management, in the phrase of a document from early 1970, was "near panic."

In October 1970, Intel came out with its third product, the 1-kilobit 1103 DRAM (for "dynamic random-access memory" and pronounced D-RAM). The 1103 was so problematic it became legendary. When asked by an interviewer in 1979 whether there had been production problems with the 1103, Grove's response was "Oh, God." Even the calm Moore observed that this "was one of the most difficult-to-use integrated circuits ever produced."

Nevertheless, the 1103 put Intel on the map. The company turned a profit for the first time in 1971 and also had its IPO. "There was a lot of resistance to semiconductor technology on the part of core-memory engineers," Moore said, but they eventually embraced it.

Intel became the memory company, and on that basis it experienced an outstanding decade. Sales and profits in 1971 were $9.41 million and $1.02 million respectively. In 1980, they were $854.56 million and $96.74 million.

Sales had grown at a compound annual rate of 65 percent and profits at 65.8 percent. By 1980, Intel was a big company.

This growth was certainly not without potholes in the road. The last half of 1974 was especially difficult, and the industrywide slowdown persisted into 1975. By the end of 1974, Intel had fired almost a third of its thirty-five hundred employees. Profits declined in 1975, the only year during this decade that happened.

Another down year was 1981, as the whole nation endured the Reagan recession, the worst economic downturn between the Great Depression and the economic crisis of 2008.

Sales and especially profits skyrocketed between 1981 and 1984, however. The rebound had its roots in a product other than memory chips: the microprocessor. Developed at Intel in 1971 to satisfy a Japanese customer in the calculator business, this was a "logic" as opposed to a memory chip that found sundry niche markets during the 1970s. Its real value only became apparent with the birth and growth of the personal computer market in the late 1970s and early 1980s.

In 1979, Robert Noyce stepped down as chairman of Intel's board to become vice chairman. The move was more than symbolic. Noyce liked to start new things and wanted more out of life than he could get from managing a big company. Gordon Moore became chairman of the board and CEO. Andy Grove, forty-three years old and as aggressive as ever, became president and chief operating officer.

The microprocessor sales force was by the end of the year getting clobbered by the competition. Why? The basic problem was that Intel's microprocessor, the 8086, was inferior to the competition. Jean-Claude Rivet, Intel's microprocessor marketing manager, called his flagship product "the Edsel of microprocessors." Not much of an endorsement.

The most menacing of the competitors was Motorola. Far larger than Intel, it was a proud company with a rich history. The microprocessor which it positioned against the 8086 was the technically superior 68000.

Intel's field sales force was aware of the problem, and morale was low. The sales force was frustrated because while it was getting beaten up in the real world, no one at Intel's home office in Santa Clara in Silicon Valley was paying much attention. On November 2, 1979, the sales manager of Intel's

Atlantic region fired off an eight-page telex to headquarters detailing the difficulties. Another such message came in from Denver at about the same time.

Grove always paid special attention to middle management and particularly to the sales force. They were out on the front lines while top management was ensconced at the home office, cushioned from the daily rough-and-tumble of the marketplace. "Snow," he wrote in *Only the Paranoid Survive*, "melts first at the periphery." Problems, in other words, appear initially at the borders.

The result was an angry staff meeting at which Grove—a combative man who both hated and feared to lose—decreed Operation Crush. Note that the response was immediate. Less than a week after he understands the predicament in the field, Grove, Intel's newly minted president, lobs a missile at the enemy.

The name of his initiative says it all. No weasel words. Nothing about continuous improvement. The goal was to crush, not compromise. To annihilate the enemy. The captain of the team was Bill Davidow, Intel's senior vice president for marketing and sales. Davidow remembered that staff meeting vividly. It "couldn't have been more unpleasant." Grove unchained is something to see.

Davidow found himself in charge of Crush, and since "subtlety is not one of Andy's strengths," Davidow knew that failure would not be tolerated. Success, however, was not going to be easy. Grove established what seemed like an impossible goal: two thousand "design wins." (An example of a design win would be Dell choosing an Intel microprocessor for a new line of computers.) These design wins had to be achieved hawking a product that was by consensus technically inferior to the competition. How was this to be accomplished?

Davidow leveraged the strength of Intel, which lay in its field-application engineers. What mattered in the last analysis was not the technical capability of a chip but the total bundle of benefits the customer received with the purchase. The winner would be the company with the best augmented product, not the best core product, and in this area Intel had an edge. "Intel had great customer service and support," Davidow wrote. "We could assure a customer's success with our device. By comparison, choosing the Motorola path clearly presented a risk to the customer."

The audacious goal of two thousand design wins was surpassed. There were twenty-five hundred. Of these, one changed the history of the company and the whole computer industry. IBM chose Intel's 8086 as the microprocessor for the PC it was hurrying to market. When the IBM PC finally hit the market in 1981, the magnitude of its success surpassed everybody's expectations. "With the IBM contract," journalist Michael Malone has written, "Intel won the microprocessor wars. And the victory was due to Operation Crush."

Largely because of this spectacular performance, Intel's sales rose from $788.68 million in 1981 to $1.629 billion in 1984. Profits took off into the stratosphere, from $27.36 million to $198.19 million. The microprocessor franchise became one of the most valuable in twentieth-century business history. Intel owned it.

Yet Intel failed to appreciate fully what it had. Like the rest of the world, Intel's executives marched backward into the future. Even into the mid-1980s, the company conceived of itself as a memory company. It was to memory that the talent and the investment continued to be channeled. DRAM chips would shortly become nothing more than their name—memory—to Intel. As Grove was soon to declare triumphantly, "The PC is it."

The struggle to migrate from a memory to a microprocessor company provides as vivid an illustration as you are likely to find of denial at work, even at a hyperrational, no-nonsense company managed by engineers.

Although Intel's financial performance in 1984 was spectacular—sales up 45 percent, profits up 71 percent, over the records set in 1983—clouds were clearly evident on the horizon. The year ended poorly as demand suddenly softened. Intel, in fact, was on the edge of a precipice. It fell off it the following year.

According to Intel's 1985 annual report, "It was a miserable year for Intel and for the rest of the semiconductor industry." Caught up in the euphoria of the PC boom, Intel overbuilt. It created "an overhead structure appropriate to the $2–3 billion company we wanted to be rather than [the] $1.0–1.5 billion company we were becoming." A projected 22 percent growth in the global semiconductor industry had turned into a 17 percent decline.

The fact that times were tough for the whole industry did not make things any easier for Intel. Overcapacity in this high-fixed-cost industry was a plague in 1985. Prices went into free fall. Intel found itself attacked from all sides. From Europe and especially from Asia, large electronics companies were muscling into its markets. Domestically, small start-ups—potentially new Intels—were carving out their own niches. Layoffs, plant closings, and unpaid vacations resulted. All Intel's budgets were cut with the exception of R&D. There, even though Intel actually lost money on an operating basis, spending was increased. (Intel posted a profit of $1.57 million in 1985 because of $54.7 million in interest and a $7 million tax credit.)

No one could accuse the company of denying reality in its public statements in 1985. The news was grim, and there was no happy talk about what the future looked like. The prediction was that 1986 "will probably be another tough year."

That turned out to be quite an understatement. Sales slid to $1.265 billion, off more than a fifth from the record year of 1984. As for profits, they were nowhere to be found. Intel lost $173.13 million, its only year in red ink as a public company. The 1986 annual report began with a touch of gallows humor: "We're pleased to report that 1986 is over." The report contained an important postscript as well. Moore informed shareholders and the public that although he would remain chairman of the board of directors, Grove would become chief executive officer in April 1987. "Andy has been at Intel since the beginning, and as president and chief operating officer, he has been one of the chief architects of this company's growth, direction, and character. . . . He is an extraordinarily talented manager."

Early in 1986, Grove had been enjoying the seven-week sabbatical that Intel gave its top management, skiing in Austria and at Lake Tahoe. Moore asked him to cut it short. The two suffered through 1986 together.

Now Grove's management talent would be put to the test. The financial situation had to be remedied. If 1987 bore the same relation to 1986 as 1986 had to 1985, Intel would lose almost a million dollars a day and find itself on the road to bankruptcy.

There were serious barriers to Intel's return to health. The biggest of all appeared to be the threat from Japanese competitors.

In Grove's assessment, Japanese semiconductor manufacturers were a pleasure to have around in the late 1970s. They helped out when Intel could not keep up with demand. Seemingly overnight, however, Japanese suppliers transformed themselves from docile puppies into ferocious pit bulls. In one paragraph of *Only the Paranoid Survive,* Grove twice describes them as "scary." Huge facilities housing floor after floor of skilled engineers working on tomorrow's technology. Rock-bottom cost of capital made possible by the intricacies of what at the time was called Japan Inc.

During the 1980s, Japanese manufacturing prowess became, in many industries, the envy of the United States. Semiconductor firms thought they were immune. The industry had started here, and the people in it convinced themselves that no one could challenge their expertise. They were wrong. By 1985, some lines of Japanese semiconductors were not only less expensive than American, they were of higher quality. This came as a real shock. For Grove, the "insidious" Japanese attack on the American economy was the story of "these humongous companies with their humongous factories trying to take a major share of whatever we have left away from us."

As if all this were not menacing enough, the Japanese had learned what aggressive marketing was all about. They were once thought to be weak in this regard. Not anymore. "Win with the 10% rule," one Japanese semiconductor manufacturer advised its sales force in a memorandum. "Find AMD [Advanced Micro Devices, a Silicon Valley semiconductor manufacturer] and Intel sockets. . . . Quote 10% below this price. . . . If they requote, go 10% AGAIN. . . . Don't quit until you WIN!" Intel had been so proud of its Operation Crush. Now the shoe was on the other foot. Giant Japanese firms with superb products, high volumes, and privileged access to capital were mounting their own version of Operation Crush. In 1985, the Japanese suppliers overtook the American industry in global share of market for semiconductors. The Japanese seemed to have discovered a whole new way to compete. Market share was everything. Profit could wait.

Think, now, of Intel. A rational company managed by rational executives. At the helm, Andy Grove, a man born into an environment that demanded that he discover the truth no matter how hidden and act on it no matter how painful and difficult. That these people and this company fell prey to denial is testimony to how magnetic denial can be.

How do people react when they find themselves facing a fact that is too terrible to be true? We have already encountered the answer to this question. They deny it. If something is too terrible to be true, then it cannot be true, because if it were, things would be too terrible. Their high IQs notwithstanding, Intel executives were no different from anyone else in this regard. Grove put it well: "As people so often do in this kind of situation, we vigorously attacked the ominous data."

Intel's self-conception may have been as a memory company, but if you look at the numbers, you can see that as a percentage of Intel's sales volume, memory chips began to decline relative to microprocessors; and that decline became steep in 1975. In 1982, microprocessors accounted for greater sales volume than memories. By the crisis year of 1985, microprocessors were outselling memories at Intel by about two to one.

An explanation of this trend requires a brief discussion of the differences between memory chips and microprocessor chips. Both are semiconductors. However, the memory semiconductors on which Intel was built—DRAMs—were more in the nature of a commodity than microprocessors. Low-cost manufacturing played perhaps as important a role in a successful DRAM business as it does in any commodity business.

In contrast, the microprocessor, also known as a logic chip, was not a commodity. It was more customized to the needs of the purchaser. Product and process design played a relatively larger role in its creation, as did marketing. The microprocessor was a relationship business far more than the memory chip. That is why sales and marketing are so important, and that is why Intel was able to win the IBM PC design.

All this was known in the 1970s and 1980s. It is not being offered with the benefit of hindsight. The numbers indicate that Intel was more a microprocessor than a memory company as of 1982. As early as 1980, its global share of the DRAM business was under 3 percent. Ironically, this was good news. The real Japanese competitive advantage was with those "humongous" and highly efficient factories. Manufacturing was far more important in DRAMs than in microprocessors.

With perspective, what was at the time Intel's great drama does not make a lot of sense. The company was being forced out of a commodity business in which it could not compete and into a specialty business with far more precise and individual product characteristics for which it could charge higher prices and compete quite well.

Why, then, was it so difficult to exit the DRAM market and focus all

energy on microprocessors? And make no mistake, it was hard as hell—
"traumatic" is the word usually associated with it by the people who lived
through it. You can, to paraphrase Benjamin Franklin, always find a principle to justify your inclinations; and Intel's leadership took every rationalization out for a test drive.

"Managing," Grove has rightly observed, "especially managing through
a crisis, is an extremely personal affair." You need data-driven emotional
intelligence. But what happens when the data push you in one direction
and your emotions pull you in another?

DRAMs were the spoiled darling of Intel's product line. "The bulk of
the memory chip [i.e., DRAM] development," Grove explained, "took place
in a spanking new facility in Oregon. The microprocessor technology
developers had to share a production facility—not even a new one at that—
with the manufacturing folks at a remote site. Our priorities were formed
by our identity; after all, memories *were* us."

Just at the moment when decisiveness and vision were most needed, they
were missing in action. "We had meetings and more meetings, bickering
and arguments, resulting in nothing but conflicting proposals," Grove recalled. Some favored a "go for it" strategy, which meant building a gigantic
factory dedicated to only memories and going toe-to-toe with the Japanese.
Others wanted to "go for it" in a different way—Intel should develop a new
technology and manufacture something that the Japanese could not. Yet
another school of thought favored investment in "special-purpose memories," an increasingly unlikely possibility as memories became globally com-
moditized. Though focus was vital, according to Grove, "We had lost our
bearings. We were wandering in the valley of death."

Two beliefs had the power of "religious dogmas" in Grove's view and
served to wed Intel to memories. One was that memory was Intel's "technology driver" and therefore should be looked at through a different lens
from other products. Memory devices were easier to test than other Intel
products, and they were therefore debugged first. The technical lessons
learned could then be applied to more complicated products. By this route,
executives convinced themselves that technical excellence and memory
were inextricably intertwined.

The DRAM technology-development group "led the company in linewidth reduction. They were already developing a 1-micron process while

the logic [i.e., the microprocessor] group was still developing a 1.5-micron process. Sunlin Chou and his group were widely regarded as Intel's best resource for process development." Grove hired Chou back at Fairchild in 1964 and always held him in the highest regard.

The second religious dogma dealt with marketing. Intel, executives told themselves, owed it to its customers and therefore to its sales force to field a full line of products. The customers demanded one-stop shopping, and if Intel could not provide that service, someone else would.

• • •

How do you extricate yourself from this kind of argumentative trap?

Here is how Grove recalls the breakthrough moment:

> I remember a time in the middle of 1985 after this aimless wandering had been going on for almost a year.
> I was in my office with Intel's chairman and CEO, Gordon Moore, and we were discussing our quandary. Our mood was downbeat.
> I looked out the window at the Ferris wheel of the Great America amusement park revolving in the distance, then I turned back to Gordon and I asked, "If we got kicked out and the board brought in a new CEO, what do you think he would do?"
> Gordon answered without hesitation. "He would get us out of memories."
> I stared at him, numb, then said, "Why shouldn't you and I walk out the door, come back, and do it ourselves?"

Something critical happened that broke the intellectual logjam and allowed Grove and Moore to discern the truth clearly and to liberate themselves from denial. What was this dramatic something? Moore and Grove were the same people before the question was asked as they were after it. Their IQs did not suddenly change. Denial is not a matter of intelligence. It is a matter of point of view.

It is difficult to make a critical business decision when you are as emotionally entangled in the issue as were Moore and Grove. What Grove did in a cognitive tour de force was to create a virtual person who had all the intelligence necessary to evaluate the situation dispassionately.

"History," says Stephen Dedalus in James Joyce's *Ulysses*, "is a nightmare from which I am trying to escape." This "new CEO"—and it goes without

saying that this person would be from outside Intel, not a colleague—
would be disinterested in his evaluation, not burdened by Intel's glorious
"we are memories" history.

We do not know why Moore answered so assuredly, "without hesitation," that memory would have to go. But we can guess. Grove had given
him a new point of view, that of the disinterested, intelligent outsider. The
scales fell from his eyes as a result. All the reasons for remaining in memory
were revealed for what they were, not true reasons but rationalizations.

Surely, one of the lessons here is that a different point of view can in-
oculate you from denial. Way back in this book's first chapter, we saw Ernest
Kanzler offer Henry Ford a different point of view. For reasons we can only
guess about, however, Ford rejected this golden opportunity. That is why
he got it wrong while Moore and Grove got it right.

Without knowing it or having it on his mind, Grove reached back into
his own life story to generate this device. In December of 1956, he and his
parents had stalled out on the question of whether he should attempt to
escape to the Austrian border. The clouds parted when an outsider in the
person of Aunt Manci walked in the door of the Kiraly Street apartment.
Grove and his family were galvanized then as Grove and Moore were in
1985. In both cases, the people in question, after fruitlessly looking and
looking and looking, had come to the right conclusion because they had
been provided with a new point of view.

. . .

Why was Grove "numb" in response to Moore's observation about getting
out of memories? Because after all the "aimless wandering," he knew that
this was the answer. On some level, he'd known it before he asked the question. Or, better put, he knew-but-didn't-know it. Grove's question and
Moore's response forced Grove to strip away his own denial and look facts
in the face. You will note that Grove did not argue with Moore. Suddenly,
he knew-and-did-know the answer.

The answer was painful for any number of reasons. In business, it is
easier to get into something than to get out of it, and it fell to Grove to
extricate Intel from memories. "It's natural to say, 'The problem is just a
distraction. My strategy still works,'" Grove later told a reporter. "If you end
up being right, you're praised for being steadfast in the face of change. If

you're wrong, people say you've been in denial." When Grove started talking about jettisoning memories, he said, "I had a hard time getting the words out of my mouth without equivocation."

The answer was clear. Speed and decisiveness were called for. Hesitation resulted instead. Intel moved in stages, as if its executives were working their way through a trance. At one point, to his own amazement, Grove allowed another executive to persuade him "to continue R&D for a [memory] product that he and I both knew we had no plans to sell."

Such denial, Grove says, is prevalent in the early stages of nearly every fundamental shift in business conditions (or to use his terminology, strategic inflection point). In this case, he recalls thinking, "If we had just started our development of [a pivotal] memory chip earlier, the Japanese wouldn't have made any headway."

Snow, however, was melting at the periphery, to repeat Grove's phrase. As at DuPont, and previously at Intel with Operation Crush, denial was an unaffordable luxury for the hands-on middle managers who had to deal with the hard truth every single day. As a result, Intel knowingly (in the middle) but not knowingly (at the top) was easing itself out of memories long before the shift was officially sanctioned. How did this happen? How, Grove asks, did "the memory company" get to where only one factory out of eight was producing memory chips by the mid-1980s, thus making the formal exit from memories less traumatic?

> It got there by the autonomous actions of the finance and production planning people, who sat around painstakingly allocating wafer production capacity month by month, moving silicon wafers from products where they seemed wasteful—memories were the prime example of this—to other products which seemed to generate better margins, such as microprocessors. These people didn't have the authority to get us out of memories but they had the authority to fine-tune the production allocation process by lots of little steps. Over the course of many months, their actions made it easier to eventually pull the plug on our memory participation.

Still, there was a lot of pain involved. For eighteen months, Intel engaged in a "process of shutting down factories, letting people go, telling customers we are no longer in the business, and facing the employees who all grew up in the memory business, who all prided themselves on their skills, and those skills were no longer appropriate for the direction that we were going to take with microprocessors."

At length, Grove went up to Oregon, headquarters of the DRAM team, and delivered a speech, the theme of which was "Welcome to the mainstream." Intel was making the transition from memories to microprocessors, and there was plenty of room for talented people willing to learn new skills.

The speech was received better than Grove had expected. Grove's audience knew the situation. They craved resolution. They wanted an end to ambiguity. Any decision was better than indecision. Grove himself did not realize this until after his speech. The DRAM team knew something had to be done. The CEO was the last to know.

But he found out in time.

11

Data-Driven Emotional Intelligence: Tylenol's Comeback

On Wednesday, September 29, 1982, in Elk Grove Village, Illinois, a suburb of Chicago, a twelve-year-old girl named Mary Kellerman died unexpectedly of an unknown cause. That same day, a twenty-seven-year-old postal worker named Adam Janus who lived in Arlington Heights, just north of Elk Grove Village, also died suddenly, without explanation. His brother Stanley and sister-in-law Theresa came to Janus's home to mourn his death. Stanley also died suddenly. Theresa fell into a coma and died on October 1. Three more deaths followed quickly. On September 30, Mary McFarland of Elmhurst, south of Elk Grove Village, Mary Reiner, a twenty-seven-year-old mother of four from Winfield, west of Elmhurst, and Paula Prince of Chicago, all died suddenly.

The cause of the first three deaths and the comatose patient were complete mysteries. Medical authorities were considering quarantining the entire geographic area in which the incidents occurred. But then paramedics spotted a common attribute. All four of the September 29 victims had recently taken Extra Strength Tylenol capsules. The three victims the following day had used the same product.

Tragically, these seven people thought they were taking Tylenol, but they were not. They were taking cyanide, one of the deadliest of poisons. News of the product tampering and subsequent deaths reached the headquarters of Johnson & Johnson, which owned McNeil Consumer Products, manufacturers of Tylenol, on September 30. This event defined a crisis. Nothing remotely similar had happened in the company's history, which stretched back to 1886. Tylenol was the leading analgesic in the United States. A hundred million Americans had taken the product in 1981. How many of them were at risk?

The fate of one particular company in the face of a menace of this magnitude may seem trivial. But it didn't to the people running Johnson & Johnson. It was they whose decisions in the days and weeks to come would have potentially vast public health consequences. They were, not incidentally, responsible for the welfare of seventy-five thousand employees and their families. They were responsible to hundreds of thousands of investors. They had to make a lot of big decisions quickly. And they had none of the information they needed and no precedent to guide them.

Yet, they got it right. Against all odds, the Tylenol brand survived. Today, Johnson & Johnson's handling of this catastrophe stands as a textbook case of successful crisis management. For our purposes, this is a telling example of how *not* to fall prey to denial.

Denial occurs when we push aside hard truths in favor of more palatable or convenient narratives. As we discovered in chapter 2, these narratives are often stories that we tell ourselves. But they can also be stories that others tell us. It is this second form of denial that Johnson & Johnson and its CEO, James E. Burke, managed to avoid. They refused to capitulate to the near unanimous verdict of pundits, analysts, and experts that Tylenol was finished as a product and a brand. Instead, they insisted on gathering and examining the data to make their own determination of exactly what the facts were. They understood, at least implicitly, that blind acceptance of something that is not a fact is as much an act of denial as evasion of something that is. That understanding led them to a conclusion that was radically different from the conventional wisdom. Ultimately, it enabled them to save Tylenol.

They also avoided another denial trap into which so many other companies have fallen: denying the human and emotional dimensions of their business. As we will see, Jim Burke, who became the public face of the company throughout the poisoning episode, never attempted to minimize or sugarcoat the suffering of the victims and their families—or, remarkably, his remorse at his company's role, however innocent, in the tragedy. Burke refused to deny the fundamental humanity at the core of the crisis, including his own. This too would prove crucial to saving the brand.

In rejecting denial in these two different ways, Johnson & Johnson adopted an approach that might be called data-driven emotional intelligence—the willingness to ignore conventional wisdom, gather facts in an objective, hardheaded manner, and face up to the full implications of those facts in both marketing and human terms.

In the initial desperate hours of the crisis, Johnson & Johnson's first order of business was to find out precisely what had happened and how it had happened. If the cause was in the control of J&J, then obviously the company had to fix it immediately. Johnson & Johnson was in 1982 and is today a highly decentralized company. Thus the division responsible for Tylenol (J&J referred to its divisions as "companies" in order to push as much responsibility down to the operating level as possible) was McNeil Consumer Products. On September 30, Burke contacted Wayne K. Nelson, the McNeil Company group chairman. Burke was at J&J's headquarters in New Brunswick, New Jersey, about thirty-five miles south of New York City. Nelson was traveling in Australia.

"I remember him saying that he would bet his bonus and a year's salary that the contamination did not occur in the plant because of the controls they had there," Burke recalled. "That made me somewhat relieved, but I was still very concerned because we did not know at that point in time that the poisonings were isolated in the Chicago area."

On September 30, things started to happen fast. At noon, officials of Cook County (encompassing Chicago and some nearby suburbs) held a press conference at which they confirmed that cyanide was the cause of death and that random capsules of Extra Strength Tylenol that contained cyanide had been found near the victims. In the case of Mary Reiner, for example, there were six Tylenol capsules found in her purse. Four of them had been emptied of the medication and filled with the poison. All bottles found containing cyanide came from batch number MC 2880. This batch consisted of ninety-three thousand bottles containing 4.7 million capsules distributed to thirty-one states. The potential size of the calamity was obvious.

The poisonings were attracting an avalanche of publicity. It is said that they received more news coverage than any other event since the assassination of President John F. Kennedy nineteen years previously. Rumors were flying around the country.

J&J decided to manage the crisis from its headquarters in New Brunswick. This seems obvious, but it was not at the time. If you looked at a container of Tylenol in 1982, you would have seen no mention of Johnson & Johnson, in conformance with the company's strict policy of decentralization. The same is true today. Burke at first thought that the public didn't associate Tylenol with Johnson & Johnson. He guessed they hardly thought of it in conjunction with McNeil either. He was probably right, but Larry Foster, who founded J&J's public relations department in 1957 and ran it from 1973 to 1989, made it clear to Burke that the media were going to run with this as a Johnson & Johnson story. Burke was squarely in the headlights of the onrushing locomotive.

On the afternoon of September 30, Johnson & Johnson created a toll-free line to handle the flood of inquiries coming from consumers. More than twenty-five hundred media inquiries were received in the early days of the crisis. The company made every effort to field each one. It wasn't easy, because at first J&J had little to say. Information was scarce. Indeed, the company actually asked the media to keep it informed of any reliable information they uncovered.

Staffing all the phones receiving these calls was not easy. The company recruited volunteers from among its employees. Even employees' family members pitched in. Remember, this was before the Internet. No corporation had a webpage for distributing information to the world with one voice. The people having thousands of phone conversations on behalf of the company had to be as accurate as possible, which meant the company had to keep them up-to-date on breaking news.

One of the first company bulletins to the media turned out to be inaccurate. David Collins, the forty-eight-year-old chairman of McNeil Consumer Products (who reported to Wayne Nelson, the company group chairman) was on a helicopter heading for the manufacturing facility in Fort Washington, Pennsylvania, less than a half hour after learning of the crisis. When he arrived, he found managers racing between phone banks and the office of the president, Joseph Chiesa.

The first thing Collins wanted to find out was whether there was any cyanide on the premises of that plant. Everyone assured him that there was not, and he so informed J&J headquarters back in New Brunswick, which relayed the news to the voracious media.

Unfortunately, this was incorrect. Small amounts of cyanide were present at the plant as part of a quality-assurance procedure, required by the U.S. Food and Drug Administration (FDA), designed to test the purity of the ingredients in Tylenol. Collins was not happy to learn of this, but he immediately informed J&J's public relations department in New Brunswick, which in turn told the media.

The Tylenol poisoning is one of those public events that are so startling and riveting that if you were old enough to appreciate its significance at the time, you may still remember where you were and what you were doing when you heard the news. I was in Palm Springs, California, facilitating a corporate meeting. When I had a moment, I would turn on the television to see the latest developments.

Put yourself in the context of the times. Terrorists were not unknown, but we did not tend to look for them under every bush as we have since 9/11. If something like this were to happen today, one would immediately assume that Al Qaeda or some other group from, to use a phrase popularized by Theodore Roosevelt, the "lunatic fringe" was behind it. No such assumption was made then. Everyone felt that something genuinely malevolent had happened (this wasn't merely an accident), and no one had a clue as to what it was. The mystery heightened the drama.

So also did the strange nature of the act. Why put cyanide in Tylenol? What could the motive of the perpetrator have been? It could hardly have been to murder a particular individual. No one could know who would swallow the tampered capsules. Did someone really want to kill Adam Janus? Did that same person figure his brother and sister-in-law would also lose their lives because of poisoned Tylenol?

One theory, at least, was not completely crazy. Perhaps a disgruntled employee of Johnson & Johnson wanted to strike at the company. Tylenol was its most profitable product. Poisoning it would be a way to achieve that goal. Seventy-five thousand employees is a big number. Surely someone in that group was mentally unbalanced. Possibly the issue was personal—a grudge against some individual at J&J. I once asked Burke whether he ever felt threatened himself during this period. He did not.

The plausibility that the cause of this tragedy lay within the company served to intensify the public focus upon it. That is one reason that the admission, following the denial, that there was indeed cyanide at McNeil's

Fort Washington plant was important. The admission and the speed with which it was made served to bolster the company's credibility. I remember feeling at the time that if they were willing to make this fact public and do so without hesitation, then surely they were committed to telling the truth.

All advertising for Tylenol was suspended on September 30. Once again, this seems an obvious thing to do. However, it would have been easy to overlook doing, and it might not have been that easy to execute. The advertising had proven remarkably effective and was doubtless one of the reasons that Tylenol's share of the profitable and highly competitive analgesic market had skyrocketed from 11 percent to a commanding 35 percent.

The number of items on the to-do list was long. All were important, and all had to be executed as soon as possible.

Later in the day on September 30, it was discovered that Mary McFarland, a mother of two from Elmhurst, had a bottle of Extra-Strength Tylenol capsules in her home with the code designation of 1910 MD. Cyanide was found in one of three capsules in this container. An immediate recall was initiated for the 172,000 bottles making up that batch, and clerks started removing them from store shelves.

The discovery of product from this new lot number turned out to be a critical clue in determining where the tampering had taken place. Lot 1910 MD originated not in Fort Washington, Pennsylvania, but in Round Rock, Texas. This batch had been distributed entirely to western states with the exception of one shipment to Chicago. It was highly unlikely that sabotage such as this or an unprecedented accident would have occurred at two separate plants at about the same time. The odds of this catastrophe having been caused by an accident in the plant in the course of manufacturing Tylenol rather than somewhere in the retail system were suddenly greatly diminished.

Also on September 30, 450,000 telexes were sent to doctors, hospitals, and retailers warning against the use of Tylenol until more was known about the situation in Chicago. Meanwhile, the company began a recall of all Extra Strength Tylenol capsules in the Chicago area. It issued a nationwide press release warning against the use of its capsules. It closed the plants at Fort Washington and Round Rock.

With all this done, Friday, October 1, still found J&J starved for information and faced with tough decisions. Who had done this? Why? Was the problem restricted to the Chicago area? How many more poisoned capsules were on retail shelves or in private hands?

Johnson & Johnson had a "corporate credo" well before such documents became de rigueur. It was originally written by General Robert Wood Johnson, the son of the company's founder, in 1943, and it was revised in 1976 when Burke became CEO. The Credo said that the company was responsible to four constituencies in the following order: to "the doctors, nurses and patients, . . . mothers and all others who use our products and services"; to its employees; to "the communities in which we live and work and to the world community as well"; and to its stockholders.

Executives in the quickly constituted Tylenol Strategy Committee met at Burke's office and sat at a rectangular table. Formal meetings took place every day at eight in the morning and six in the evening, but in fact many of those executives spent much of each day there, discussing and arguing with each other. There was a good deal of shouting too. There was complete freedom of speech. It was essential "to let the debate rage," Burke said, to release the tension of the situation. In words of one syllable: "We were all scared to death."

For six weeks, each day that the eight men who constituted the Tylenol Strategy Committee arrived at work for the morning meeting following the brief sleep the previous night, there was a fresh copy of the Credo on the table in front of their chair. Unlike most such statements, this document was revered. Burke described it as profound in its simplicity. All it says is that "everybody is responsible to all those that are dependent upon them." The complete text is merely a page long.

The Credo is a statement of general principles. The question facing the decision makers was how to put these principles into action. On October 1, Burke began to discuss the possibility of a nationwide product recall with COO Dave Clare. There were good arguments both for and against such a move. In favor was the fact that a recall would enable Johnson & Johnson to get ahead of events. Retailers even outside the Chicago area were beginning to remove Tylenol from their shelves. False alarms concerning deaths from Tylenol abounded. A total, nationwide recall would be a decisive action that would enable J&J to be proactive rather than reactive.

But what Tylenol products should be recalled? Should the recall be restricted to capsules (which were, perhaps, 40 percent of the business at the time), or should all products with the Tylenol brand be recalled? The distinction between capsules and pills—which would become critically important as the drama unfolded—was not at all clear in the early days. Dan Rather, the CBS evening-news anchorman at a time when network news was far more important than it is today, used the word "pills" on the air to describe the tampered Tylenol products. Was this a Tylenol problem, a capsule problem, an industry problem, or a problem for all of American retailing? Without having the central issues defined and bounded, any action was potentially counterproductive. The poisoner or poisoners might be emboldened by a Tylenol recall and move on to other products. The sensation of bringing a giant corporation to its knees could provide a lot of encouragement to the lunatic(s) responsible for the tampering.

What was the right thing to do? No one knew. There were multiple points of view to be taken into consideration. The Credo offered guiding principles, But it did not provide practical advice at the ground level on what to do today and tomorrow about this crisis. Nevertheless, violating its spirit would be to sacrifice something of fundamental value in the eyes of the men making the decisions.

During the course of the weekend, Burke became convinced that the crisis was a matter of national concern. All of American retailing, in his view and Clare's, was being jeopardized by anonymous terrorism.

On Monday morning, Burke flew to Washington, D.C., to meet with William Webster, the director of the FBI, and Arthur Hayes, the director of the Food and Drug Administration. Burke was anxious to impress upon them both his alarm at the dire implications of a madman loose in America's stores. He had concluded, albeit reluctantly and not without second thoughts, that Tylenol should be recalled nationally.

It is worth noting that this product recall was quite different from most others. First, in this case it was the company suggesting the recall. Usually, the suggestion—or rather the demand—for the recall of a product comes from the government. Second, Tylenol was not going to be recalled because the product caused harm when used as directed—the usual reason. In this case, the product itself did not present any difficulties. The problem was that some person(s) had decided to use the product's packaging—box, bottle, and capsule—as a vehicle for delivering cyanide to what appeared to be random victims.

Burke didn't like the decision to recall nationally but he saw no way around it. The first words in the Credo dealt with serving the customer. To Burke, that meant there was little alternative to withdrawal, whether the reasons for doing so were strictly rational and logical or not. The Tylenol tampering was something new and carried with it the swift wind of hidden menace and mystery. The very fact that the whole episode was so senseless made withdrawal seem the thing to do.

Moreover, no one knew what was going to happen tomorrow or the next day. What if someone else died from poisoned Tylenol? What would that do to the morale of the employees of what was, after all, a health-care company and one that, because of products such as its baby powder, had always been associated with children? What would it mean to the Credo? At the time, Burke wondered, "How the hell after we'd had everybody in the world challenge the system, buy into it, and say, 'Yes, we believe in it,' could we sit in our offices and say, 'Well, in this case we're just not going to do it?'"

Burke went to Washington to inform the appropriate governmental agencies of his company's decision to conduct a nationwide product recall. So he was more than a little surprised when, in his first meeting with the FBI's William Webster, he learned that the FBI preferred that Tylenol remain on the market. Webster was chiefly worried about Halloween, a few weeks away. In his view, an action as drastic as pulling Tylenol nationally would serve to stimulate the "crazies" with whom law enforcement and other agencies had to contend each year on that night.

Arthur Hayes, head of the FDA, joined Webster and Burke and, if anything, was even more opposed to a national withdrawal. "I listened and was sympathetic," Burke recalled, "but I was still very concerned that this was not the right solution, either from the point of view of the public, or from the point of view of my company's business. I knew legally I had the right to pull the product, but I hated to be in the position of making two regulatory agencies uncomfortable."

Once again, we encounter another oddity of the Tylenol episode. In almost every product recall situation, it is a government agency demanding a product's removal from the market and the manufacturer fighting back.

This time it was the other way around. Halloween and the problems it caused law enforcement and a possible intensification of those problems by the removal of Tylenol had never entered Burke's mind.

Burke must have felt as if he had stepped into a parallel universe. The previous Monday, things could not have looked better. Johnson & Johnson had been heading for a terrific year. Burke had singled out Tylenol as having great potential years earlier, and it had performed outstandingly since he became CEO and could control how it was marketed. Now, he found himself arguing with the government for the right to pull it off the shelves entirely.

Burke was still in Washington on the evening of Tuesday, October 5, discussing the potential recall with Webster and Hayes over warm Pepsi and cold pizza when they were informed that another poison, strychnine, had been discovered in an Extra Strength Tylenol capsule in Oroville, California, about seventy miles north of Sacramento. This was the first poisoning outside the Chicago area and the first not using cyanide. The copycats were on the loose.

That was all Webster and Hayes needed to hear. They agreed with Burke that the brand had to be withdrawn. It was announced on Wednesday, October 6, that 31 million bottles of Tylenol capsules were being removed from retail shelves nationwide.

Meanwhile, J&J with the help of the FDA and FBI tested more than 8 million Tylenol capsules. Almost seventy-five contained cyanide. The cost of the testing, withdrawal, and destruction was covered by J&J, and the price came to about $100 million.

To say that the outlook for the future of the brand in the fall of 1982 was not good is to understate the case. The senselessness of the poisonings made them more frightening than if they had had a clear purpose. A front-page article in *The Wall Street Journal* on October 8 noted that "as time passes without a suspect being caught or a motive for the seemingly random killings assigned, damage to the Tylenol name is mounting." According to Jerry Della Femina, a well-known advertising agent of the time, "I would say that a year from now it's going to be very difficult to find any product with the name Tylenol on it, unfortunately." That was a consensus view in advertising and marketing both in practice and in academia.

The reasons were obvious. The sinister nature of the act seemed right out of the Lucrezia Borgia playbook. A brand is said to be a promise, and what more shattering violation of a promise can be imagined than this? If and when the brand, having been pulled from retail shelves, were reintroduced, what would the company say about it? There were plenty of other headache remedies on the market. Why take a chance with one that had proven fatal?

Perhaps most problematic was that the perpetrator had not been apprehended. To this day, no one knows who was responsible for any of the Tylenol poisonings. As a result, rumors were rampant. Burke remembered one in particular. A member of the Mafia fingered another member of the Mafia as the culprit. "We were convinced we had it solved," Burke said. "We got the FBI involved and everything. But it turned out he was just trying to get rid of one of his friends." From J&J's point of view, such incidents "heightened the drama, clouded the issues, and made it difficult to maintain focus" on the problem at hand.

Executives at Johnson & Johnson weren't quite as hopeless about the brand's future as outside commentators. The active ingredient in Tylenol is acetaminophen, and there were some suggestions within the company that an acetaminophen compound might be marketed under a different name or that the color of the packaging be changed. Discontinuing the product altogether was also considered.

"We discussed pulling the total product," Burke recalled. "And we went through all those options. We went through the technical question of how do you poison a tablet, and all the other issues, but I never for one minute thought that [pulling the product permanently] was the right thing to do."

From his start at Johnson & Johnson as product director for Band-Aids in 1953 to his ascendancy to the top of the corporation, Burke lived and breathed consumer-product marketing and branding. He became close to Bobby Johnson, General Robert Wood Johnson's son, and to the General himself. Father and son did not get along, and Burke's ability to maintain close relations with both—he became a surrogate son to the General without exciting the resentment of his biological son—speaks volumes about the finesse with which he approached human relations. In the corporation itself, his rise was steady and marked by important lessons about product integrity that remained with him. He managed to play the soul-destroying game of company politics without having his soul destroyed.

When the Tylenol disaster struck, Burke was as ready for it as any person could have been, even though he had undergone no formal preparation for such an unexpected occurrence. He knew who he was. He knew about products and consumers. More important, he knew what he did not know and what could not be known by anyone else. That is why he was not overwhelmed by the views of others that the Tylenol brand was through. That was not a fact. It was a conclusion based on nothing in particular.

Burke wanted facts directly from consumers. Looking facts in the face is essential to avoiding denial, and before you can do so, you must ascertain what the "facts" are. This exercise requires considerable intellectual subtlety and, in a phrase we have encountered before, emotional intelligence.

Johnson & Johnson embarked on its quest for facts less than a week after the first poisonings. Videotapes of some of the interviews it conducted are still available at the Baker Library at the Harvard Business School, and they tell a remarkable story. A core of consumers were Tylenol loyalists, people who would stick with the product through the crisis. Even more important, many people did not blame Tylenol for the poisonings. Rather, they blamed capsules, or even, in the words of one interviewee, "all pain relievers over the counter."

This finding was not intuitive, and it was not understood by outside commentators. However, Burke suspected it from the beginning. People, he believed, have a lot of loyalty to brands that mean something to them, and Tylenol meant a great deal to them. If the average consumers were willing to conceive of the poisonings not as a problem with Tylenol as a brand but rather with capsules as a product form, that was vital to know. If this was true, Johnson & Johnson had a chance to snatch victory from what seemed to be the jaws of unavoidable failure.

To be sure, not all the news was good. Independent surveys showed that almost half of Tylenol users said they would not use the brand again. But many of these people did not realize that the poisonings had involved only capsules, not pills. Might their opinions change if the distinction was made clear? Meanwhile, Tylenol's competitors were trying to fill the gap left by its removal and regain some of the market share they had lost over the past decade. To muddy the waters yet further, there occurred an outbreak of copycat product tampering, featuring mercuric chloride in Extra Strength Excedrin, rat poison in Maximum Strength Anacin, and hydrochloric acid in Visine eyedrops.

On Thursday, October 7, J&J took a step toward convincing the public that the problem was product form and not brand. It announced a plan to exchange Tylenol capsules for Tylenol pills. Burke was quoted in *The Wall Street Journal* as "sensing a tremendous reservoir of good will, of trust toward Johnson & Johnson and the brand. . . . They feel we are being victimized just like everyone else."

Burke believed that this "reservoir of trust in Johnson & Johnson" arose in large part from the fact that for decades, thanks to products such as J&J's baby powder, the firm had been known around the world as the baby company—*the* baby company. "There is no greater trust than between mother and child," Burke said. "It's just the nature of our lives. So there was an element of trust built into everybody's attitude toward Johnson & Johnson that is not built into many other companies." Everything could be risked except that trust.

On October 11, the company made the decision to save the brand. Burke said to his people that he thought the company could save 70 percent to 80 percent of the business if they did their job right. This was a pure guess. Burke voiced it to encourage his troops. It turned out to be an underestimate.

Some reasons for guarded optimism included an announcement from the FDA on October 15 officially exonerating the company from any negligence or wrongdoing with regard to the poisonings. In addition, competitive products were finding it difficult to exploit Tylenol's situation. Shelf space vacated by Tylenol was, more often than not, left empty or filled by private-label or generic products. The major nationally branded competitors did not have the production capacity to make up for the shortfall. Nor could they figure out how to capitalize on Tylenol's troubles without seeming malicious or, worse, inviting some lunatic to tamper with one of their own products.

On October 22, a little more than three weeks after the crisis broke, the first new television advertisements for Tylenol were aired. What do you say about the product? How do you say it? Who says it? This had never been done before, so there was no template, no guide to best practice.

The advertisement was sober and straightforward, businesslike without being cold. Burke said, "All we did was put on our medical director—who looked like central casting's idea of a medical director . . . just happened to—and all he did was say, 'Trust us.'"

The advertisement was brilliant. Burke could not have been more accurate about the self-presentation of the fatherly, reassuring, deep-voiced, gray-haired but not elderly Dr. Thomas N. Gates, McNeil's medical director. In a 151-word advertisement, Gates used the word *trust* five times.

Burke felt that time would play a key role in the fate of the brand. Having withdrawn it from the market, J&J had to reintroduce it as quickly as possible lest its loyalists drift away to the competition. As McNeil's David Collins said, to restore consumer confidence in the brand "we have to get Tylenol back into our customers' homes." When Burke discussed the reintroduction privately, his admiration for the people involved in the development of the new packaging was boundless. This sort of thing, so often taken for granted, had to be handled perfectly. Burke said a book could be written about how well this part of the process was managed.

On November 4, the FDA announced new drug-packaging requirements which provided that by February 1983, products deemed to be "tamper-susceptible"—such as capsules—had to be packaged in containers that both discouraged tampering and, if tampered with, made it obvious that the product had been handled inappropriately. The Proprietary Association, the trade association that represented companies selling pharmaceuticals over the counter, came up with ten safety precautions. The FDA required that one of these ten be used, accompanied by a warning on the package that consumers not use the product if there was evidence of tampering.

Thus the federal government was endorsing the interpretation of events put forward by Johnson & Johnson. The poisoning was not an issue associated with a particular brand. This was not a Tylenol problem. Rather, it extended to products that were "tamper-susceptible." This meant the issue was packaging.

Since J&J had been working on packaging with feverish intensity for more than a month, it was actually ahead of the game. It was beginning to emerge from the shadow of seemingly unavoidable total competitive disaster to a position of leadership. On November 11, J&J became the first company to act on the FDA's directive. Burke chaired a closed-circuit video press conference to announce that within weeks Tylenol would be reintroduced in a triple-safety-sealed package, with three times the protection mandated by the FDA. The cost of the new packaging (2.5 cents per bottle) would not be passed along to the consumer but rather absorbed by the company.

In addition, Burke announced that J&J would run advertisements offering consumers a $2.50 coupon to replace any Tylenol product they might have discarded. What is more, no proof of prior purchase was necessary since few if any people would have kept a suspect product in their possession for a month.

Essentially, this was a new product launch of a product already on the market. Over 40 million coupons were distributed. Doubtless some of these went to people who had not purchased the product previously, but that was fine with J&J. Trial might lead to repurchase, and before you knew it, you would have a new customer.

Burke appeared on this closed-circuit telecast wearing a light-colored suit. The mood was decidedly upbeat. The packaging and coupons were "our response to our loyal consumers who have given us their trust."

By the end of November, Tylenol had recaptured 55 percent of its pre-poisoning market share, up from 20 percent at the end of October. This is all the more remarkable because capsules, which accounted for 40 percent of Tylenol's prepoisoning business, were only beginning to be shipped. *The Wall Street Journal* called this performance a marketing miracle.

The miracle wasn't over. In 1983, Tylenol regained 85 percent of its market share. This recovery did not come cheaply. Marketing expenditures were about $62 million, twice what they had been in 1981. But look what was being achieved! Johnson & Johnson was proving to the nation, to the world, and most importantly to itself that it could do anything. The trinity that made up Burke's approach to business—the Credo, decentralization, and management for the long term—was receiving as powerful an endorsement as one could wish for.

By September 1984, Tylenol's market share had increased to 33 percent.

In 1985 the FDA approved the over-the-counter sale of products containing ibuprofen. Now there was a third type of mass-marketed painkiller in addition to aspirin and acetaminophen. If ibuprofen did to acetaminophen what acetaminophen had done to aspirin, it represented an important threat to Tylenol.

Nevertheless, by mid-1985, the management of Tylenol had succeeded in the face of what so many had thought was inevitable failure. Its market share once again reached its prepoisoning level, 35 percent. Moreover, the market was growing. It was a third larger in dollars than it had been before the poisonings.

What explains this extraordinary performance? For Burke, the answer was trust. "All of the previous managements who built this corporation handed us on a silver platter the most powerful tool you could possibly have—institutional trust. . . . All of that hundred years of trust works to help solve problems no matter how serious they may be."

At last the book seemed closed. One of the most difficult challenges in the history of American business had been met with a degree of success greater than anyone could have imagined. "We didn't believe it could happen again," Burke said, "and nobody else did either."

■ ■ ■

It did happen again.

On Friday evening, February 7, 1986, a twenty-three-year-old woman named Diane Elsroth was visiting her boyfriend, Michael Notarnicola, at the home of his family in Yonkers, New York, just over the Westchester County line from New York City. Ms. Elsroth, a stenographer and the daughter of a New York State trooper, was feeling under the weather, so her boyfriend brought her two Extra Strength Tylenol capsules from a previously unopened bottle that his mother had purchased the week before at an A&P in nearby Bronxville.

Twelve hours later, Ms. Elsroth was dead. The cause of death was revealed by an autopsy to be cyanide. The source of the cyanide was Tylenol.

Word that another Tylenol poisoning had taken place hit headquarters in New Brunswick with the force of a physical blow. Some of the features of the 1982 incident were repeated. For example, it quickly became apparent that the poisoning did not take place in a McNeil plant. Television advertising for all forms of Tylenol was suspended indefinitely. Once again no culprit was apprehended (the Notarnicola family was quickly ruled out as suspects). This appeared to be another local event.

As soon as he was informed, Burke immediately alerted the FBI and the FDA. Within hours, the two agencies in conjunction with county officials began collecting Tylenol capsules from stores within a three-mile radius of the A&P from which the poisoned capsules had been purchased. J&J immediately began consumer surveys designed to determine people's feelings toward all Tylenol products. A lot was at stake. Tylenol in its various forms accounted for 20 percent of J&J's profits.

Burke held the first of three press conferences during this crisis in New Brunswick on Tuesday, February 11. He was adamant that this was a local situation that did not warrant a national recall. The company intended to continue to market its product without changing its name.

On Thursday, February 13, the FBI notified Johnson & Johnson that another bottle of tampered Tylenol had been found at a Woolworth's less than two blocks away from where the first had been purchased. Five capsules were poisoned. The factory seals appeared to be in place. Soon thereafter, however, it became clear that somehow—the method has never been made public—the criminal who poisoned the medication managed to reseal the packaging and to replicate the original, untouched version. The "fingerprint" of the cyanide was the same that had killed Diane Elsroth but different from that used for testing purposes in McNeil plants and also different from that used in the 1982 poisonings.

Part of the genius of the company's 1982 response was that it had stayed ahead of events. In 1986, events were moving more quickly. For example, on Monday, February 10, the A&P ordered all Tylenol capsules removed from the shelves of its more than a thousand stores in twenty-six states. The New York City Health Department televised an announcement that consumers should avoid using any Tylenol capsule products. In addition to producing Extra Strength and Regular Strength Tylenol, McNeil at the time of the second poisoning also marketed Co-Tylenol, a cold remedy; Maximum Strength Tylenol Sinus Medication; and various other products in capsules that did not carry the Tylenol name.

Both these actions were taken prior to Burke's first press conference. The A&P's action was especially troubling because it contradicted the narrative that J&J was trying to establish for the second tampering. That narrative was that this incident was "strictly a local situation," "an act of terrorism. Pure and simple." Burke strongly discouraged the media from turning the event "into a national nightmare until it is." But the A&P had already pulled the product from all of its stores. It had stores in twenty-six states.

A third bottle of tampered Tylenol was found in a store in the tiny, unincorporated hamlet of Yorktown, New York. Yorktown is in northern Westchester County, up the Hudson from Yonkers. This seems to have been an amateurish copycat effort, and whatever was put in the capsule was not cyanide.

By the time of his first press conference, Burke was clearly unhappy with the way the media were handling the poisoning. He chastised reporters for sensationalism, for "turn[ing] this thing into a circus," rather than telling the truth in a sober fashion.

Burke is a smart man and superb in front of a group, but his anger both at fate for this second challenge and at the media for what he viewed as their hyping of the story was barely concealed. The media had been his steadfast ally during the first poisoning. If he allowed an adversarial relationship to develop, that alliance would come to an end. He could have slipped into the kind of situation that Roberto Goizueta created for himself just the previous year at Lincoln Center when announcing New Coke.

The mass media deal in stereotypes. An individual, a company, a country, is either good or bad. Stories are then viewed through the good or bad lens. There is not a lot of room for shades of gray. Burke was under enormous pressure. He could be immensely charming, but he could also become enraged. He had to control that rage if he wanted media cooperation. Lecturing reporters on how to do their job or pointing out their mistakes either of fact or in emphasis would not help his cause even if objectively he was right and they were wrong.

On Friday, February 14, Burke held his second press conference. Fourteen states had already indefinitely postponed the sale of Tylenol capsules. Burke was beginning to feel pressure from outside the company to get out of the capsule business over the counter. The company's stock had taken a hit.

Inside the company, however, especially at McNeil, the feeling was quite the opposite. Executives felt a national recall was not indicated and that it would do more harm than good. A new product form had recently been developed. It was dubbed a "caplet." It was the same shape as a capsule but hard like a pill and thus tougher to tamper with. But McNeil chairman David Collins believed it would be more difficult to persuade consumers to migrate from capsules to caplets in 1986 than it had been to persuade capsule consumers in 1982 to migrate to capsules in triple-safety-sealed containers.

At the second press conference, Burke had a rather testy exchange with a well-known New York reporter, Gloria Rojas. "If you say that this is strictly a local problem but somebody has penetrated that bottle and is very bright," Rojas asked, "what's to stop that same somebody from going anywhere in this country and repeating the act?" The answer was "Nothing." Given that truth, the idea that the poisoning could be considered a local problem disappeared.

Rojas, reacting to Burke's criticism of the media, quickly responded, "So then why do you expect the local media to reassure people that it's okay?" Burke hotly answered that he had not made that request. He and Rojas then began arguing about whether J&J had ordered the product off the market. The point here is not that one person was right and the other wrong. This was actually a legitimate misunderstanding. The point is that an argument was taking place. A "we versus they" situation was intolerable for Johnson & Johnson. Burke could have lost Tylenol that day.

Over the weekend of February 15 and 16, less than a week after J&J had learned of the Elsroth tragedy, the Tylenol Strategy Committee held meetings. The committee concluded that it would discontinue all sales of Tylenol capsules over the counter. It was a tough and painful decision, but Burke decided that he and the company couldn't live with capsules any more.

On Monday, February 17, Burke held the third and final press conference concerning Tylenol. It was remarkable and should be viewed by every businessperson in the world.

Dressed in a dark blue suit, somber and serious, Burke said:

> I wish to make the following opening statement. Johnson & Johnson
> will no longer manufacture or sell any capsule products made directly

available to the consumer. We feel the company can no longer guarantee the safety of capsules to a degree consistent with Johnson & Johnson's standards of responsibility to its consumers.

We urge our consumers who use Tylenol capsules to convert to the new Extra Strength Tylenol Caplets, which were specifically designed by the company as a substitute for the capsules. [At this point, Burke held up in his right hand before the cameras an oversize mock-up of a caplet.] We estimate that the cost of this decision will be about one hundred and fifty million dollars. While this decision is a financial burden to us, it does not begin to compare to the loss suffered by the family and friends of Diane Elsroth.

This seemingly simple, straightforward statement was in fact highly nuanced and complex. When I have shown it to executives and to MBA students, someone always raises an objection to Burke's display of the caplet. Some feel that it should have been delayed for another time. Indeed one contemporary newspaper columnist said that Burke was "blessed" by an ability "to mix decency with cunning." This charge was picked up directly and put to Burke on live television. He was unapologetic. "I had a job to do," and part of the job was protecting his company.

There is also an interesting issue with regard to mention of a dollar figure for the recall. One number, $150 million, has different meanings to different constituencies. To the general public, it seems like a fortune. But to professional investors and Wall Street securities analysts, when thought of in the context of a company with $7 billion in sales and a history of a century of outperforming the market averages, it was a noteworthy amount of money but represented no threat to the underlying value of the firm.

Burke's statement that $150 million "does not begin to compare to the loss suffered by the family and friends of Diane Elsroth" deserves special note. Not only were the words perfect, but the way Burke spoke them could not have been improved upon. He obviously had to exercise considerable self-control at this passage, and when he pronounced Ms. Elsroth's name, he came close to breaking down. Yet it was vital for him to keep his composure, and it was vital for him actually to mention the name of Ms. Elsroth. The death of a million people is a statistic; the death of a single individual is a tragedy—a tragedy that no amount of money can buy you out of.

Burke was speaking to the whole world. Everyone was watching him—

the general public, his company's employees, and Ms. Elsroth's family. Everyone associated with Johnson & Johnson had reason to be pleased.

The day after this announcement, Burke appeared on a live television interview during the evening news. He was on the set alone with two newspeople. There was no public relations advisor with him from J&J. No lawyer. That singleness and vulnerability had been a theme of Burke's handling of both poisoning crises. He could say in images, not in words, that Johnson & Johnson was not shrouded in bureaupathology. The buck stopped with him.

One reporter began the interview by saying that "the mother of Diane Elsroth, the girl who was killed, said that she feels that Johnson & Johnson was three years too late." In other words, Mrs. Elsroth said that Johnson & Johnson should have canceled their capsule business after the first poisonings. Doing it now wouldn't bring her daughter back.

What does one say in response to a cri de coeur such as this? Put yourself in Burke's position. What would *you* say?

If you hesitated in responding to that question, you are lost. Five seconds is an eternity on live television. Here is what Burke said: "My response is that if I was the mother of Diane Elsroth, I'd say the same thing. And I'd feel the same thing. And with the benefit of hindsight, which is twenty-twenty, I wish we had never gone back into the market with capsules."

There must have been lawyers back at headquarters in New Brunswick who died the death of the thousand cuts when they heard those words. In this most litigious of societies, Burke was admitting a mistake and inviting a lawsuit. The Elsroth family did in fact sue Johnson & Johnson for $100 million. The suit went to trial. Johnson & Johnson prevailed because the plaintiff did not demonstrate that the defendant had been negligent.

Think once again of Burke's televised admission of responsibility. It was the essence of acceptance and the opposite of denial. The Elsroth family did not have legal recourse because Johnson & Johnson was more the victim than the perpetrator of this still unsolved crime. But Burke, after doing everything possible to insure the integrity of this product, including providing three times the protection that the law required, understood that he was dealing with emotion, not legalisms. When he said what he said, he could not have known J&J would be sued or how the case would turn out if it was.

What he did know was that this was a moment of truth and a moment for truth. He spoke the truth, and that was astonishingly liberating for everyone who heard it because we have all become so accustomed to public figures telling less than the truth or lying.

By casting denial aside and looking facts in the face, Burke did more than save a brand that was important to his company. He also provided a memorable moment in American public life.

12

A New Point of View

This book begins in the early twentieth century, when Henry Ford refused to accept a new reality (changing market, growing competition) that was literally staring him in the face from outside his office window. But of course, the dilemma of denial goes back much further. In the fourth century B.C., the Greek statesman Demosthenes declared, "Nothing is easier than self-deception. For what each man wishes, that he also believes to be true." This tendency is part of human nature.

Given how long denial has been with us, it would be unrealistic to expect it to go away anytime soon. Despite the best efforts of psychologists, sociologists, and management consultants, denial will remain a pitfall of business life. To think that even the most persuasive advice, studies, or cautionary tales can eliminate the all-too-human proclivity to shield oneself from bad news would itself be an exercise in denial.

Denial operates in all institutions and in all individuals. It is present at the Harvard Business School and at your company or organization. It is present in me and in you. It can never be completely defeated because we can't fully know or face the truth about ourselves. It is impossible to be both subject and object. The writer and critic Granville Hicks published his autobiography in 1965. He chose the perfect title: *Part of the Truth.* An autobiography that tells the whole truth can never be written. Denial afflicts us all.

That said, denial is not an all-or-nothing proposition. It is a continuum. Individuals and organizations have the power to determine where on that continuum they fall. Both the cautionary and exemplary stories in this book demonstrate that human beings and companies are capable of positioning themselves further toward the "facing facts" end of the spectrum than the "denial" end. We all deny, but as we have seen, some people deny less than others. How can you be one of them?

There are no easy answers or twelve-step programs. History shows that resisting denial is a battle that must be fought every day on many fronts. There are, however, some general rules of thumb that arise from the narratives in this book. I will share them with you momentarily. But first, a warning.

Many of the incidents just recounted focus on crises—flash points in which a clear decision has to be made. My warning is that beneath these "moments of truth" lie the history and culture of the corporation. The decision point shows what happens when that culture is challenged. But the decision arrived at is, if not predetermined, at least heavily weighted in one direction or the other prior to that point.

There are weeks, months, in some cases years of history that go far toward explaining why people acted the way they did when pressed. Surely it was no accident that Ernest Kanzler was fired at Ford while the Young Turks at DuPont did not lose their jobs. It was no accident that Roberto Goizueta (an honorable man and as honest as most people who reach the top of American corporations) put himself into a position in which he had to lie while Andy Grove was desperately trying to discover the truth.

It was no accident that Jim Burke saved Tylenol at Johnson & Johnson. He said to me that "people keep telling me what a wonderful job I did. . . . But what if this had been the James E. Burke Company?" In his view, the brand would have been lost. It was Johnson & Johnson's history and its Credo which in Burke's view were really responsible for the Tylenol comeback.

The first lesson is that the time to deal with denial is right now, this very day. Don't wait for a crisis. It will be too late.

Some companies are "lucky" enough to suffer crises that shake them out of denial and into awareness and action while there is still time. For example, Intel's game-changing move from memories to microprocessors was occasioned by surging Japanese competition that threatened to destroy the company. DuPont's leadership might not have adopted the proposal to reinvent the company as a decentralized, multidivisional enterprise—a development that economist Oliver Williamson has called "the most significant organizational innovation of the twentieth century"—if its profit-and-loss statement hadn't been decimated by a depression.

The A&P, however, never enjoyed the luxury of an eye-opening crisis. Instead it was like the proverbial frog being boiled in a gradually warming pot of water. There was no sudden shock forcing it to face reality. By the time it realized what was happening, the opportunity for confronting the facts and doing something about them had passed.

Denial-avoidance is a life's work, not an agenda item. Every company reveals itself every day, wittingly or not. The same is true of every individual. During crises, companies don't suddenly change. They are what they are, only more so.

Think about the phrase "deferred maintenance," a term often used to describe needed repairs or upkeep that are delayed for financial or other reasons. This is not a happy phrase, especially to those of us who fly a lot. What does it mean? Does it mean that a mechanic decided not to use his wrench to tighten a bolt one more time because he felt like knocking off early to have a smoke? Doubtless in the history of aviation (to choose just one industry at random) there have been irresponsible mechanics whose laziness has resulted in disaster. That, however, is not the real problem.

The real problem signified by deferred maintenance is a point of view woven into the fabric of a company. A firm that once might have focused on *getting the job done* now is concerned with *getting done with the job*. In her brilliant analysis of the disastrous decision to launch the space shuttle *Challenger* in January 1986, Columbia University sociologist Diane Vaughan uses the phrase "normalization of deviance." Normalizing deviance is a long, drawn-out, incremental process. In order for Vaughan to discover and document it, she had to explore the history of the space program for years prior to the fatal miscalculation on the night before the launch.

How much do you really want to know the truth about your company even if the news is bad? How often do you challenge yourself and your colleagues by asking what is the worst plausible reality that could befall your organization? How much freedom of speech do you really encourage? Demand?

When discussing the true origins of the Challenger tragedy, Vaughan located its genesis in "routine and taken-for-granted aspects of organizational life that created a way of seeing that was simultaneously a way of not seeing." She independently arrived at a formulation strikingly similar to Freud's "knowing-with-not-knowing." Denial is the rule, not the exception.

The fact that denial is the rule rather than the exception leads to our second lesson. If you have read this far, you know that it is vital to acknowledge and confront whatever facts are facing you. No matter how brutal those facts may be, ignoring, dismissing, rationalizing, or twisting them will not make them less so.

Advising someone to avoid denial by facing facts is a little like suggesting that someone lose weight by eating less. Both statements are unarguably true yet not easily implemented. If one could simply resolve to wake up tomorrow and unflinchingly confront reality, denial would hardly be the problem that it is.

What you can endeavor to be more aware of, however, is denial itself. The stories of self-delusion (and its opposite) in this book can help readers to be more attentive to denial's pervasiveness and perniciousness. Simply being aware that you and your company are capable of lying to yourselves and tailoring facts to fit your preconceptions is important. You can't avoid blind spots when you drive. However, good drivers know those blind spots exist and take them into account when they get behind the wheel. So it should be with denial.

Our third lesson involves the difficulty yet importance of encouraging straight talk in an organization. Lord Acton's famous dictum about power corrupting is known to all. It does. But it does something even more dangerous because it is so easy to deny. Power deranges. That is our third lesson. Powerful people are routinely surrounded by yes-men, but that is not the real problem because they are relatively easy to spot. The real problem is the courtier who is sufficiently clever not to be detected.

The room changes, the feeling changes the geography changes, in the presence of a man or woman with power. They see the world through a different lens from the rest of us. They don't really know as much as they may think about their own organization because people stop telling them the truth. Consider the king in the following cartoon:

*"Then we're in agreement. There's nothing rotten in Denmark.
Something is rotten everywhere else."*

This syndrome makes denial easy and common. You can believe what you want to until it is too late. A leader has to be profoundly committed to the truth to ferret out the facts that he or she must look in the face to make informed decisions. Such leaders are all too rare.

Speaking truth to power is invariably praised and just as rarely practiced. In *Only the Paranoid Survive*, Andy Grove asserts the importance of what he calls "Cassandras" within an organization. Cassandra, in Greek mythology, was the prophetess who warned of the fall of Troy. Cassandras, Grove says, are people "who are quick to recognize impending change and cry out an early warning." They are the antidotes to groupthink. Most often they are middle managers, people who "usually know more about upcoming change than the senior management because they spend so much time 'outdoors' where the winds of the real world blow in their faces. In other words their genes have not been selected to achieve perfection in the old way." The Young Turks who warned DuPont of its structural flaws after World War I and persevered until they were finally heeded provide compelling evidence for Grove's thesis.

The challenging of assumptions can spring from the top, middle, or even bottom of an organization. If denial is to be warded off, such challenges have to come from somewhere. They have to be listened to. Remember that the original Cassandra was cursed. She was destined always to speak the truth but never to be believed.

This leads to our fourth lesson, which deals with the responsibilities of top management in conquering denial. The more I study denial, the more impressed I am by the necessity of the top decision maker in a company to be able to listen. Cassandra will not speak if she will not be heard. Cassandras will leave companies that shut them up. These companies get reputations as places where what matters most is the party line and flattering the boss. No Cassandra would choose to work at such a place, so you have created an adverse-selection problem. Sycophants welcome! Job description: help the CEO enjoy the denial in which he basks.

Is your company such a place? One quick test: are the private conversations that follow meetings usually more frank and honest than the public discussions in the meetings themselves? The energy level is often greater after a meeting than in it, notes Babson College management professor Allan Cohen. Why? Because "everybody talks about what didn't get said."

Andy Grove combated groupthink and cultivated Cassandras by listening to the salesmen who told him that Motorola was beating Intel in the marketplace. He was able to play the role of Cassandra himself in the memory exit because he knew Gordon Moore would listen to him.

The derangement of power makes cultivating Cassandras problematic. They need to be encouraged and sometimes provoked. Here was Alfred P. Sloan Jr.'s approach. At a meeting of one of GM's top committees in the 1920s, he is reported to have said, "Gentlemen, I take it we are all in complete agreement on the subject here." Heads nodded. Sloan continued, "We postpone further discussion of this matter until our next meeting, to give ourselves time to develop disagreement and perhaps gain some understanding of what the decision is all about."

The failure of leadership led directly to the denial of reality at both the A&P and Sears. Look at John and George Hartford in 1950. John was seventy-eight, and George was eighty-six. These childless widowers were devoted to the A&P. They seemed immortal. Their business model in a rapidly changing world was not. Who was there inside or outside the company who could tell these immensely wealthy men that they had to adapt?

They chose their own successor. He was a timeserver. The worst thing in the world took place early on his watch: the company continued to coast uphill. By carefully looking at the numbers you liked, it was easy to deny that the A&P was in decline.

The story at Sears is strikingly similar, with a few intriguing twists. Robert Wood was a great businessman, whose greatness allowed him to deny the importance of selfless succession planning. Wood was sixty in 1939. That was the mandatory retirement age. He rigged the system so that in his case retirement was waived. This is invariably problematic.

Wood hung on until he was seventy-five in 1954. He drooled, ate cigarettes, didn't unwrap his candy, and didn't zip his fly. Clearly there was a lot of denial at Sears. It was the "emperor's new clothes." Everyone saw these unfortunate habits but no one could mention them. He must have seemed like an apparition, the ghost of Wood past.

Just as bad, Wood chose his successors and the successors of his successors. The same problem arose as at the A&P. Sears kept seeming to do well. This made its actual descent easy to deny.

Sears, under Wood's successors, did what Coca-Cola did and what so many other big companies do when they become idea-free zones. They build big buildings. As tall as the Sears Tower was, it seemed to mock any suggestion of the descent into which the company had in fact embarked. The ditch Wood's "organization man" successors were digging was deeper than the height of that tower.

In both cases, leadership failure made Cassandras impossible. People just kept doing their jobs day after day. The market kept leaving them day after day. The days left to both firms now are numbered as a result. There is no denying that.

Our fifth lesson involves the oft-stated but frequently ignored admonition to adopt a long-term perspective. We have seen that denial goes hand in hand with short-term thinking. It is an unconscious choice to dodge a hard reality and the inevitable discomfort, hardship, or pain it promises. The present may be better than it would have been had the truth been faced, but the future holds avoidable failure in store.

Many of the companies in this book discovered this the hard way. For example, we saw how the U.S. tire industry steadfastly refused to admit to itself both the coming of radial technology and the long-term havoc that change would inevitably wreak on its business model. Recall that IBM lost its grip on the emerging PC market by failing to ask itself, "Am I doing today what will enable me to succeed tomorrow?" And who knows what would have happened had Webvan's management and investors taken a cold, hard look at whether the company's business model was sustainable over the long run?

Our nation's recent financial woes are only the latest reminder that there are innumerable reasons why organizations should adopt structures and incentives that promote and reward long-term thinking. Avoiding denial ranks high among them.

Our sixth lesson deals with vocabulary. Remember how the U.S. tire companies haughtily dismissed clearly superior radial tires as a second-rate technology for wimpy foreigners? Trash-talking can be a tip-off to denial. In *The Ego and the Mechanisms of Defense*, Anna Freud, who extended much of her father's work on the psychology of denial, told of a young girl who came to her suffering from debilitating anxiety attacks. The girl was unfailingly "friendly and frank" in analysis. But when Freud raised the subject of the anxiety attacks directly, the girl would lash out at her with a "volley of contemptuous and mocking remarks." Freud interpreted this as a classic defense mechanism—"defense by means of ridicule and scorn." If you find yourself trash-talking your competition, take a moment to think about what you're doing. What am I using this derision to hide—perhaps from myself?

Another vocabulary lesson. When people are doing things they ought not to be doing, they often relabel their actions rather than change them. It's easier to do that. It's quicker. It's pure denial. When they don't like reality, they change its name rather than its factual basis.

Think of *The Godfather*. The phrase "I'll make him an offer he can't refuse" means something entirely different from what it does in common parlance.

Think of the hapless John Akers as IBM was unraveling in the 1980s. He labeled 1987 the *Year of the Customer*. A phrase without meaning. What would 1988 be? What had all the other years been?

Think of Ford, which when confronted with a product defect that led to blowouts and deaths in Explorers equipped with Firestone tires, issued not a recall but a "customer notification enhancement action." When Johnson & Johnson recalled Tylenol, it called the move what it was: a recall. Which company is more deserving of your trust?

Think of the vocabulary used about the 2008 economic crisis. *Troubled assets* aren't "troubled assets." They are worthless pieces of junk. But think how much more difficult it would have been to pass a Worthless Junk Repurchase Program.

The economic disaster of 2008 was touched off by the subprime-mortgage debacle. Once again, look at the vocabulary. Is the term "subprime mortgage" really meaningful? A mortgage used to be a loan that your friendly local banker made to a family in good financial condition for a house that looked like it was worth it. Subprime mortgages were nothing like this. They were loans made to people who had no chance of repaying them. One mortgage company, Long Beach Financial, writer Michael Lewis reports, "was moving money out the door as fast as it could, few questions asked, in loans built to self-destruct. It specialized in asking homeowners with bad credit and no proof of income to put no money down and defer interest payments for as long as possible." Lewis cites the example of one agricultural worker in California who received a $720,000 "mortgage." His annual income was $14,000. The only way such a transaction could not end in foreclosure is if housing prices continued to rise. This is not a mortgage in the time-honored sense of the word. It is a fraud.

Mortgages had been bundled together and turned into securities since the Great Depression. This practice worked fine for decades. When, however, subprime mortgages were bundled together with solid ones, the housing market became a device for producing AAA-rated securities out of junk. Collapse was inevitable.

The mangling of language and Orwellian doublespeak suffused the catastrophe. The result, as Orwell himself said, is to "perform the important service of partially concealing your meaning even from yourself." You know but you don't know. You see but you don't see.

My personal favorite in this category is the hedge fund. I remember first hearing that term and assuming that it was a fund designed to balance risks. "To hedge your bets" is a phrase that has long been in common parlance. My assumption was wrong.

Economist Paul Krugman, one of the few people who has been able to think straight during these years, explained that "hedge funds don't hedge." (Note the straightforward language.) They do the opposite. They are more risky, not less risky, than an average investment. Why were they incorrectly labeled? Would they have done less damage if their managers had been as blunt as Krugman, choosing to call themselves Funds for Gamblers or something else along those lines?

Therefore, watch your language.

Our seventh lesson is deceptively simple: tell the truth. Doing so can help you to avoid denial. Says Warren Buffett, "The CEO who misleads others in public may eventually mislead himself in private." In his handling of the Tylenol poisoning crisis, Jim Burke of Johnson & Johnson understood implicitly that deceit and self-deceit are flip sides of the same coin. He opted for neither. This helps explain his success. To misquote Sir Walter Scott, "Oh, what a tangled web we weave, when first we practice to deceive ourselves."

For our eighth and final lesson, let me ask you to consider the following question. Would you and would your company rather be conventionally wrong or unconventionally right? Most (not all) of the people who were right in predicting the 2008 economic crisis are unconventional. Because of that unconventionality, their message was easy to deny, and it was denied. Almost all the Nobel Prize–winning economists have been wrong about our economy. The oddballs have been right.

By way of illustration, let us contrast two economists. Robert E. Lucas was born on September 15, 1937, and educated at the University of Chicago. Lucas was a member of the economics department at his alma mater when he won the Nobel Prize in 1995. He doubtless has a very high IQ.

Lucas was and is a leading figure in his profession. He is widely cited, and I gather he is a superb mathematical modeler. He served as president of the American Economics Association in 2002. Lucas delivered his presidential address to the AEA on January 10, 2003, and this is how it began: "Macroeconomics was born as a distinct field in the 1940s, as part of the intellectual response to the Great Depression. The term then referred to the body of knowledge and expertise that we hoped would prevent the recurrence of that economic disaster. My thesis in this lecture is that macroeconomics in this original sense has succeeded. Its central problem of depression-prevention has been solved, for all practical purposes, and has in fact been solved for many decades."'

We now know that the "central problem of depression-prevention" has been anything but solved. Lucas uses the phrase "for all practical purposes." I don't know if he wanted these words to have real meaning or whether he merely used them for the sake of the rhythm of the sentence.

It is an unfortunate phrase. The problem of depression-prevention may indeed have been solved for "theoretical" purposes. Lucas is a leading theorist, and we could probably take his word for that. However, in practice, in the real world, depression-prevention is the biggest problem there is.

"Looking back from only a few years later," Krugman has written, "with much of the world in the throes of a financial and economic crisis all too reminiscent of the 1930s, these optimistic pronouncements [not only by Lucas but by Ben Bernanke, the chairman of the Federal Reserve] sound almost incredibly smug. What was especially strange about this optimism was the fact that during the 1990s, economic problems reminiscent of the Great Depression *had*, in fact, popped up in a number of countries—including Japan, the world's second-largest economy."

Let us now consider another economist. Nouriel Roubini's background is quite different from Lucas's. He was born to Iranian Jewish parents in Istanbul in 1959. Early in life, he began his career as a self-described "global nomad." The family moved to Tehran and thence to Israel, Italy, and the United States. His accented English is hard for a native speaker to pin down, perhaps because he also speaks Farsi, Hebrew, and Italian. Roubini has been involved with numerous academic and policy-making institutions of the first rank. However, his career path and indeed his whole approach to the acquisition and dissemination of economic knowledge have been idiosyncratic, to say the least.

What he lacks in mathematical modeling, Roubini has more than made up for by combining his undoubted intellectual ability with an understanding of the world thoroughly grounded in reality. "You have to be there," he has said. "You have to see it, smell it, and live it. You have to see people, travel, and interact." In other words, you have to be able to see clearly what is in front of you and not allow yourself to be blinded by theory. If there is a conflict between theory and reality, you have got to get rid of the former, not ignore the latter. The academic world dispenses little credit for such things.

As early as 2004, a year after Robert Lucas was telling the world that modern macroeconomics had solved the problem of depression "for all practical purposes," Roubini began warning of the dangers of the huge deficit in America's balance of trade. By late 2004, he was writing about a "nightmare hard-landing scenario" for the U.S. economy. No one wanted to hear it. He became known as Dr. Doom.

On September 7, 2006, Roubini addressed a group of economists assembled at the International Monetary Fund. He warned of a housing collapse, mortgage defaults, and other disasters. "The audience seemed skeptical, even dismissive," according to The New York Times. "When the economist Amirvan Banerji delivered his response to Roubini's talk, he noted that Roubini's predictions did not make use of mathematical models." As late as August 2008, Banerji continued to dismiss Roubini as the proverbial stopped clock that was right twice a day.

Most of us cleave to the conventional even when it is wrong. Roubini comprehends the technology of economics, but he leavens it with a healthy dose of keen observation and common sense. That is unacceptable to conventional thinkers. Who could call economics "economic science" if people comported themselves thus?

In the words of John Maynard Keynes, "A 'sound' banker, alas! is not one who foresees danger and avoids it, but one who, when he is ruined, is ruined in a conventional and orthodox way along with his fellows, so that no one can really blame him."

In the glory days of IBM back in the 1960s and 1970s, it was often said that "nobody ever got fired for buying IBM." In other words, no purchasing manager or IT expert would ever lose his or her job because of buying Big Blue. This was true even if the product was not the best for the company, even if it malfunctioned. The buyer always had a powerful response: "Gee, after all, it was IBM." He or she was conventionally wrong.

Denial is simultaneously the safe and the wrong way to handle a problem. Suggesting the right and the risky way will get you into trouble.

You will therefore never defeat denial, but you had better battle it. As James Baldwin once wrote, "Not everything that is faced can be changed, but nothing can be changed until it is faced."

Acknowledgments

Books don't spring into existence by themselves. You need help.

I owe a great debt to David Ruben. David and I talked about this book endlessly. He became so much a part of it that he wrote the first draft of some passages, including all of chapter 2. While working on this book, I had the pleasure of coauthoring three op-ed pieces with David; and his commitment to *Denial* was a powerful factor in keeping it focused and completing it on time and to specifications.

As I observe in the text, this book is the product of a whole career devoted to the study of business history. It has been my great good fortune to have as my mentors during my professional career the late Alfred D. Chandler Jr. and Thomas K. McCraw. Both Straus Professor Emeriti at the Harvard Business School and both Pulitzer Prize–winning historians, Al and Tom led a remarkable efflorescence of the discipline from the mid-1970s to the end of the century. Today, there are more than a half dozen historians at HBS. Our courses are oversubmitted. And this is at an institution that no one attends because he or she wants to study history.

Also at HBS, my gratitude goes to innumerable staff people who helped check facts and saved me from errors. The Business Information Analysts, led by Sarah Ericksen, are the best in the world at what they do. One can't say enough good things about Baker Library. I also must thank Dave Frieze, my administrative assistant, for all the work he did on this manuscript.

In the business world, my most important help came from two people with whom I did not actually discuss this book, Jim Burke and Andy Grove.

Burke gave generously of his time years ago to discuss the Tylenol tamperings with me. The result was teaching material used at the Harvard Business School and indeed around the world. Grove, perhaps more than any other executive, has been able to intellectualize about the work he has done. His unique knowledge of his job and ability to communicate that knowledge combined with his interest in the problem of denial in business explain why his influence on this book extends beyond the chapter devoted to Intel.

Many friends have contributed to this book. Kim and Andy Scott discussed it with me at length (as well as providing me with a place to stay at their beautiful home in Silicon Valley). Both work at Google, Andy as an engineer and Kim as the director of AdSense. Both read widely. Andy suggested that I read *The Challenger Launch Decision*, the brilliant study by Columbia University sociologist Diane Vaughan. I also benefited from discussions with Silicon Valley entrepreneur Michael Dearing and Rakesh Khurana, the Marvin Bower Professor of Leadership Development at the Harvard Business School, both former students.

Reed E. Hundt, lawyer and professional board member, supported this project from its inception. He saved me from many an error and helped keep the book securely anchored in the real world. Maurizio Fava, M.D., the vice chair of psychiatry at the Massachusetts General Hospital, gave me an idea of the extent of the psychiatric literature on denial. I am also indebted to him for his judgment, his optimism, and also his cooking. I was the dinner guest of him and his wife, Stefania Lamon-Fava, M.D., Ph.D., on innumerable occasions. Such a gift matters a lot in the life of a widower.

This is my fourth book handled by the incomparable literary agent Helen Rees. Helen first put me in touch with Adrian Zackheim, the founder and publisher of Portfolio, an imprint of Penguin Group, USA. It was fortunate indeed for me that she did.

At Portfolio, my editor, David Moldawer, added a great deal of value to this project. His skill and his good cheer are much appreciated.

Needless to say, any errors in this book are my responsibility alone.

My late wife, Joyce R. Tedlow, M.D., was a woman capable of looking facts in the face even when they were grim. To her memory I owe any contribution to knowledge this book may make.

Notes

The principal source for this book is my four decades of research into business history in general and many of the companies discussed here in particular. Much of that research has found its way into books, articles, and other outlets. Whenever possible, I have chosen to cite the original sources rather than my own works, so that readers who are interested in pursuing quotations and data may do so more easily.

This volume has been informed by the work of many scholars, journalists, and others. In these notes, I want to acknowledge with gratitude and give credit to them all.

Preface to the Paperback Edition

p. xiv: "culture of ethical failure": Wikipedia entry on MMS, accessed July 21, 2010.

p. xiv: "We made a few little mistakes early on": Tim Webb, "BP Boss Admits Job on the Line Over Gulf Oil Spill," *Guardian*, May 14, 2010.

p. xiv: "in relation to the total water volume": Webb, *Guardian*.

p. xv: "lives were being ruined along the coast": Ann Gerhart, "BP Chairman Talks About the 'Small People,' Further Angering Gulf," *Washington Post*, June 17, 2010.

p. xvi: "assume that extremely unlikely events will never occur": James G. March, *A Primer on Decision Making: How Decisions Happen* (New York: Free Press, 1994), 47.

p. xvi: the thirteenth most influential businessperson of all time: Forbes.com Staff, "Twenty Most Influential Businessmen: Sakichi Toyoda," Forbes.com, July 13, 2005.

p. xvi: "Why not make it your life's work?": Jeffrey R. Bernstein, "Toyoda Automatic

Looms and Toyota Automobiles," in Thomas K. McCraw, ed., *Creating Modern Capitalism* (Cambridge: Harvard University Press, 1997), 407.

p. xvii: "Only when the problem is resolved is the line restarted": www.toyotageorge town.com/qualdex.asp, viewed on the Internet July 23, 2010.

p. xviii: "thereby jeopardizing the company's legendary quality": Garry Emmons, "American Auto's Troubled Road," Harvard Business School Working Knowledge, April 10, 2006. Viewed on the Internet on July 24, 2010.

p. xviii: quality suffered commensurately: Paul Ingrassia, "Toyota: Too Big, Too Fast: Consumer Reports, the Bible of the Car Buying Public, Now Rates Ford's Quality Higher Than Toyota's," January 28, 2010.

p. xix: rather than heeding the message: Ingrassia, "Too Big."

p. xix: "rolling multiple times, and bursting into flames": "Toyota Recall Lawsuits Mount Over Sudden Acceleration Problems," AboutLawsuits.com, January 29, 2010. Viewed on the Internet January 28, 2010.

p. xx: "defects linked to unintended acceleration": "Lexus Risks Ceding Decade-Long Lead to Mercedes, BMW," *BusinessWeek*, July 23, 2010.

p. xx: this most public of products would pass by unnoticed? Some of the material in the paragraphs above first appeared in Richard S. Tedlow, "Toyota was in Denial, How About You?" *BusinessWeek*, April 8, 2010.

p. xxi: He thinks so: Silverman, "Should J&J Replace The McNeil Management Team?" Pharmalot, July 16, 2010. See also Jim Edwards, "Why Hasn't McNeil's President Resigned Over the Tylenol Recall (Among Other Unsolved Mysteries)?" BNET, July 9, 2010.

p. xxi: "stellar reputation": See Silverman, Pharmalot.

p. xxi: not easy to find on the corporate Web site: http://jnjbtw.com/2010/05/to-all-who-use-our-products-from-bill-weldon/.

Introduction

p. 2: "[Being caught] crossed my mind": Danny Hakim, "On TV, Spitzer Says Getting Caught 'Crossed My Mind,'" *New York Times*, April 7, 2009.

p. 2: "knowing with not knowing": Sigmund Freud, "On Beginning the Treatment" (1913), in *The Freud Reader*, ed. Peter Gay (New York: W. W. Norton, 1989), 376.

p. 2: "protective stupidity": George Orwell, *1984* (New York: Alfred A. Knopf, 1992), 221.

p. 3: "When do people pay attention?": Stanley Cohen, *States of Denial: Knowing About Atrocities and Suffering* (Cambridge: Polity Press, 2001), 249.

1. Shooting the Messenger: Henry Ford and the Model T

I have over the years written essays, reviews, a business-school case, and book chapters on Henry Ford and his company. Some of the material in this chapter builds on that previous work. See, for example, *New and Improved: The Story of Mass Marketing in America* (New York: Basic Books, 1990) and *Giants of Enterprise: Seven Business Innovators and the Empires They Built* (New York: HarperCollins, 2001).

p. 7: Model T voted "car of the century": James G. Cobb, "This Just In: Model T Gets Award," *New York Times*, December 24, 1999.

p. 7: "the most widely discussed man of his time": David L. Lewis, *The Public Image of Henry Ford: An American Folk Hero and His Company* (Detroit: Wayne State University Press, 1976), 216. This outstanding book was somewhat underestimated by, among others, me. See my "The Wise Old Fool Who Founded Ford," *Business and Society Review* 19 (Fall 1976): 92–93.

p. 8: "my father taking my [younger] brother and myself": Allan Nevins and Frank Ernest Hill, *Ford: The Times, the Man, the Company* (New York: Scribner's, 1954), 42.

p. 8: "I never had any particular love": Ibid., 51.

p. 8: "I have tried to live my life": Ibid.

p. 8: like a watch without the mainspring: Ibid.

p. 8: "a sight almost as astounding": Ibid., 54.

p. 8: "Dave, you'll grow with the business": Ibid., 177.

p. 9: "a fallacy too absurd": Donald T. Critchlow, *Studebaker: The Life and Death of an American Corporation* (Bloomington: Indiana University Press, 1996), 44–45.

p. 9: "That a time should come when horses would be a rare sight": Mark Sullivan, *The Turn of the Century*, vol. 1, *Our Times: The United States, 1900–1925* (New York: Scribner's, 1928), 26n.

p. 9: In 1900, horses deposited 2.5 million pounds of manure: James J. Flink, *The Automobile Age* (Cambridge, MA: MIT Press, 1988), 136.

p. 9: More than 1 million bicycles were sold: David A. Hounshell, *From the American System to Mass Production, 1800–1932: The Development of Manufacturing Technology in the United States* (Baltimore: Johns Hopkins University Press, 1984), 192.

p. 10: Kettering and the self-starter: James M. Rubenstein, *Making and Selling Cars* (Baltimore: Johns Hopkins University Press, 2002), 77.

p. 13: Ford press release: Lewis, *Public Image of Henry Ford*, 70.

p. 22: "We had no stake in the old ways of the automobile business": Alfred P. Sloan Jr., *My Years with General Motors* (New York: Doubleday, 1963), 171. "better and better cars, with a bigger package beyond basic transportation": Ibid., 176

p. 22: "Ford's share declined relatively": Ibid.

p. 23: Chart: James Dalton, "What Will Ford Do Next?" *Motor*, May 1926, reprinted in Alfred D. Chandler Jr., ed. and comp. *Giant Enterprise: Ford, General Motors, and the Automobile Industry* (New York: Harcourt, Brace, and World, 1964), 107.

p. 24: "Chevrolet for the *hoi polloi*": "General Motors I," *Fortune*, December 1938.

p. 25: "Most of your troubles at the present time" and R. L. Polk & Co.: Anne Jardim, *The First Henry Ford: A Study in Personality and Business Leadership* (Cambridge MA: MIT Press, 1970), 217.

p. 25: Ernest Kanzler memorandum: Ibid., 217–219.

p. 26: "But me no buts": Henry Fielding, *Rape upon Rape; or The Justice Caught in His Own Trap, a Comedy* (1730; repr., Whitefish, MT: Kessinger Publishing, 2004), Act 2, Scene 2.

p. 27: "The Ford car will continue to be made in the same way": Jardim, *First Henry Ford*, 219.

p. 27: "The old master had failed to master change": Sloan, *My Years*, 186.

p. 27: "Not many observers expected as catastrophic" Ibid., 187.

p. 28: Shutting down the River Rouge for a year cost: For the shutdown at the Rouge, see Hounshell, *Mass Production*, 281–82.

p. 28: "The measure of the worth of a business enterprise": Sloan, *My Years*, 213.

2. What Denial Is, and Is Not

The psychological literature on denial is deep and rich. Three good starting points for those who wish to explore that literature are E. L. Edelstein, Donald L. Nathanson, and Andrew M. Stone, eds., *Denial: A Clarification of Concepts and Research* (New York: Plenum Press, 1989); David Shapiro, "On the Psychology of Self-Deception," *Social Research* 63 (Fall 1996); and Benedict Carey, "Denial Makes the World Go Round," *New York Times*, November 20, 2007.

Much of the research on the psychology of denial has been captured and distilled in four enlightening, accessible books, each of which helped to inform this chapter: Stanley Cohen, *States of Denial: Knowing About Atrocities and Suffering* (Cambridge: Polity Press, 2001); Daniel Goleman, *Vital Lies, Simple Truths: The Psychology of Self-Deception* (New York : Simon and Schuster, 1985); Herbert Fingarette, *Self-Deception* (London: Routledge & Kegan Paul, 1969); and David Livingstone Smith, *Why We Lie: The Evolutionary Roots of Deception and the Unconscious Mind* (New York: St. Martin's Press, 2004). Cohen is a sociologist, Goleman a psychologist and journalist, and Fingarette and Smith philosophers.

Two other recommended works on the subject for general readers are Eviatar Zerubavel, *The Elephant in the Room: Silence and Denial in Everyday Life* (New York: Oxford University Press, 2006); and Carol Tavris and Elliot Aronson, *Mistakes Were Made (but not by me): Why We Justify Foolish Beliefs, Bad Decisions, and Hurtful Acts* (New York: Harcourt, 2007).

For more on denial in a medical context, see Shlomo Breznitz, ed., *The Denial of Stress* (New York: International Universities Press, 1983). For Michael Kinsley's endorsement of denial as a positive coping strategy, see "In Defense of Denial: A Noted Journalist, Given a Diagnosis of Parkinson's, Makes the Case for Kidding Yourself about Bad News," *Time*, December 17, 2001. For a brief discussion of anosognosia, a syndrome in which patients deny the existence of their illness or disability, see Sandra Blakeslee, "Figuring Out the Brain from Its Acts of Denial," *New York Times*, January 23, 1996.

The leading contributor to the evolutionary perspective on denial is Robert L. Trivers, a professor of anthropology and biological sciences at Rutgers University. His arguments are best summarized in his article "The Elements of a Scientific Theory of Self-Deception," *Annals of the New York Academy of Sciences* 907 (April 2000), 114–31, and his introduction to Joan S. Lockard, *Self-Deception: An Adaptive Mechanism* (New York: Prentice Hall, 1988).

The seminal work on the phenomenon known as groupthink is Irving L. Janis's *Victims of Groupthink: A Psychological Study of Foreign-Policy Decisions and Fiascoes* (Boston: Houghton Mifflin Company, 1972).

One reason for writing this book was the fact that relatively little has been published on the problem of denial in business. Among the exceptions are Walter Kiechell III, "Facing up to Denial," *Fortune*, October 18, 1993; Patricia Sellers, "CEOs in Denial," *Fortune*, June 21, 1999; Reginald L. Litz, "Cheating at Solitaire: Self-Deception, Executive Mental Health, and Organizational Performance," *Business and Society Review* 108, no. 2 (Summer 2003); and Andrew S. Grove, *Only the Paranoid Survive: How to Manage the Crisis Points That Challenge Every Company* (New York: Doubleday, 1996), which is not specifically about denial but addresses it at various points both implicitly and explicitly.

p. 30: sociologist Stanley Cohen refers to a scene: Cohen, *States of Denial*, 50.

p. 30: "Elya would die of a hemorrhage": Saul Bellow, *Mr. Sammler's Planet* (New York: Viking, 1970), 66.

p. 30: "The ability to deny is an amazing human phenomenon": Cohen, *States of Denial*, 50.

p. 31: Freud and cancer: Peter Gay, *Freud: A Life for Our Time* (New York: W. W. Norton, 1988), 418–27.

p. 31: Freud and denial (*Verleugnung*): Cohen, *States of Denial*, 25–30, and Leo Goldberger, "The Concept and Mechanisms of Denial: A Selective Overview," in Breznitz, *Denial of Stress*, 83–95.

p. 31: Freud on *"knowing-with-not-knowing"*: Sigmund Freud, "On Beginning the Treatment" (1913), in *The Freud Reader*, ed. Peter Gay (New York: W. W. Norton, 1989), 376.

p. 32: "To deceive oneself on purpose seems": Immanuel Kant, *The Metaphysics of Morals*, ed. and trans. Mary J. Gregor (Cambridge: Cambridge University Press, 1996), 183.

p. 32: "In order to avoid looking, some element of the mind": Goleman, *Vital Lies*, 107.

p. 32: self-deception "is as ordinary and familiar": Fingarette, *Self-Deception*, 162.

p. 33: "I will look at any additional evidence to confirm": Robert Andrews, *The Routledge Dictionary of Quotations* (London: Routledge & Kegan Paul, 1987), 27.

p. 33: "Insensibly, one begins to twist facts to suit theories": Arthur Conan Doyle, *The Adventures of Sherlock Holmes* (New York: Oxford University Press, 1993), 8.

p. 33: The term was coined by sociologist William H. Whyte Jr.: William H. Whyte Jr., "Groupthink," *Fortune*, March 1952.

p. 33: more fully developed two decades later by Yale psychologist Irving L. Janis: Janis, *Victims of Groupthink*.

p. 34: "mutually assured delusion": Roland Bénabou, "Groupthink: Collective Delusions in Organizations and Markets," National Bureau of Economic Research Working Paper No. 14764 (March 2009).

p. 34: "Denial functions as a buffer": Elisabeth Kübler-Ross, *On Death and Dying* (London: Routledge, 1973), 34.

p. 34: some studies have found that patients who avoid thinking about surgery: Daniel Goleman, "Insights into Self-Deception," *New York Times*, May 12, 1985.

p. 35: "Disconnected remarks and chance meetings": Stendhal, *The Red and the Black* (New York: Bantam Books, 1958), 325, attributed by Stendhal to Schiller.

3. The Technological Chasm: Denial in the Tire Industry

I began research on the tire industry in 1990. Many of the facts in this chapter are derived from work I did for an unpublished paper that year and have continued doing on the industry since then. I am deeply indebted to my coauthors of an article in *Industrial and Corporate Change* referenced below. Professor Donald N. Sull, formerly at the Harvard Business School and now at the London Business School, generously shared his unrivaled knowledge of the American tire industry with Richard S. Rosenbloom, professor emeritus at the Harvard Business School, and me. Don participated in the leveraged buyout of the Uniroyal Goodrich Tire Company in the late 1980s. He has written extensively on the industry.

p. 39: "The major tire companies have a virtually unthreatened hold": "The Tire Industry: Skidding out of Control?" *Sales Management*, April 1, 1970.

p. 39: For Akron and the tire industry, see Daniel Nelson, *Farm and Factory: Workers in the Midwest, 1880–1990* (Bloomington: Indiana University Press, 1995), and Steve Love, David Giffels, and Debbie Van Tassel, *Wheels of Fortune: The Story of Rubber in Akron* (Akron: University of Akron Press, 1998).

p. 41: In 1966, the Federal Trade Commission found: Donald N. Sull, Richard S. Tedlow, and Richard S. Rosenbloom, "Managerial Commitments and Technological Change in the U.S. Tire Industry," *Industrial and Corporate Change* 6, no. 2 (March 1997): 467–68.

p. 41: "On Friday and Saturday night": Ibid., 468.

p. 41: "no-brainer" industry: Ibid.

p. 42: Firestone, for example actually lost $1.1 million: Ibid., 470.

p. 42: Porter introduced the "five forces" framework in his article "How Competitive Forces Shape Strategy" in the March/April 1979 *Harvard Business Review*. He has since discussed and refined it in numerous books and articles.

p. 42: "There is no substitute for the pneumatic tire": "Tire and Rubber Industry," *Value Line*, March 23, 1990, 126.

p. 44: In 1968, *Consumer Reports* awarded five of its top six ratings to radials: "Tires," *Consumer Reports*, August 1968.

p. 44: Akron . . . "tended to sniff at the belted radial as a 'European' tire": "The Michelin Man Rolls into Akron's Backyard," *Fortune*, December 1974.

p. 45: The radial was . . . "a sophisticated tire": "Are You Going to Buy Radials?" *Forbes*, June 15, 1974.

p. 45: "You could leave out one of the plies of a four-ply tire by mistake": D. A. Wyckoff, "Firestone Tire and Rubber Company," Harvard Business School Publishing Case No. 9-684-044 (Boston: HBS Publishing, 1984).

p. 45: it would cost between $600 million and $900 million . . . to convert to radials: "Radials Seen as OE Soon," *Modern Tire Dealer*, May 1971.

p. 46: "In the rubber industry there are two good big companies": "What's a Uniroyal?" *Forbes*, November 15, 1972.

p. 46: "most revolutionary automotive development by BFGoodrich": BFGoodrich *Annual Report* (1965).

p. 46: The company's "research pioneering": "Profiles of Big Five," *Forbes*, September 15, 1980.

p. 46: "one of the major errors ever made": "Riding with Radials," *Dun's Review*, October 1971.

p. 46: "The tire industry is in a period of extensive change": BFGoodrich *Annual Report* (1972).

p. 46: "one of the most popular radials in Europe": Uniroyal *Annual Report* (1972).

p. 46: "bias-ply" rather than radial tires: Sull, Tedlow, and Rosenbloom, "Managerial Commitments," 471.

p. 47: Many experts, however, including *Consumer Reports*, disputed that claim: "Tires: Bias Ply and Belted-Bias," *Consumer Reports*, October 1974.

p. 49: "Who put those damn Frog tires on the Lincoln?": Don Frey, "Learning the Ropes: My Life as a Product Champion," *Harvard Business Review* 69, no. 5 (September/October 1991): 46–52.

p. 49: "successfully faced and overcome major challenges": Firestone *Annual Report* (1973).

p. 50: "Growth": Firestone, *Annual Report* (1974).

p. 50: "it appears that Firestone is coming apart at the seams": "Forewarnings of Fatal Flaws," *Time*, June 25, 1979.

p. 50: "We are making an inferior quality tire": Ibid.

p. 50: "The company just kept churning out the 500 tires": Ibid.

p. 51: "The published information didn't convey the severity of what was happening": R. W. Ackerman, "Firestone, Inc.," Harvard Business School Case No. 9-388-127 (Boston: HBS Publishing, 1988).

p. 51: "astonished the financial community": W. Carl Kester, *Japanese Takeovers:*

The Global Contest for Corporate Control (Boston: Harvard Business School Press, 1991), 127.

p. 52: "Ford and Bridgestone/Firestone are writing the most important chapter": Robert L. Simison, Norihiko Shirouzu, Timothy Aeppel, and Todd Zaun, "Pressure Points: Tension Between Ford and Firestone Mounts Amid Recall Efforts," *Wall Street Journal*, August 28, 2000.

p. 52: Ford labeled its move a "customer notification enhancement action": *Firestone Tire Recall: Hearing Before the Committee on Commerce, Science, and Transportation, United States Senate, One Hundred Sixth Congress, second session, September 12, 2000* (Washington, DC: United States Government Printing Office, 2003), 84.

p. 53: "A man with great intelligence and a sharp analytical mind": Mansel G. Blackford and K. Austin Kerr, *BFGoodrich: Tradition and Transformation, 1870–1995* (Columbus: Ohio State University Press, 1996), 294.

p. 54: "Who would want to buy an ailing tire company?": "Nice Try," *Forbes*, December 1, 1975.

p. 54: Keener arranged a secret meeting in Paris: The account of this episode is based on Blackford and Kerr, *BFGoodrich*, 278–280.

p. 55: "returns are substantially higher": BFGoodrich *Annual Report* (1981).

p. 56: Gibara turned down $40 million: Zachary Schiller, "Stan Gault's Designated Driver," *Business Week*, April 8, 1996.

4. "They Just Didn't Believe These Things Were Happening": Denial at the A&P

Much of the factual material for this chapter was first published in my book *New and Improved*. The interpretation of those facts is wholly new with this volume.

p. 58: "If we had it to do all over again, we wouldn't do it": "A&P Looks like Tengelmann's Vietnam," *Business Week*, February 1, 1982.

p. 58: "strategic inflection point": Andrew S. Grove, *Only the Paranoid Survive* (New York: Doubleday, 1996), 32–33.

p. 59: "We first got into baking powder": Roy J. Bullock, "A History of the Great Atlantic and Pacific Tea Company Since 1878," *Harvard Business Review* 12 (October 1933): 62.

p. 60: "Unless we can operate in the future along economy lines": William I. Walsh, *The Rise & Decline of the Great Atlantic & Pacific Tea Company* (Secaucus, NJ: Lyle Stuart, 1986), 41–42.

p. 61: Wheel of Retailing: Malcolm McNair first observed the pattern that would later become known as the Wheel of Retailing in *Expenses and Profits in the Chain Grocery Business in 1929*, published in June 1931 as Bulletin no. 84 of the Bureau of Business Research at what was then called the Harvard Graduate School of Business Administration (as opposed to its present name, Harvard Business School). He elaborated on the phenomenon in his 1937 introduction to the casebook *Problems in Retailing* (New York: McGraw-Hill), which he coauthored with his Harvard Business School colleagues Charles Gragg and Stanley Teele. But he did not return to the theory in any substantive way until a 1957 speech at the University of Pittsburgh's Graduate School of Retailing. The address, "Significant Trends and Developments in the Postwar Period," marked McNair's first explicit use of the wheel metaphor. It was published the following year in Albert D. Smith, ed., *Competitive Distribution in a Free High-Level Economy and Its Implications for the University* (Pittsburgh: University of Pittsburgh Press, 1958). McNair did not employ the exact phrase "wheel of retailing" until 1976, when he and Eleanor May used it in their monograph *The Evolution of Retail Institutions in the United States* (Cambridge: Marketing Science Institute, 1976).

p. 61: The Wheel of Retailing concept can be seen as an ancestor to the theory of disruptive innovation advanced by Harvard Business School professor Clayton M. Christensen in *The Innovator's Dilemma: When New Technologies Cause Great Firms to Fail* (Boston: Harvard Business School Press, 1997) and many of his other works as well. See also Clayton M. Christensen and Richard S. Tedlow, "Patterns of Disruption in Retailing," *Harvard Business Review* 78, no. 1 (January-February 2000): 42–45.

p. 61: "It seems to me that there is more or less a definite cycle in American distribution": McNair, "Significant Trends," in Smith, *Competitive Distribution*, 17–18.

p. 62: "From an established, successful fifty-three-year-old chain": Walsh, *Rise & Decline*, 28.

p. 63: "The typical independent grocer": Neil M. Clark, "The Independent Grocer Finds 'A Way Out!'" *Forbes*, September 1, 1930.

p. 63: A&P stores were visited only by A&P representatives": "The A&P in Fairfield, Conn.," *Fortune*, July 1930.

p. 64: "One great asset in being away from the business section" and Cullen's remarks in the following paragraph: M. M. Zimmerman, *The Super Market: A Revolution in Distribution* (New York: Mass Distribution, 1955), 32–35.

p. 65: Sylvan Goldman and the shopping cart: Terry P. Wilson, *The Cart That Changed the World: The Career of Sylvan N. Goldman* (Norman: University of Oklahoma Press, 1978). See also Richard S. Tedlow's review of *Cart* in *Business History Review* 54, no. 1 (Spring 1980): 135–36.

p. 66: On December 8, 1936: Zimmerman, *Revolution*, 40–43.

p. 66: "could profitably sell goods at prices which would be ruinous": Morris A. Adelman, *A&P: A Study in Price-Cost Behavior and Public Policy* (Cambridge, MA: Harvard University Press, 1959), 61.

p. 66: "We did not take it very seriously" and "In a very short space of time": District Court of the United States for the Eastern District of Illinois, *United States v. The New York Great Atlantic and Pacific Tea Company, Inc. et al.*, no. 16153 (criminal), testimony of John A. Hartford, p. 20,438.

p. 66: This paternalism . . . "has taken the tangible form of high wages": "A&P Goes to the Wars," *Fortune*, April 1938.

p. 67: "Basically, the supermarket represents the complete antithesis": O. Fred Rost, "A Super Market X-Ray," *Advertising and Selling*, April 13, 1933.

p. 68: "It has always been our idea—we have been volume": *U.S. v. A&P*, testimony of John A. Hartford, p. 20,439.

p. 68: "It is easy to build up a complicated and expensive structure": Adelman, *A&P*, 81.

p. 69: "We're just a couple of grocery boys": Walsh, *Rise & Decline*, 86.

p. 69: the "secret" road to profit "lies almost entirely": Ibid., 75–76.

p. 69: Mr. John and Mr. George graced the cover of *Time* magazine: "Retail Trade: Red Circle and Gold Leaf," *Time*, November 13, 1950.

p. 69: The company had about 110,000 employees: Edwin P. Hoyt, *That Wonderful A&P!* (New York: Hawthorn, 1969), 205.

p. 69: "When at home, both these lonely old men": Ibid., 206.

p. 70: The Hartford brothers were "heartsick": Walsh, *Rise & Decline*, 66.

p. 71: "such thoughts were never expressed": Ibid., 79.

p. 71: "The company was prospering" and John Hartford's death: Ibid., 76.

p. 72: the foundation's 7 million shares of A&P were worth: Hoyt, *A&P!*, 217.

p. 72: In the late 1920s, the company was selling 600 million loaves: John A. Rentz, *The Death of Grandma: The Hartfords' Great Atlantic and Pacific Tea Company, A&P* (self-published, 1983), 53–54.

p. 73: For the A&P's store leases: William E. Fruhan Jr., *Financial Strategy: Studies in the Creation, Transfer, and Destruction of Shareholder Value* (Homewood, II: R. D. Irwin, 1979), 213–214.

p. 73: "Grandma has rarely been an innovator": "The Great A&P," *Fortune*, November 1947.

p. 74: With less than half of A&P's volume: Walsh, *Rise & Decline*, 90, 94.

p. 74: In an instance of candor rare on corporate websites: http://www.aptea.com/history_timeline.asp, accessed July 20, 2009.

p. 75: "After almost twenty years of steady decline and cutbacks": Walsh, *Rise & Decline*, 132.

p. 76: "They just didn't believe these things were happening": "A&P vs. G&W: Lethargic Food Giant Has Glamorous History—and Balance Sheet," *Wall Street Journal*, February 14, 1973.

p. 77: "Not with a bang but a whimper": T. S. Eliot, "The Hollow Men," *Collected Poems, 1909–1962* (New York: Houghton Mifflin Harcourt, 1963), 79.

5. The Edifice Complex: Denial at Sears

As with chapter 4, a considerable amount of the evidence presented in this chapter was originally developed for *New and Improved*. Once again, the use of those facts is unique to this book.

p. 78: The Chicago Club: Take a look at its home page at http://www.thechicagoclub
.org. Looks nice, doesn't it?

p. 78: Wood had developed an "odd passion": Alfred D. Chandler Jr., *Strategy and Structure: Chapters in the History of the American Industrial Enterprise* (Cambridge, MA: MIT Press, 1962), 233.

p. 79: "I believe there still lingers": Talk to be given by R. E. Wood, August 30, 1938, Buying and Cataloging Forces, Sears file, Wood papers, Herbert Hoover Presidential Library, West Branch, Iowa.

p. 79: "This country's going into a tailspin within two years": Robert E. Wood, "Reminiscences," Oral History Collection, Columbia University, 1961, p. 98.

p. 79: "the biggest gamble of his career": "Young Sears, Roebuck," *Fortune*, August 1948.

p. 80: "Go west, young man": Though the remark is famously attributed to Greeley and expresses a sentiment that he clearly endorsed, he may never have written or said it. In a succinct history of the "Go west" quote, Fred R. Shapiro in *The Yale Book of Quotations* (New Haven: Yale University Press, 2006), 322–23, calls it "one of the great examples of the prevalence of misinformation about famous quotations." See also Robert Chadwell Williams, *Horace Greeley: Champion of American Freedom* (New York: NYU Press, 2006), 40–41.

p. 80: By 1959, Sears had seventeen stores in the burgeoning Los Angeles market: Robert Brooker with John McDonald, "The Strategy That Saved Montgomery Ward," *Fortune*, May 1970.

p. 80: "show up Avery as weak, confused, and nearly senile": Cecil C. Hoge Sr., *The First Hundred Years Are the Toughest: What We Can Learn from the Century of Competition Between Sears and Wards* (Berkeley: Ten Speed Press, 1988), 165.

p. 81: during the 1950s and 1960s, about one in five citizens moved in any given year: Steven A. Holmes, "U.S. No Longer a Land Steeped in Wanderlust," *New York Times*, September 12, 1995.

p. 82: grabbed the suits that he wore "off the pile": "General Robert E. Wood, President," *Fortune*, May 1938.

p. 82: "Hercules in the cradle": Hamilton to Washington, April 14, 1794, in John Church Hamilton, ed., *The Works of Alexander Hamilton: Comprising His Correspondence, and His Political and Official Writings, Exclusive of the Federalist, Civil and Military,* vol 4 (New York: John F. Trow, 1850), 525.

p. 82: "American century": H. R. Luce, "The American Century," *Life*, February 17, 1941.

p. 82: Roosevelt was asked during World War II what American book he would put in the hands of every Russian: David M. Potter, *People of Plenty: Economic Abundance and the American Character* (Chicago: University of Chicago Press, 1954), 80.

p. 83: Roosevelt called Stalin "Uncle Joe": James MacGregor Burns, *Roosevelt: The Soldier of Freedom, 1940–1945* (New York: Harcourt, 1970), 412.

p. 83: "Sears guaranteed [its] cookstove to cook": Boris Emmet and John E. Jeuck, *Catalogues and Counters: A History of Sears, Roebuck and Company* (Chicago: University of Chicago Press, 1950), 113.

p. 83: "the humbling of products": Donald R. Katz, *The Big Store: Inside the Crisis and Revolution at Sears* (New York: Viking, 1987), 301.

p. 83: Sears "could sell a breath of air": Morris Robert Werner, *Julius Rosenwald: The Life of a Practical Humanitarian* (New York: Harper, 1939), 44.

p. 83: "In my humble opinion, we must have volume": Emmet and Jeuck, *Catalogues and Counters*, 180.

p. 84: "violated every rule of good advertising except one": Louis E. Asher and Edith Heal, *Send No Money* (Chicago: Argus, 1942), 3–4. See also Francis Sill Wickwire, "We Like Corn, on or off the Cob," *Collier's*, December 10, 1949.

p. 85: Sears had consistently placed first in surveys of the nation's most trusted companies: Katz, *Big Store*, vii.

p. 85: "Honesty is the best policy": Werner, *Rosenwald*, 36–37.

p. 85: Louis Asher dispatched a man named J. H. Jeffries into the field: Jeffries to Asher, letter, November 7, 1906; Asher to Jeffries, letter, November 9, 1906; box 1, folder 12, Asher papers, University of Chicago.

p. 85: An executive talked about it at a dinner: The executive was James M. Barker, who in remarks at the March 25, 1968, dinner related that Rosenwald had offered to refund the purchase price of Sears's electric belts and other such dubious devices (Sears file, Wood papers, Herbert Hoover Presidential Library).

p. 86: Lessing Rosenwald broke with Wood over this prejudice: James C. Worthy, *Shaping an American Institution: Robert E. Wood and Sears, Roebuck* (Urbana: University of Illinois Press, 1984), 49.

p. 86: "A good night's sleep, a good appetite, and a sound elimination": "General Robert E. Wood, President," *Fortune*, May 1938.

p. 86: "There is a deeper conflict between Sears, Roebuck and Co. and Montgomery Ward and Co.": Robert E. Wood, talk given before buyers, November 5, 1936, Sears file, Wood papers, Herbert Hoover Presidential Library.

p. 86: In 1964, *Fortune* ran a cover story whose praise was unstinting: John McDonald, "Sears Makes It Look Easy," *Fortune*, May 1964.

p. 87: "There is no better illustration of the practice of management": Peter Drucker, *The Practice of Management* (New York: Harper & Row, 1954), 27.

p. 87: "one of the most alert management groups in the country": William H. Whyte Jr., "The Fallacies of 'Personality' Testing," *Fortune*, September 1954.

p. 87: "I could not have this feeling of pride": Worthy, *American Institution*, epigraph.

p. 88: "This he did with reluctance but good grace": Ibid., 53.

p. 88: He "drooled, ate cigarettes": Katz, *Big Store*, 19.

p. 88: "As late as 1973": Ibid.

p. 89: "The chief executive office [had become] a revolving door"; Houser "bitterly resented"; and "the candidate with the shortest time to go": Worthy, *American Institution*, 252–53.

p. 89: "[Wood] had trouble seeing in advance" and "Wood deliberately chose as his successors": Ibid., 255.

p. 89: Peter Principle: Laurence J. Peter and Raymond Hull, *The Peter Principle* (New York: W. Morrow, 1969).

p. 90: "like an animal or a plant": Worthy, *American Institution*, 126.

p. 92: "Ozymandias": *The Complete Poems of Percy Bysshe Shelley* (New York: Modern Library, 1994).

p. 92: "Being the largest retailer in the world": Rovert Enstad, "Girder Tops Sears 'Rock,'" *Chicago Tribune*, May 4, 1973.

p. 92: "Gordon Metcalf's last erection": Katz, *Big Store*, 23. See also Richard S. Tedlow and David Ruben, "Sears' Edifice Complex," Forbes.com, July 10, 2009, http://www.forbes.com/2009/07/10/sears-tower-willis-opinions-contributors-chicago.html, accessed August 7, 2009.

p. 93: return to shareholders per square foot of CEO's office: Rick Tetzeli, "What Chief Executives Return to Shareholders per Square Foot of Office Space," *Fortune*, April 19, 1993.

p. 93: Wood as "consummate old-world gentleman-businessman": Katz, *Big Store*, 5–6.

p. 93: he would be fired: Ibid., 24.

p. 94: "As lifelong Sears employees carried their belongings": Ibid.

p. 95: "store of the future" campaign: Ibid., 399.

6. Success Today vs. Success Tomorrow: Denial and the IBM PC

My principal previous publications on IBM and the sources of some of the material in this chapter are the passage on Thomas J. Watson Sr. in *Giants of Enterprise* and *The Watson Dynasty: The Fiery Reign and Troubled Legacy of IBM's Founding Father and Son* (New York: HarperBusiness, 2003).

p. 96: "the most important product announcement": Thomas J. Watson Jr. and Peter Petre, *Father, Son & Co.: My Life at IBM and Beyond* (New York: Bantam Books, 1990), p. 351.

p. 97: "always had a regal aura about him": Paul Carroll, *Big Blues: The Unmaking of IBM* (New York: Crown, 1993), 153.

p. 97: "good looks and manners": Gerald Breckenridge, "Salesman No. 1," *Saturday Evening Post*, May 24, 1941.

p. 98: Akers "was a forceful speaker " and "carried himself with a confidence born of total success": Carroll, *Big Blues*, 153.

p. 98: "stony-faced" Akers: Ibid., 350.

p. 98: "a depth of experience, toughness, and energy": Kent Gibbons, "Gerstner's Selection as IBM Boss Shows Desire for Manager," *Washington Times*, March 27, 1993.

p. 98: "retired to a chair at the edge of the stage": Carroll, *Big Blues*, 331.

p. 99: Those interested in a more detailed treatment of the System/360—or who prefer watching to reading—can view a video of a presentation I gave on the subject at the Computer History Museum in Mountain View, California, in August 2008, at http://www.youtube.com/watch?v=DcqganpWfd8&feature=channel_page.

p. 100: T. Vincent Learson . . . expressed "no real objections": Carliss Y. Baldwin and Kim B. Clark, *Design Rules: The Power of Modularity* (Cambridge, MA: MIT Press, 2000), 179.

p. 101: "There is a growing market for any device": Arthur D. Little Inc., *The Electronic Data Processing Industry: Present Equipment, Technological Trends, Potential Market* (New York: White, Weld, 1956), 33.

p. 101: "Below the surface, IBM's organization didn't fit the changing markets": Thomas A. Wise, "IBM's $5,000,000,000 Gamble," *Fortune*, September 1966.

p. 101: "People began to speculate that we'd gotten so big": Watson and Petre, *My Life*, 347.

p. 102: "I thought it was probably our own fault": Ibid.

p. 102: "Mr. Watson, I am looking at your son's record" and "He's not very good": Ibid., 37–38.

p. 102: "I had to be assigned a tutor": Ibid., 71.

p. 103: "The most important role of managers": Andrew S. Grove, *Only the Paranoid Survive* (New York: Doubleday, 1996), 107.

p. 103: "Fear of failure became the most powerful force": Watson and Petre, *My Life*, 284.

p. 103: "wildly disorganized": Ibid., 347.

p. 104: "User migration from one architecture to another": Bob O. Evans, "Introduction to SPREAD Report," *Annals of the History of Computing* 72, no. 4 (Winter 1998).

p. 104: "Building this new line meant putting IBM through tremendous upheavals": Watson and Petre, *My Life*, 364.

p. 104: "We made two miscalculations": Rowena Olegario, "IBM and the Two Thomas J. Watsons," in Thomas K. McCraw, ed., *Creating Modern Capitalism: How Entrepreneurs, Companies, and Countries Triumphed in Three Industrial Revolutions* (Cambridge, MA: Harvard University Press, 1997), 392.

p. 105: "It was the biggest privately financed commercial project": Watson and Petre, *My Life*, 346–47.

p. 105: "My anxiety was misplaced": Ibid., 352.

p. 106: director Kubrick and author Arthur C. Clarke always denied the connection: Arthur C. Clarke, *Greetings, Carbon-Based Bipeds!: Collected Essays, 1934–1998* (New York: St. Martin's Press, 2000), 482; Vincent Lobrutto, *Stanley Kubrick: A Biography* (New York: D. I. Fine, 1997), 267–68.

p. 106: "the most successful capitalist who ever lived": Max Ways, "The Hall of Fame for Business Leadership—1976," *Fortune*, January 1976.

p. 106: "The Greatest Capitalist in History": *Fortune*, August 31, 1987.

p. 106: "Objectively, it was the greatest triumph of my business career": Watson and Petre, *My Life*, 360.

p. 107: "Ever Onward": As befitting a company with a rich history, IBM has a rich historical website at http://www.ibm.com/ibm/history/. This and other IBM songs may be heard by clicking on "Multimedia."

p. 108: "The president called me back to Washington": Watson and Petre, *My Life*, 432–33.

p. 109: mission was slowly, inexorably transformed into momentum: I have here borrowed Daniel J. Boorstin's memorable phrase "Mission and Momentum" from *The Americans: The Democratic Experience* (New York: Viking, 1973), 557–98.

p. 109: "IBM has been built on problems": Olegario, "IBM," in McCraw, ed., *Creating Modern Capitalism*, 392.

p. 110: "With competitors seemingly vanquished": Carroll, *Big Blues*, 82.

p. 110: Former IBM executive Sam Albert recalled: *Triumph of the Nerds: The Rise of Accidental Empires* (PBS, aired June 1996), Part II transcript, http://www.pbs.org/nerds/part2.html.

p. 111: IBM's dress code . . . made the *New York Times*: Joseph Berger, "Black Jeans Invade Big Blue," *New York Times*, February 7, 1995.

p. 111: the company from which products were not launched. They escaped: Louis V. Gerstner, *Who Says Elephants Can't Dance? Inside IBM's Historic Turnaround* (New York: HarperBusiness, 2002), 186.

p. 112: it would have ranked seventy-fourth on the Fortune 500: Carroll, *Big Blues*, 75.

p. 113: "Why would computer executives who had proven themselves to be brilliant": Grove, *Only the Paranoid Survive*, 64–65.

p. 114: "There are no second acts": F. Scott Fitzgerald, *The Last Tycoon: An Unfinished Novel* (New York: Charles Scribner's Sons, 1941), 163. The quotation actually appears in "Hollywood, Etc.," one of Fitzgerald's notes for the unfinished novel that was published with the work by editor Edmund Wilson in 1941.

p. 114: "Only a handful of people understand": Gerstner, *Elephants*, 66.

p. 114: By 2004, IBM's services unit alone had higher revenues: David Kirkpatrick, "Inside Sam's $100 Billion Growth Machine," *Fortune*, June 14, 2004.

p. 115: "I think that you have to have more than just a machine": Available in both audio and written formats on the IBM Archives website, http://www-03.ibm.com/ibm/history/multimedia/ibmservice_trans.html.

p. 115: Georg Simmel on the value of outsiders in organizations: Georg Simmel and Kurt H. Wolff (editor and translator), *The Sociology of Georg Simmel* (Glencoe, Il: Free Press, 1950), 405.

7. Coke's New Formula for Denial

As the notes below indicate, this chapter is much indebted to Thomas Oliver's *The Real Coke, the Real Story* (New York: Random House, 1986) and to Roger Enrico and Jesse Kornbluth's *The Other Guy Blinked: How Pepsi Won the Cola Wars* (New York: Bantam, 1986).

p. 116: "Never": Thomas Oliver, *the Real Coke, the Real Story* (New York: Random House, 1986), 177.

p. 117: New Coke product announcement: The account of and quotations from this event are based on Oliver, *Real Coke*, 131–34.

p. 117: "I have climbed to the top of the greasy pole": Robert Blake, *Disraeli* (London: Eyre & Spottiswoode, 1966), 487.

p. 119: Goizueta's awkward attempt to describe the taste of New Coke can be seen and heard on the MSNBC website as part of an archived *NBC Nightly News* report from April 23, 1985, http://www.msnbc.msn.com/id/7209828/.

p. 120: "They're actually going to do it!": Roger Enrico and Jesse Kornbluth, *The Other Guy Blinked: How Pepsi Won the Cola Wars* (New York: Bantam, 1986), 199.

p. 121: "TO ALL PEPSI BOTTLERS": Ibid., 200–201.

p. 121: "Look at it this way": Ibid., 201.

p. 122: "That classic American hero": E. L. Doctorow, *Ragtime* (New York: Random House, 1975), 158–59. The particular object of Doctorow's words was J. P. Morgan.

p. 122: "Unlike the auto or refrigerator": "Bob Woodruff of Coca-Cola," *Fortune*, September 1945.

p. 123: "World & Friend": "The Sun Never Sets on Cacoola," *Time*, May 15, 1950.

p. 123: "The relationship between Woodruff and Austin": Mark Pendergrast, *For God, Country and Coca-Cola: The Definitive History of the Great American Soft Drink and the Company That Makes It* (New York: Basic Books, 2000), 309.

p. 124: "I knew Paul was drinking a little": Ibid., 315.

p. 124: The tallest building in its Atlanta neighborhood: Ibid.

p. 124: This further alienated Austin from the aging Woodruff: Ibid., 334.

p. 124: from 1962 to 1981, great things did happen at Coca-Cola: Ibid., 341–42.

p. 124: he actually said "Pepsi": Ibid., 324.

p. 124–25: "Coca-Cola is a delightful, palatable, healthful beverage": This advertisement appeared in the *Delineator* in July 1905. It is available in Advertising Copy, vol. 1, Coca-Cola Archives.

p. 125: "Pepsi-Cola aids digestion": This advertisement appeared in the *Greensboro Daily News Sunday*, December 19, 1915. It is part of a large collection of Pepsi-Cola advertising that has been donated to the National Museum of American History of the Smithsonian Institution in Washington, D.C.

p. 125: "Texas was a disaster": Oliver, *Real Coke*, 50.

p. 125: "We had a joke": Ibid., 51.

p. 126: "It wasn't allowed": Ibid., 53.

p. 126: "sublimated essence of all that America stands for": Pendergrast, *For God, Country and Coca-Cola*, 198.

p. 126: "no sacred cows": Oliver, *Real Coke*, 74.

p. 127: Goizueta himself was publicly quoted in 1984 expressing concern: Ibid., 112.

p. 127: "To my mind, I am in this damn mess": E. J. Kahn Jr., *The Big Drink: The Story of Coca-Cola* (New York: Random House, 1960), 15.

p. 127: "Rum and Coca-Cola": There is a long and not uninteresting story behind this song, much of it unearthed and presented by Kevin Burke, a freelance photographer and self-described calypsophile from Cambridge, Massachusetts, at http://www.rumandcocacolareader.com/.

8. The Madness of Crowds: Delivering Denial at Webvan

As the notes below indicate, this chapter is much indebted to John Cassidy's *dot.con: How America Lost Its Mind and Money in the Internet Era* (New York: HarperCollins, 2002).

p. 129: "What experience and history teaches us": Georg Wilhelm Friedrich Hegel, *Lectures on the Philosophy of World History* (1837; repr., Cambridge, England: Cambridge University Press, 1975), 21.

p. 130: "madness of crowds": Charles Mackay, *Extraordinary Popular Delusions and the Madness of Crowds* (1841; repr., New York: Harmony Books, 1980).

p. 131: "It was the spark that touched off the Internet boom" and "Netscape mesmerized investors": Adam Lashinsky, "Remembering Netscape: The Birth of the Web," *Fortune,* July 12, 2005.

p. 132: "I was walking down the hallway": Sam Wyly, *1,000 Dollars and an Idea: Entrepreneur to Billionaire* (New York: Newmarket Press, 2008), 111.

p. 133: *F'd Companies*: Philip J. Kaplan, *F'd Companies: Spectacular Dot-Com Flameouts* (New York: Simon & Schuster, 2002).

p. 133: "Self-promoting technology 'gurus'": John Cassidy, *dot.con: How America Lost Its Mind and Money in the Internet Era* (New York: HarperCollins, 2002), 39.

p. 134: using companies to create stocks: Ibid., 247.

p. 135: case study . . . "in the illusions of the dot-com boom": "Webvan's Billion-Dollar Mistake," *Financial Times,* July 9, 2001.

p. 135: "gave up a retirement package worth": Cassidy, *dot.con*, 243.

p. 135: This package "would have kicked in"; "all about leveraging technology"; "This is not going to be a free ride"; and "would be sitting on a paper profit": Robert Lenzner, "Bagging Groceries," *Forbes,* October 18, 1999.

p. 136: "Of all the follies of the Internet boom": Cassidy, *dot.con*, 241.

p. 137: In its IPO filing, Webvan promised: Webvan Group, prospectus filed with SEC, November 5, 1999.

p. 137: Webvan "could be the biggest company": Kevin Maney, "Webvan Lugs a Dream: Company Hopes Food Will Whet Appetites for a Retail Revolution," *USA Today,* June 27, 2000.

p. 137: "We view Webvan as one of the few true e-tailing enablers": Connie Guglielmo, "Can Webvan Deliver?" *Inter@ctive Week,* January 31, 2000.

p. 139: Webvan's own banker, Goldman Sachs, expected it to lose half a billion dollars: Cassidy, *dot.con*, 244.

p. 139: "I believe they were doomed from the start": "Webvan's Billion-Dollar Mistake," *Financial Times.*

p. 139: "It's hard to understand why Wall Street analysts love [Webvan]": Guglielmo, "Can Webvan Deliver?"

p. 140: "Something out of a Fritz Lang movie": Cassidy, *dot.con*, 242.

p. 141: "Maybe we have one of the great flameouts in history": "George Shaheen, President and CEO, Webvan," Kellogg School of Business Cyber Symposium, February 2000. Transcript at http://www.fantastictranscripts.com/transcription/ shaheen00.html, accessed July 27, 2009.

p. 141: "When I talk to my old friends in the book business": George Anders, "Co-Founder of Borders to Launch Online Megagrocer," *Wall Street Journal*, April 22, 1999.

p. 141: "Naw. It's going to be ten billion": Randall E. Stross, "Only a Bold Gamble Can Save Webvan Now," *Wall Street Journal*, February 2, 2001.

9. Strategy, Structure, and Facing Facts at DuPont

The facts for this chapter rely heavily on Alfred D. Chandler Jr., *Strategy and Structure: Chapters in the History of the American Industrial Enterprise* (Cambridge, MA: MIT Press, 1962). Chandler's superb chapter on DuPont in that book is among his finest work. Supplemental to the book have been innumerable discussions between the late Professor Chandler and me. I have also examined numerous documents relevant to this subject because of work I have done for DuPont. See also my paper presented at the Academy of Management in August 2008, "From 'Universalistic Rather Than Particularistic' to 'The Treasure of the Sierra Madre': Another Look at Chapter 2 of Alfred D. Chandler, Jr.'s *Strategy and Structure*."

I have followed the convention embraced by Alfred D. Chandler Jr. and Stephen Salsbury in *Pierre S. du Pont and the Making of the Modern Corporation* (New York: Harper & Row, 1971) of using a lowercase "d" for the du Pont family and uppercase "D" for the DuPont corporation.

p. 146: "this felicitous union of fall-line power": Joseph Frazier Wall, *Alfred I. du Pont: The Man and His Family* (New York: Oxford University Press, 1990), 41.

p. 147: "There had developed a tradition of what might be called 'family communism'": Alfred D. Chandler Jr. and Stephen Salsbury, *Pierre S. du Pont and the Making of the Modern Corporation* (New York: Harper & Row, 1971), 5.

p. 147: Their "ancient and friendly competitor": Chandler, *Strategy and Structure*, 52.

p. 147: "The conversation was brief—very brief": Wall, *du Pont*, 192.

p. 147: "I think there is going to be some tall hustling to get everything reorganized": Chandler, *Strategy and Structure*, 55.

p. 148: "the less said, the sooner mended": Wall, *du Pont*, 312.

p. 148: "At the time we made the purchase of the properties": Chandler, *Strategy and Structure*, 55.

p. 149: Alfred's "failure as an administrator"; "increasing deafness"; and health "broke": Ibid., 63.

p. 150: Pierre . . . "had been branded deceitful": Wall, *du Pont*, 351.

p. 151: Employment skyrocketed along with the spectacular increase: The data in this paragraph are from Chandler, *Strategy and Structure*, 84.

p. 151: "Coleman's shares": Wall, *du Pont*, 342.

p. 152: The Unitary (or U form) of organization "proved admirably suited": Chandler, *Strategy and Structure*, 66.

p. 152: "By the summer of 1919": Ibid., 78.

p. 153: In 1957, *Fortune* estimated: Richard Austin Smith, "The Fifty-Million-Dollar Man" (sidebar, "America's Biggest Fortunes"), *Fortune*, November 1957.

p. 153: "We must be careful that our point of view is not entirely warped": Chandler, *Strategy and Structure*, 84.

p. 153: "only a portion of the present equipment will be useful": Ibid., 85.

p. 153: "advantages of careful business management on a large scale": Ibid., 92.

p. 155: "The more paint and varnish we sold": Ibid.

p. 155: The problem seemed to reside in sales: Ibid., 93.

p. 156: The real problem was . . . "entirely within ourselves": Ibid., 95.

p. 157: "In no case do they have a divided control": Ibid., 96.

p. 157: Here are some of the penciled objections: Ibid., 98–99.

p. 158: It violated the "principle of specialization": Ibid., 99.

p. 160: "A Plan to Make 10% on Our Paint and Varnish Net Sales": A copy of this report is in my possession. The original can be found in the Hagley Museum and Library in Wilmington, Delaware.

pp. 160, 161: "What is needed" and "The trouble with the Company is right here in Wilmington": Chandler, *Strategy and Structure*, 165.

p. 161: "Losses soon converted into profits": Ibid., 112.

p. 161: "major watershed": Charles W. Cheape, *Strictly Business: Walter Carpenter at Du Pont and General Motors* (Baltimore: Johns Hopkins University Press, 1995), 49.

10. "Why Shouldn't You and I Walk Out the Door . . . ?": A New Perspective at Intel

Much of the material in this chapter draws on my biography of Andy Grove, *Andy Grove: The Life and Times of an American* (New York: Portfolio, 2006).

p. 163: more than 550,000 Jews living in Hungary . . . perished during the Holocaust: "Hungary," *Encyclopedia Judaica*, 616.

p. 163: "Living under a Communist regime and being told what to think": Tedlow, *Grove*, 1.

p. 164: "I listened to Rajk's examination with morbid fascination": Andrew S. Grove, *Swimming Across: A Memoir* (New York: Warner, 2001), 109.

p. 164: "Eager to cultivate an interest in a new profession": Ibid., 152.

p. 164: "Two men are ogling a spanking new Western car": Ibid., 167.

pp. 165–66: The account of Grove's escape from Hungary: Ibid., 225–36.

p. 166: "let chaos reign and then rein in chaos": Andrew S. Grove, *Only the Paranoid Survive: How to Manage the Crisis Points That Challenge Every Company* (New York: Doubleday, 1996), 121–64.

p. 167: Moore "asked me about my thesis": Tedlow, *Grove*, 81.

p. 167: "truly outstanding technical person": Ibid., 80.

p. 168: "Changing jobs in our industry is fairly common": Leslie Berlin, "Entrepreneurship and the Rise of Silicon Valley: The Career of Robert Noyce, 1956–1990" (Ph. D. diss., Stanford University, 2001), 150.

p. 169: "imagination of disaster": Henry James, Arthur Christopher Benson, Auguste Monod, and E. F. Benson, *Henry James: Letters to A. C. Benson and Auguste Monod* (New York: Charles Scribner's Sons, 1930), 35.

p. 169: "I was scared to death": Peter Botticelli, David Collis, and Gary Pisano, "Intel Corporation: 1986–1997," Harvard Business School Publishing Case No. 9-797-137 (Boston: HBS Publishing, rev. 1998).

p. 169: "I went from chemistry to chemical engineering": Margaret Grove Radford, "Technology Is Impossible to Hold Back," *Destiny*, Summer 1997.

p. 170: "an outside man, a man of thought": Interview of Andrew S. Grove by Arnold Thackray and David C. Brock, September 1, 2004, 12–13, Oral History Collection, Chemical Heritage Foundation, http://www.chemheritage.org. Interview in my possession. Drucker's exact characterization of the trio to which Grove refers is "the 'thought man,' the 'man of action' and the 'front man'": Peter Drucker, *The Practice of Management*, (New York: Harper & Row, 1954), 168.

p. 170: "If at Intel we can't make it": Tedlow, *Grove*, 137.

p. 170: 1103 production problems: Ibid., 138.

p. 171: "the Edsel of microprocessors": Ibid., 337.

p. 172: "Snow melts first at the periphery": Grove, *Only the Paranoid Survive*, 110.

p. 172: Bill Davidow and Operation Crush: William H. Davidow, *Marketing High Technology: An Insider's View* (New York: Free Press, 1986), 4–11.

p. 173: "With the IBM contract, Intel won the microprocessor wars": Michael Malone, *Infinite Loop: How the World's Most Insanely Great Computer Company Went Insane* (New York: Doubleday, 1999), 218.

p. 175: "scary": Grove, *Only the Paranoid Survive*, 85.

p. 175: "these humongous companies with their humongous factories": Richard Mackenzie, "'The Industry Has Stopped Growing,'" *Insight*, October 7, 1985.

p. 175: "Win with the 10% rule": Grove, *Only the Paranoid Survive*, 87.

p. 176: "we vigorously attacked the ominous data": Ibid., 86.

p. 176: [Intel's] global share of the DRAM business was under 3 percent: Robert A. Burgelman, *Strategy Is Destiny: How Strategy-Making Shapes a Company's Future* (New York: Free Press, 2002), 35, 63.

p. 177: "Managing, especially managing through a crisis": Grove, *Only the Paranoid Survive*, 81.

p. 177: "The bulk of the memory chip [i.e., DRAM] development": Ibid., 87–88.

p. 177: "We had meetings and more meetings" and "We had lost our bearings": Ibid., 88–89.

p. 177: "led the company in linewidth reduction": Burgelman, *Strategy Is Destiny*, 37.

p. 178: "I remember a time in the middle of 1985": Grove, *Only the Paranoid Survive*, 89.

p. 178: "History is a nightmare from which I am trying to escape": James Joyce, *Ulysses* (1922; repr., New York: Penguin Classics, 2000), 42.

p. 179: "It's natural to say, 'The problem is just a distraction'": Patricia Sellers, "CEOs in Denial," *Fortune*, June 21, 1999.

p. 180: "I had a hard time getting the words out of my mouth": Grove, *Only the Paranoid Survive*, 89.

p. 180: "to continue R&D for a [memory] product": Ibid., 91.

p. 180: "If we had just started our development": Ibid., 124.

p. 180: "It got there by the autonomous actions": Ibid., 111.

p. 180: "process of shutting down factories, letting people go": Video Monitoring Services of America, *Technopolitics*, KCSM-TV San Francisco, September 22, 1996, 5:30 p.m.

11. Data-Driven Emotional Intelligence: Tylenol's Comeback

Except where noted below, the facts and quotations in this chapter were gathered by me in interviews with James Burke and other principals for an extensive research project on the Tylenol tamperings. That research resulted in two Harvard Business School cases authored by me and Wendy K. Smith, "James Burke: A Career in American Business (A)," Harvard Business School Publishing Case No. 9-389-177 (Boston: HBS Publishing, rev. 2005), and "James Burke: A Career in American Business (B)," Harvard Business School Publishing Case No. 9-390-030 (Boston: HBS Publishing, rev. 2005). My Tylenol research also generated an hour-long film on this subject for HBS classroom use, which included video material made available by Johnson & Johnson. My understanding of this episode was greatly enhanced by discussions with Johnson & Johnson executive Lawrence G. Foster, author of *Robert Wood Johnson: The Gentleman Rebel* (State College, PA: Lillian Press, 1999).

p. 186: Theodore Roosevelt and the "lunatic fringe": William Safire, *Safire's Political Dictionary* (New York: Oxford University Press, 2008), 405.

p. 191: "As time passes without a suspect being caught": Michael Waldholz and Dennis Kneale, "Growing Headache: Tylenol's Maker Tries to Regain Good Image in Wake of Tragedy," *Wall Street Journal*, October 8, 1982.

p. 192: To this day, no one knows for sure who was responsible for any of the Tylenol poisonings: The cases remain unsolved but continue to make headlines. For instance, in February 2009, FBI agents searched the Cambridge, Massachusetts, residence of James W. Lewis, who was convicted in 1983 and served more than twelve years in prison for attempting to extort $1 million from Johnson & Johnson "to stop the killing." Lewis was and remains a suspect in the murders, but he has never been charged. Neither is he the only suspect. Jamie Sotonoff, "Six Months after FBI Raids, Still No Arrests in Tylenol Murders," *Chicago Daily Herald*, August 4, 2009.

p. 194: "Sensing a tremendous reservoir of good will" ": Waldholz and Kneale, "Growing Headache."

p. 196: *The Wall Street Journal* called this performance a marketing miracle: "Speedy Recovery: Tylenol Regains Most of No. 1 Market Share, Amazing Doomsayers," *Wall Street Journal*, December 24, 1982.

p. 201: Burke was "blessed" by an ability "to mix decency with cunning": Murray Kempton, "The Tylenol Case and Our Wish for a Happy Ending," *Newsday*, February 19, 1986.

p. 202: The Elsroth family did in fact sue Johnson & Johnson: United States District Court for the Southern District of New York, *Elsroth v. Johnson & Johnson*, 700 F. Supp. 151 (S.D.N.Y. 1988).

12. A New Point of View

p. 204: "Nothing is easier than self-deception": Harvey Yunis, *Taming Democracy: Models of Political Rhetoric in Classical Athens* (Ithaca, NY: Cornell University Press, 1996), 265.

p. 204: Granville Hicks: *Part of the Truth: An Autobiography* (New York: Harcourt, Brace and World, 1965).

p. 206: "the most significant organizational innovation of the twentieth century": Oliver E. Williamson, *The Economic Institutions of Capitalism* (New York: Free Press, 1985), 279.

p. 206: "normalization of deviance": Diane Vaughan, *The Challenger Launch Decision: Risky Technology, Culture, and Deviance at NASA* (Chicago: University of Chicago Press, 1996), 75 and throughout.

p. 207: "routine and taken-for-granted aspects of organizational life": Ibid., 394.

p. 207: Power deranges: The phrase "power deranges" was first suggested to me by the Honorable Sandra L. Lynch, chief judge of the United States Court of Appeals for the First Circuit. I used this phrase in *Giants of Enterprise* (New York: HarperCollins, 2001), 60.

p. 207: Andy Grove on "Cassandras": Andrew S. Grove, *Only the Paranoid Survive* (New York: Doubleday, 1996), 108–9.

p. 209: "everybody talks about what didn't get said": Walter Kiechel III, "Facing Up to Denial," *Fortune*, October 18, 1993.

p. 209: "Gentlemen, I take it we are all in complete agreement on the subject here": Irving L. Janis, *Victims of Groupthink: A Psychological Study of Foreign-Policy Decisions and Fiascoes* (Boston: Houghton Mifflin, 1972), 218–19.

p. 211: Anna Freud . . . told of a young girl: Anna Freud, *The Ego and the Mechanisms of Defense* (New York: International Universities Press, 1966), 35–37.

p. 212: *The Year of the Customer*: Jeremy Main, *Quality Wars: The Triumphs and Defeats of American Business* (New York: Simon & Schuster, 1994), 191.

p. 212: "loans built to self-destruct": Michael Lewis, "The End," *Condé Nast Portfolio*, December 2008.

p. 212: "the important service of partially concealing your meaning even from yourself": George Orwell, "Politics and the English Language" (1946), in *The Orwell Reader* (New York: Harcourt, 1984), 362.

p. 213: "Hedge funds don't hedge": Paul Krugman, *The Return of Depression Economics and the Crisis of 2008* (New York: W. W. Norton, 2009), 120.

p. 213: "The CEO who misleads others in public may eventually mislead himself in private": *An Owner's Manual: A Message from Warren E. Buffett, Chairman and CEO*, January 1999, http://www.berkshirehathaway.com/owners.html, accessed May 6, 2009.

p. 213: "Macroeconomics was born as a distinct field in the 1940s": Robert E. Lucas, "Macroeconomic Priorities," *American Economic Review* 93, no. 1 (March 2003).

p. 214: "Looking back from only a few years later": Krugman, *Depression Economics*, 10.

p. 214: "You have to be there": Janera Soerel, "Talking to Nouriel Roubini," *Janera*, May 2, 2007, http://www.janera.com/janera_words.php?id=44, accessed July 30, 2009.

p. 215: "nightmare hard-landing scenario"; "The audience seemed skeptical, even dismissive"; and Banerji continued to dismiss Roubini . . . : Stephen Mihm, "Dr. Doom," *New York Times Magazine*, August 17, 2008.

p. 215: "A 'sound' banker, alas! is not one who foresees": Nick Paumgarten, "Annals of Finance: The Death of Kings," *New Yorker*, May 18, 2009. The quote originally comes from Keynes's August 1931, essay, "The Consequences to the Banks of the Collapse of Money Values," in John Maynard Keynes, *Essays in Persuasion* (New York: W. W. Norton, 1963), 176.

p. 216: "Not everything that is faced can be changed": James Baldwin, "As Much Truth as One Can Bear," *New York Times Book Review*, January 14, 1962, 38.

Bibliography

Books

Adelman, Morris A. *A&P: A Study in Price-Cost Behavior and Public Policy*. Cambridge MA: Harvard University Press, 1959.

Andrews, Robert. *The Routledge Dictionary of Quotations*. London: Routledge & Kegan Paul, 1987.

Applebaum, William. *Supermarketing: The Past, the Present, a Projection*. Chicago: Super Market Institute, 1969.

Asher, Louis E., and Edith Heal. *Send No Money*. Chicago: Argus, 1942.

Baldwin, Carliss Young, and Kim B. Clark. *Design Rules: The Power of Modularity*. Cambridge, MA: MIT Press, 2000.

Bellow, Saul. *Mr. Sammler's Planet*. New York: Viking, 1970.

Berlin, Leslie. *The Man Behind the Microchip: Robert Noyce and the Invention of Silicon Valley*. New York: Oxford University Press, 2005.

Blackford, Mansel G., and K. Austin Kerr. *BFGoodrich: Tradition and Transformation, 1870–1995*. Columbus: Ohio State University Press, 1996.

Blake, Robert. *Disraeli*. London: Eyre & Spottiswoode, 1966.

Boorstin, Daniel J. *The Americans: The Democratic Experience*. New York: Viking, 1973.

Breznitz, Shlomo, ed. *The Denial of Stress*. New York: International Universities Press, 1983.

Burgelman, Robert A. *Strategy Is Destiny: How Strategy-Making Shapes a Company's Future*. New York: Free Press, 2002.

Burns, James MacGregor. *Roosevelt: The Soldier of Freedom, 1940–1945*. New York: Harcourt Brace Jovanovich, 1970.

Carroll, Paul. *Big Blues: The Unmaking of IBM*. New York: Crown, 1993.

Cassidy, John. *dot.con: How America Lost Its Mind and Money in the Internet Era*. New York: HarperCollins, 2002.

Chandler, Alfred D., Jr. *Strategy and Structure: Chapters in the History of the American Industrial Enterprise.* Cambridge, MA: MIT Press, 1962.

————, ed. *Giant Enterprise: Ford, General Motors, and the Automobile Industry.* New York: Harcourt, Brace, and World, 1964.

Chandler, Alfred D., Jr., and Stephen Salsbury. *Pierre S. du Pont and the Making of the Modern Corporation.* New York: Harper & Row, 1971.

Cheape, Charles W. *Strictly Business: Walter Carpenter at Du Pont and General Motors.* Baltimore: Johns Hopkins University Press, 1995.

Christensen, Clayton M. *The Innovator's Dilemma: When New Technologies Cause Great Firms to Fail.* Boston: Harvard Business School Press, 1997.

Clarke, Arthur C. *Greetings, Carbon-Based Bipeds!: Collected Essays, 1934–1998.* New York: St. Martin's Press, 2000.

Cohen, Stanley. *States of Denial: Knowing About Atrocities and Suffering.* Cambridge, England: Polity Press, 2001.

Critchlow, Donald T. *Studebaker: The Life and Death of an American Corporation.* Bloomington: Indiana University Press, 1996.

Davidow, William H. *Marketing High Technology: An Insider's View.* New York: Free Press, 1986.

Davis, Donald Finlay. *Conspicuous Production: Automobiles and Elites in Detroit, 1899–1933.* Philadelphia: Temple University Press, 1988.

Doctorow, E. L. *Ragtime.* New York: Random House, 1975.

Doyle, Arthur Conan. *The Adventures of Sherlock Holmes.* New York: Oxford University Press, 1993.

Drucker, Peter. *The Practice of Management.* New York: Harper & Row, 1954.

Edelstein, E. L., Donald L. Nathanson, and Andrew M. Stone, eds. *Denial: A Clarification of Concepts and Research.* New York: Plenum Press, 1989.

Eliot, T. S. *Collected Poems, 1909–1962.* New York: Houghton Mifflin Harcourt, 1963.

Emmet, Boris, and John E. Jeuck. *Catalogues and Counters: A History of Sears, Roebuck and Company.* Chicago: University of Chicago Press, 1950.

Enrico, Roger, and Jesse Kornbluth. *The Other Guy Blinked: How Pepsi Won the Cola Wars.* New York: Bantam, 1986.

Epstein, Ralph C. *The Automobile Industry: Its Economic and Commercial Development.* Chicago: A. W. Shaw, 1928.

Fielding, Henry. *Rape upon Rape; or, The Justice Caught in His Own Trap, a Comedy.* Whitefish, MT: Kessinger Publishing, 2004.

Fingarette, Herbert. *Self-Deception.* London: Routledge & Kegan Paul, 1969.

Fitzgerald, F. Scott. *The Last Tycoon: An Unfinished Novel.* New York: Charles Scribner's Sons, 1941.

Flink, James J. *America Adopts the Automobile, 1895–1910.* Cambridge, MA: MIT Press, 1970.

————. *The Automobile Age.* Cambridge, MA: MIT Press, 1988.

————. *The Car Culture.* Cambridge, MA: MIT Press, 1976.

Ford, Henry, with Samuel Crowther. *My Life and Work*. Garden City, NY: Doubleday, 1922.

Foster, Lawrence G. *Robert Wood Johnson: The Gentleman Rebel*. State College, PA: Lillian Press, 1999.

Freud, Anna. *The Ego and the Mechanisms of Defense*. New York: International Universities Press, 1966.

Fruhan, William E., Jr. *Financial Strategy: Studies in the Creation, Transfer, and Destruction of Shareholder Value*. Homewood, II: R. D. Irwin, 1979.

Gay, Peter. *Freud: A Life for Our Time*. New York: W. W. Norton, 1988.

————, ed., *The Freud Reader*. New York: W. W. Norton, 1989.

Gerstner, Louis V. *Who Says Elephants Can't Dance? Inside IBM's Historic Turnaround*. New York: HarperBusiness, 2002.

Goleman, Daniel. *Vital Lies, Simple Truths: The Psychology of Self-Deception*. New York: Simon & Schuster, 1985.

Grove, Andrew S. *Only the Paranoid Survive: How to Manage the Crisis Points That Challenge Every Company*. New York: Doubleday, 1996.

————. *Swimming Across: A Memoir*. New York: Warner, 2001.

Hamilton, John Church, ed. *The Works of Alexander Hamilton: Comprising His Correspondence, and His Political and Official Writings, Exclusive of the Federalist, Civil and Military*. New York: John F. Trow, 1850.

Hegel, Georg Wilhelm Friedrich. *Lectures on the Philosophy of World History*. Cambridge, England: Cambridge University Press, 1975.

Hicks, Granville. *Part of the Truth: An Autobiography*. New York: Harcourt, Brace and World, 1965.

Hitler, Adolf. *Mein Kampf*. Unabridged American edition. New York: Reynal & Hitchcock, 1939.

Hoge, Cecil C., Sr. *The First Hundred Years Are the Toughest: What We Can Learn from the Century of Competition Between Sears and Wards*. Berkeley: Ten Speed Press, 1988.

Hounshell, David A. *From the American System to Mass Production, 1800–1932: The Development of Manufacturing Technology in the United States*. Baltimore: Johns Hopkins University Press, 1984.

Hounshell, David A., and John K. Smith. *Science and Corporate Strategy: Du Pont R&D, 1902–1980*. New York: Cambridge University Press, 1988.

Hoyt, Edwin P. *That Wonderful A&P!* New York: Hawthorn, 1969.

James, Henry, Arthur Christopher Benson, Auguste Monod, and E. F. Benson. *Henry James: Letters to A. C. Benson and Auguste Monod*. New York: Charles Scribner's Sons, 1930.

Janis, Irving L. *Victims of Groupthink: A Psychological Study of Foreign-Policy Decisions and Fiascoes*. Boston: Houghton Mifflin Company, 1972.

Jardim, Anne. *The First Henry Ford: A Study in Personality and Business Leadership*. Cambridge, MA: MIT Press, 1970.

Joyce, James. *Ulysses*. New York: Penguin Classics, 2000.

Kahn, E. J., Jr. *The Big Drink: The Story of Coca-Cola*. New York: Random House, 1960.

Kant, Immanuel. *The Metaphysics of Morals*. Cambridge, England: Cambridge University Press, 1996.

Kaplan, Philip J. *F'd Companies: Spectacular Dot-Com Flameouts*. New York: Simon & Schuster, 2002.

Katz, Donald R. *The Big Store: Inside the Crisis and Revolution at Sears*. New York: Viking, 1987.

Kester, W. Carl. *Japanese Takeovers: The Global Contest for Corporate Control*. Boston: Harvard Business School Press, 1991.

Keynes, John Maynard. *Essays in Persuasion*. New York: W. W. Norton, 1963.

Krugman, Paul. *The Return of Depression Economics and the Crisis of 2008*. New York: W. W. Norton, 2009.

Kübler-Ross, Elisabeth. *On Death and Dying*. London: Routledge, 1973.

Leuchtenberg, William E. *The Perils of Prosperity, 1914–1932*. Chicago: University of Chicago Press, 1958.

Levitt, Theodore. *Marketing for Business Growth*. New York: McGraw-Hill, 1974.

———. *The Marketing Imagination*. New York: Free Press, 1983.

Lewis, David L. *The Public Image of Henry Ford: An American Folk Hero and His Company*. Detroit: Wayne State University Press, 1976.

Little, Arthur D. *The Electronic Data Processing Industry: Present Equipment, Technological Trends, Potential Market*. New York: White, Weld, 1956.

Lobrutto, Vincent. *Stanley Kubrick: A Biography*. New York: D. I. Fine, 1997.

Lockard, Joan S. *Self-Deception: An Adaptive Mechanism*. New York: Prentice Hall, 1988.

Love, Steve, David Giffels, and Debbie Van Tassel. *Wheels of Fortune: The Story of Rubber in Akron*. Akron, OH: University of Akron Press, 1998.

McCraw, Thomas K., ed. *Creating Modern Capitalism: How Entrepreneurs, Companies, and Countries Triumphed in Three Industrial Revolutions*. Cambridge, MA: Harvard University Press, 1997.

Mackay, Charles. *Extraordinary Popular Delusions and the Madness of Crowds*. New York: Harmony Books, 1980.

McNair, Malcolm. *Expenses and Profits in the Chain Grocery Business in 1929*. Boston: Harvard Graduate School of Business Administration, June 1931.

McNair, Malcolm, Charles Gragg, and Stanley Teele. *Problems in Retailing*. New York: McGraw-Hill, 1937.

McNair, Malcolm, and Eleanor May. *The Evolution of Retail Institutions in the United States*. Cambridge, MA: Marketing Science Institute, 1976.

Main, Jeremy. *Quality Wars: The Triumphs and Defeats of American Business*. New York: Simon & Schuster, 1994.

Malone, Michael. *Infinite Loop: How the World's Most Insanely Great Computer Company Went Insane*. New York: Doubleday, 1999.

Martin, Robert F. *National Income in the United States, 1799–1939.* New York: National Industrial Conference Board, 1939.

Martinez, Arthur C., with Charles Madigan. *The Hard Road to the Softer Side: Lessons from the Transformation of Sears.* New York: Crown Business, 2001.

Nelson, Daniel. *Farm and Factory: Workers in the Midwest, 1880–1990.* Bloomington: Indiana University Press, 1995.

Nevins, Allan, and Frank Ernest Hill. *Ford: Expansion and Challenge, 1915–1933.* New York: Charles Scribner's Sons, 1957.

———. *Ford: The Times, the Man, the Company.* New York: Charles Scribner's Sons, 1954.

Oliver, Thomas. *The Real Coke, the Real Story.* New York: Random House, 1986.

Orwell, George. *1984.* New York: Alfred A. Knopf, 1992.

———. *The Orwell Reader.* New York: Harcourt, Brace and World, 1984.

Pendergrast, Mark. *For God, Country and Coca Cola: The Definitive History of the Great American Soft Drink and the Company That Makes It.* New York: Basic Books, 2000.

Peter, Laurence J., and Raymond Hull. *The Peter Principle.* New York: William Morrow, 1969.

Potter, David M. *People of Plenty: Economic Abundance and the American Character.* Chicago: University of Chicago Press, 1954.

Rae, John B. *The American Automobile: A Brief History.* Chicago: University of Chicago Press, 1965.

———. *Henry Ford.* Englewood Cliffs, NJ: Prentice-Hall, 1969.

———. *The Road and the Car in American Life.* Cambridge, MA: MIT Press, 1971.

Rentz, John A. *The Death of Grandma: The Hartfords' Great Atlantic and Pacific Tea Company, A&P.* Self-published, 1983.

Rubenstein, James M. *Making and Selling Cars.* Baltimore: Johns Hopkins University Press, 2002.

Safire, William. *Safire's Political Dictionary.* New York: Oxford University Press, 2008.

Shapiro, Fred R. *The Yale Book of Quotations.* New Haven: Yale University Press, 2006.

Shelley, Percy Bysshe. *The Complete Poems of Percy Bysshe Shelley.* New York: Modern Library, 1994.

Simmel, Georg. *The Sociology of Georg Simmel.* Glencoe, II: Free Press, 1950.

Sloan, Alfred P., Jr. *My Years with General Motors.* New York: Doubleday, 1963.

Smith, Albert D., ed. *Competitive Distribution in a Free High-Level Economy and Its Implications for the University.* Pittsburgh: University of Pittsburgh Press, 1958.

Smith, David Livingstone. *Why We Lie: The Evolutionary Roots of Deception and the Unconscious Mind.* New York: St. Martin's Press, 2004.

Sorenson, Charles E., with Samuel T. Williamson. *My Forty Years with Ford.* New York: Norton, 1956.

Stendhal. *The Red and the Black.* New York: Bantam Books, 1958.

Sullivan, Mark. *Our Times: The United States, 1900–1925*. New York: Charles Scribner's Sons, 1928.

Tavris, Carol, and Elliot Aronson. *Mistakes Were Made (but not by me): Why We Justify Foolish Beliefs, Bad Decisions, and Hurtful Acts*. New York: Harcourt, 2007.

Tedlow, Richard S. *Andy Grove: The Life and Times of an American*. New York: Portfolio, 2006.

———. *Giants of Enterprise: Seven Business Innovators and the Empires They Built*. New York: HarperCollins, 2001.

———. *New and Improved: The Story of Mass Marketing in America*. New York: Basic Books, 1990.

———. *The Watson Dynasty: The Fiery Reign and Troubled Legacy of IBM's Founding Father and Son*. New York: HarperBusiness, 2003.

Vaughan, Diane. *The Challenger Launch Decision: Risky Technology, Culture, and Deviance at NASA*. Chicago: University of Chicago Press, 1996.

Wall, Joseph Frazier. *Alfred I. du Pont: The Man and His Family*. New York: Oxford University Press, 1990.

Walsh, William I. *The Rise & Decline of the Great Atlantic & Pacific Tea Company*. Secaucus, NJ: Lyle Stuart, 1986.

Walton, Sam, with John Huey. *Sam Walton, Made in America: My Story*. New York: Doubleday, 1992.

Watson, Thomas J., Jr., and Peter Petre. *Father, Son & Co.: My Life at IBM and Beyond*. New York: Bantam Books, 1990.

Werner, Morris Robert. *Julius Rosenwald: The Life of a Practical Humanitarian*. New York: Harper, 1939.

Wik, Reynold M. *Henry Ford and Grass-roots America*. Ann Arbor: University of Michigan Press, 1972.

Williams, Robert Chadwell. *Horace Greeley: Champion of American Freedom*. New York: NYU Press, 2006.

Williamson, Oliver E. *The Economic Institutions of Capitalism*. New York: Free Press, 1985.

Wilson, Terry P. *The Cart That Changed the World: The Career of Sylvan N. Goldman*. Norman: University of Oklahoma Press, 1978.

Womack, James P., Daniel T. Jones, and Daniel Roos. *The Machine That Changed the World*. New York: Harper Perennial, 1991.

Wood, John Cunnigham, and Michael C. Wood, eds. *Henry Ford: Critical Evaluations in Business and Management*, Vol. 1. New York: Routledge, 2003.

Worthy, James C. *Shaping an American Institution: Robert E. Wood and Sears, Roebuck*. Urbana: University of Illinois Press, 1984.

Wyly, Sam. *1,000 Dollars and an Idea: Entrepreneur to Billionaire*. New York: Newmarket Press, 2008.

Yunis, Harvey. *Taming Democracy: Models of Political Rhetoric in Classical Athens*. Ithaca, NY: Cornell University Press, 1996.

Zerubavel, Eviatar. *The Elephant in the Room: Silence and Denial in Everyday Life.* New York: Oxford University Press, 2006.

Zimmerman, M. M. *The Super Market: A Revolution in Distribution.* New York: Mass Distribution, 1955.

Articles

Anders, George. "Co-Founder of Borders to Launch Online Megagrocer." *Wall Street Journal,* April 22, 1999.

"A&P Goes to the Wars." *Fortune,* April 1938.

"The A&P in Fairfield, Conn." *Fortune,* July 1930.

"A&P Looks like Tengelmann's Vietnam." *Business Week,* February 1, 1982.

"A&P vs. G&W: Lethargic Food Giant Has Glamorous History—and Balance Sheet." *Wall Street Journal,* February 14, 1973.

"Are You Going to Buy Radials?" *Forbes,* June 15, 1974.

Baldwin, James. "As Much Truth as One Can Bear." *New York Times Book Review,* January 14, 1962.

Bénabou, Roland. "Groupthink: Collective Delusions in Organizations and Markets." National Bureau of Economic Research Working Paper No. 14764. March 2009.

Berger, Joseph. "Black Jeans Invade Big Blue." *New York Times,* February 7, 1995.

Blakeslee, Sandra. "Figuring Out the Brain from Its Acts of Denial." *New York Times,* January 23, 1996.

"Bob Woodruff of Coca-Cola." *Fortune,* September 1945.

Breckenridge, Gerald. "Salesman No. 1." *Saturday Evening Post,* May 24, 1941.

Brooker, Robert, with John McDonald. "The Strategy That Saved Montgomery Ward." *Fortune,* May 1970.

Bullock, Roy J. "A History of the Great Atlantic and Pacific Tea Company Since 1878." *Harvard Business Review* 12 (October 1933).

Butterfield, Roger. "Henry Ford, the Wayside Inn, and the Problem of 'History Is Bunk.'" In Wood and Wood, *Henry Ford.*

Carey, Benedict. "Denial Makes the World Go Round." *New York Times,* November 20, 2007.

Christensen, Clayton M., and Richard S. Tedlow. "Patterns of Disruption in Retailing." *Harvard Business Review* 78, no. 1 (January-February 2000).

Clark, Neil M. "The Independent Grocer Finds 'A Way Out!'" *Forbes,* September 1, 1930.

Cobb, James G. "This Just In: Model T Gets Award." *New York Times,* December 24, 1999.

Dalton, James. "What Will Ford Do Next?" *Motor,* May 1926.

Enstad, Rovert. "Girder Tops Sears 'Rock.'" *Chicago Tribune,* May 4, 1973.

Evans, Bob O. "Introduction to SPREAD Report." *Annals of the History of Computing* 72, no. 4 (Winter 1998).

"Forewarnings of Fatal Flaws." *Time*, June 25, 1979.

Freud, Sigmund. "On Beginning the Treatment." In Gay, *Freud Reader*.

Frey, Don. "Learning the Ropes: My Life as a Product Champion." *Harvard Business Review* 69, no. 5 (September/October 1991).

Garraty, John A. "U.S. Steel vs. Labor: The Early Years." *Labor History* 1, no. 1 (Winter 1960).

"General Motors I." *Fortune*, December 1938.

"General Robert E. Wood, President." *Fortune*, May 1938.

Gibbons, Kent. "Gerstner's Selection as IBM Boss Shows Desire for Manager." *Washington Times*, March 27, 1993.

Goleman, Daniel. "Insights into Self-Deception." *New York Times*, May 12, 1985.

"The Great A&P." *Fortune*, November 1947.

"The Greatest Capitalist in History." *Fortune*, August 31, 1987.

Guglielmo, Connie. "Can Webvan Deliver?" *Inter@ctive Week*, January 31, 2000.

Hakim, Danny. "On TV, Spitzer Says Getting Caught 'Crossed My Mind.'" *New York Times*, April 7, 2009.

Holmes, Steven A. "U.S. No Longer a Land Steeped in Wanderlust." *New York Times*, September 12, 1995.

"Hungary." *Encyclopedia Judaica*.

Kempton, Murray. "The Tylenol Case and Our Wish for a Happy Ending." *Newsday*, February 19, 1986.

Kiechell, Walter, III. "Facing Up to Denial." *Fortune*, October 18, 1993.

Kinsley, Michael. "In Defense of Denial: A Noted Journalist, Given a Diagnosis of Parkinson's, Makes the Case for Kidding Yourself about Bad News." *Time*, December 17, 2001.

Kirkpatrick, David. "Inside Sam's $100 Billion Growth Machine." *Fortune*, June 14, 2004.

Lashinsky, Adam. "Remembering Netscape: The Birth of the Web." *Fortune*, July 12, 2005.

Lenzner, Robert. "Bagging Groceries." *Forbes*, October 18, 1999.

Lewis, Michael. "The End." *Condé Nast Portfolio*, December 2008.

Litz, Reginald L. "Cheating at Solitaire: Self-Deception, Executive Mental Health, and Organizational Performance." *Business and Society Review* 108, no. 2 (Summer 2003).

Loomis, Carol J. "Dinosaurs?" *Fortune*, May 3, 1993.

Lucas, Robert E. "Macroeconomic Priorities." *American Economic Review* 93, no. 1 (March 2003).

Luce, H. R. "The American Century." *Life*, February 17, 1941.

McCraw, Thomas K., and Richard S. Tedlow. "Henry Ford, Alfred Sloan, and the Three Phases of Marketing." In McCraw, *Creating Modern Capitalism*.

McDonald, John. "Sears Makes It Look Easy." *Fortune*, May 1964.

Mackenzie, Richard. "'The Industry Has Stopped Growing.'" *Insight*, October 7, 1985.

McNair, Malcolm. "Significant Trends and Developments in the Postwar Period." In Smith, *Competitive Distribution*.

Maney, Kevin. "Webvan Lugs a Dream: Company Hopes Food Will Whet Appetites for a Retail Revolution." *USA Today*, June 27, 2000.

"The Michelin Man Rolls into Akron's Backyard." *Fortune*, December 1974.

Mihm, Stephen. "Dr. Doom." *New York Times Magazine*, August 17, 2008.

"Nice Try." *Forbes*, December 1, 1975.

Olegario, Rowena. "IBM and the Two Thomas J. Watsons." In McCraw, *Creating Modern Capitalism*.

Orwell, George. "Politics and the English Language." In Orwell, *Orwell Reader*.

Paumgarten, Nick. "Annals of Finance: The Death of Kings." *New Yorker*, May 18, 2009.

Porter, Michael E. "How Competitive Forces Shape Strategy." *Harvard Business Review* 57, no. 2 (March-April 1979).

"Profiles of Big Five." *Forbes*, September 15, 1980.

Radford, Margaret Grove. "Technology Is Impossible to Hold Back." *Destiny*, Summer 1997.

"Radials Seen as OE Soon." *Modern Tire Dealer*, May 1971.

Raff, Daniel M. G., and Lawrence Summers. "Did Henry Ford Pay Efficiency Wages?" *Journal of Labor Economics* 5, no. 4, pt. 2 (October 1987).

"Retail Trade: Red Circle and Gold Leaf." *Time*, November 13, 1950.

"Riding with Radials." *Dun's Review*, October 1971.

Rost, O. Fred. "A Super Market X-Ray." *Advertising and Selling*, April 13, 1933.

Schiller, Zachary. "Stan Gault's Designated Driver." *Business Week*, April 8, 1996.

Sellers, Patricia. "CEOs in Denial." *Fortune*, June 21, 1999.

Shapiro, David. "On the Psychology of Self-Deception." *Social Research* 63 (Fall 1996).

Simison, Robert L., Norihiko Shirouzu, Timothy Aeppel, and Todd Zaun. "Pressure Points: Tension Between Ford and Firestone Mounts Amid Recall Efforts." *Wall Street Journal*, August 28, 2000.

Smith, Richard Austin. "The Fifty-Million-Dollar Man" (sidebar: "America's Biggest Fortunes"). *Fortune*, November 1957.

Soerel, Janera. "Talking to Nouriel Roubini." *Janera*, May 2, 2007. http://www.janera.com/janera_words.php?id=44.

Sotonoff, Jamie. "Six Months after FBI Raids, Still No Arrests in Tylenol Murders." *Chicago Daily Herald*, August 4, 2009.

"Speedy Recovery: Tylenol Regains Most of No. 1 Market Share, Amazing Doomsayers." *Wall Street Journal*, December 24, 1982.

Stross, Randall E. "Only a Bold Gamble Can Save Webvan Now." *Wall Street Journal*, February 2, 2001.

Sull, Donald N. "The Dynamics of Standing Still: Firestone Tire & Rubber and the Radial Revolution." *Business History Review* 73, no. 3 (Autumn 1999).

Sull, Donald N., Richard S. Tedlow, and Richard S. Rosenbloom. "Managerial Commitments and Technological Change in the U.S. Tire Industry." *Industrial and Corporate Change* 6, no. 2 (March 1997).

"The Sun Never Sets on Cacoola." *Time*, May 15, 1950.

Tedlow, Richard S. "From 'Universalistic Rather Than Particularistic' to 'The Treasure of the Sierra Madre': Another Look at Chapter 2 of Alfred D. Chandler, Jr.'s *Strategy and Structure*." Paper presented at the Academy of Management, August 2008.

———. Review of *The Cart That Changed the World: The Career of Sylvan N. Goldman. Business History Review* 54, no. 1 (Spring 1980).

———. "The Wise Old Fool Who Founded Ford." *Business and Society Review* 19 (Fall 1976).

Tedlow, Richard S., and David Ruben. "Sears' Edifice Complex." Forbes com, July 10, 2009. http://www.forbes.com/2009/07/10/sears-tower-willis-opinions-contributors-chicago.html.

Tetzeli, Rick. "What Chief Executives Return to Shareholders per Square Foot of Office Space." *Fortune*, April 19, 1993.

"Tire and Rubber Industry." *Value Line*, March 23, 1990.

"The Tire Industry: Skidding out of Control?" *Sales Management*, April 1, 1970.

"Tires." *Consumer Reports*, August 1968.

"Tires: Bias Ply and Belted-Bias." *Consumer Reports*, October 1974.

Trivers, Robert L. "The Elements of a Scientific Theory of Self-Deception." *Annals of the New York Academy of Sciences* 907 (April 2000).

———. Introduction to Lockard, *Self-Deception*.

Waldholz, Michael, and Dennis Kneale. "Growing Headache: Tylenol's Maker Tries to Regain Good Image in Wake of Tragedy." *Wall Street Journal*, October 8, 1982.

Ways, Max. "The Hall of Fame for Business Leadership—1976." *Fortune*, January 1976.

"Webvan's Billion-Dollar Mistake." *Financial Times*, July 9, 2001.

"What's a Uniroyal?" *Forbes*, November 15, 1972.

Whyte, William H. Jr. "Groupthink." *Fortune*, March 1952.

———. "The Fallacies of 'Personality' Testing." *Fortune*, September 1954.

Wickwire, Francis Sill. "We Like Corn, on or off the Cob." *Collier's*, December 10, 1949.

Wise, Thomas A. "IBM's $5,000,000,000 Gamble." *Fortune*, September 1966.

"Young Sears, Roebuck." *Fortune*, August 1948.

Cases and Teaching Notes

Ackerman, R. W. "Firestone, Inc." Harvard Business School Publishing Case No. 9-388-127. Boston: HBS Publishing, 1988.

Botticelli, Peter, David Collis, and Gary Pisano. "Intel Corporation: 1986–1997."

Harvard Business School Publishing Case No. 9-797-137. Boston: HBS Publishing, rev. 1998.

Tedlow, Richard S., and Wendy K. Smith. "James Burke: A Career in American Business (A)." Harvard Business School Publishing Case No. 9-389-177. Boston: HBS Publishing, rev. 2005.

———. "James Burke: A Career in American Business (B)." Harvard Business School Publishing Case No. 9-390-030. Boston: HBS Publishing, rev. 2005.

Wyckoff, D. A. "Firestone Tire and Rubber Company." Harvard Business School Publishing Case No. 9-684-044. Boston: HBS Publishing, 1984.

Websites

The Chicago Club: http://www.thechicagoclub.org.

"The Great Atlantic & Pacific Tea Company Milestones by Decades": http://www .aptea.com/history_timeline.asp.

IBM Archives: http://www.ibm.com/ibm/history/.

"The IBM System/360 Business Case": http://www.youtube.com/watch?v=Dcqganp Wfd8&feature=channel_page.

"New Coke Launches": http://www.msnbc.msn.com/id/7209828/.

"The Rum and Coca-Cola Reader": http://www.rumandcocacolareader.com/.

Miscellaneous

Annual reports: Historical annual reports were consulted for many of the companies discussed.

Berkshire Hathaway Inc. An Owner's Manual: A Message from Warren E. Buffett, Chairman and CEO. January 1999. http://www.berkshirehathaway.com/owners.html.

Berlin, Leslie. "Entrepreneurship and the Rise of Silicon Valley: The Career of Robert Noyce, 1956–1990." Ph.D. diss., Stanford University, 2001.

Coca-Cola advertisement. Delineator, July 1905.

Firestone Tire Recall: Hearing Before the Committee on Commerce, Science, and Transportation, United States Senate, One Hundred Sixth Congress, second session, September 12, 2000. Washington, DC: United States Government Printing Office, 2003.

Grove, Andrew S. Interview by Arnold Thackray and David C. Brock, September 1, 2004. Oral History Collection. Chemical Heritage Foundation. http://www .chemheritage.org. Interview in my possession.

Hartford, John A. Testimony in the District Court of the United States for the Eastern District of Illinois. United States v. The New York Great Atlantic and Pacific Tea Company, Inc. et al. No. 16153 (criminal).

Jeffries, J. H., to Louis Asher, letter, November 7, 1906; Asher to Jeffries, letter, November 9, 1906. Box 1, folder 12, Asher papers. University of Chicago.

Pepsi-Cola advertisement. *Greensboro Daily News Sunday*, December 19, 1915.

Pickard, F. W. "A Plan to Make 10% on Our Paint and Varnish Net Sales." A copy of this report is in my possession. The original can be found in the Hagley Museum and Library in Wilmington, Delaware.

"George Shaheen, President and CEO, Webvan." Kellogg School of Business Cyber Symposium, February 2000. Transcript at http://www. fantastictranscripts.com/ transcription/shaheen00.html.

Triumph of the Nerds: The Rise of Accidental Empires. PBS, aired June 1996. Part II transcript. http://www.pbs.org/nerds/part2.html.

United States District Court for the Southern District of New York. *Elsroth v. Johnson & Johnson.* 700 F. Supp. 151 (S.D.N.Y. 1988).

Video Monitoring Services of America. *Technopolitics.* KCSM-TV San Francisco, September 22, 1996, 5:30 p.m.

Wood, Robert E. "Reminiscences." Oral History Collection. Columbia University, 1961.

————. Talk given before buyers, November 5, 1936. Sears file, Wood papers. Herbert Hoover Presidential Library, West Branch, Iowa.

————. Talk to be given August 30, 1938, "Buying and Cataloging Forces." Sears file, Wood papers. Herbert Hoover Presidential Library, West Branch, Iowa.

Index